Lecture Notes in Computer Science 15341

Founding Editors

Gerhard Goos
Juris Hartmanis

Editorial Board Members

Elisa Bertino, *Purdue University, West Lafayette, IN, USA*
Wen Gao, *Peking University, Beijing, China*
Bernhard Steffen ⓘ, *TU Dortmund University, Dortmund, Germany*
Moti Yung ⓘ, *Columbia University, New York, NY, USA*

The series Lecture Notes in Computer Science (LNCS), including its subseries Lecture Notes in Artificial Intelligence (LNAI) and Lecture Notes in Bioinformatics (LNBI), has established itself as a medium for the publication of new developments in computer science and information technology research, teaching, and education.

LNCS enjoys close cooperation with the computer science R & D community, the series counts many renowned academics among its volume editors and paper authors, and collaborates with prestigious societies. Its mission is to serve this international community by providing an invaluable service, mainly focused on the publication of conference and workshop proceedings and postproceedings. LNCS commenced publication in 1973.

Pari Delir Haghighi · Solomiia Fedushko ·
Gabriele Kotsis · Ismail Khalil
Editors

Advances in Mobile Computing and Multimedia Intelligence

22nd International Conference, MoMM 2024
Bratislava, Slovak Republic, December 2–4, 2024
Proceedings

 Springer

Editors
Pari Delir Haghighi ⓘ
Monash University
Clayton, VIC, Australia

Solomiia Fedushko
Lviv Polytechnic National University
Lviv, Ukraine

Gabriele Kotsis ⓘ
Johannes Kepler University Linz
Linz, Austria

Ismail Khalil ⓘ
Johannes Kepler University Linz
Linz, Austria

ISSN 0302-9743 ISSN 1611-3349 (electronic)
Lecture Notes in Computer Science
ISBN 978-3-031-78048-6 ISBN 978-3-031-78049-3 (eBook)
https://doi.org/10.1007/978-3-031-78049-3

© The Editor(s) (if applicable) and The Author(s), under exclusive license
to Springer Nature Switzerland AG 2025

This work is subject to copyright. All rights are solely and exclusively licensed by the Publisher, whether the whole or part of the material is concerned, specifically the rights of translation, reprinting, reuse of illustrations, recitation, broadcasting, reproduction on microfilms or in any other physical way, and transmission or information storage and retrieval, electronic adaptation, computer software, or by similar or dissimilar methodology now known or hereafter developed.
The use of general descriptive names, registered names, trademarks, service marks, etc. in this publication does not imply, even in the absence of a specific statement, that such names are exempt from the relevant protective laws and regulations and therefore free for general use.
The publisher, the authors and the editors are safe to assume that the advice and information in this book are believed to be true and accurate at the date of publication. Neither the publisher nor the authors or the editors give a warranty, expressed or implied, with respect to the material contained herein or for any errors or omissions that may have been made. The publisher remains neutral with regard to jurisdictional claims in published maps and institutional affiliations.

This Springer imprint is published by the registered company Springer Nature Switzerland AG
The registered company address is: Gewerbestrasse 11, 6330 Cham, Switzerland

If disposing of this product, please recycle the paper.

Preface

We are delighted to present the proceedings of the 22nd International Conference on Advances in Mobile Computing & Multimedia Intelligence (MoMM2024), which was held at the faculty of Management, Comenius University Bratislava, Slovakia from 2–4 December 2024.

The papers included in this volume represent an exciting collection of cutting-edge research that highlights the evolving landscape of mobile computing and multimedia intelligence. This year's conference showcases diverse and innovative contributions, focusing on wearable technologies, human-computer interaction, software intelligence, multimedia processing, and healthcare applications.

MoMM 2024 received a total of 34 paper submissions. From these, the Program Committee selected 10 as regular papers, resulting in an acceptance rate of 29%. Additionally, 8 papers were accepted as short papers to showcase pioneering research and innovative projects across various disciplines. These short papers highlight early-stage research, novel ideas, and preliminary findings, fostering meaningful discussions and potential collaborations.

The single-blind peer review process provided evaluation of each submitted paper by at least three reviewers. Their assessment not only served the purpose of quality control for the conference but also contained valuable comments for the authors and inspiring ideas for improvement or further research.

We would like to sincerely thank our Program Committee members and external reviewers for their critical and motivating reviews.

As mobile devices and multimedia systems continue to become integral parts of our daily lives, the challenges and opportunities in these fields are expanding rapidly. The selected papers for this conference exemplify the dynamic interplay between data, user experience, artificial intelligence, and sensor-based technologies, providing a glimpse into the future of intelligent systems and human interaction.

The proceedings are organized into five topics, each representing a crucial aspect of mobile computing and multimedia intelligence:

- **Wearable and Sensor-Based Data for Human Performance and Interaction:** This topic explores the analysis of motion and physiological data, advancements in wearable authentication methods, and techniques for embedding and estimating data from sensors, highlighting the growing role of smart devices in monitoring and enhancing human performance.
- **Mobile User Experience, Motivation, and Behavior:** Papers in this topic delve into user experience and motivation, examining the role of gamification, eco-friendly technologies, and the cognitive impacts of multisensory experiences in virtual environments.
- **Medical and Cognitive Health Applications:** Addressing critical issues in health and medical data, this topic focuses on predictive models for cognitive impairment,

neural networks in medical diagnostics, and optimized scheduling for healthcare professionals.
- **Image, Video, and Multimedia Processing:** With the rise of high-resolution media and the need for efficient processing methods, this topic presents solutions for detecting non-authentic images, analyzing omnidirectional videos, and evaluating geolocation-based clustering methods.
- **Software and System Intelligence:** This topic focuses on advances in software defect prediction, recommender systems, gesture recognition, and the integration of virtual objects into real-world systems, offering new perspectives on enhancing system intelligence and efficiency.

We believe the papers presented in these proceedings will not only advance the current state of research but will also inspire new directions and collaborations in mobile computing and multimedia intelligence. We thank all the authors for their valuable contributions, the reviewers for their critical insights, and the organizing committee at the Faculty of Management, Comenius University Bratislava, Slovakia for their tireless efforts in making this conference a success.

We extend our heartfelt gratitude to our keynote speakers: Toshiyuki Amagasa from the University of Tsukuba, Japan, Antonio Liotta from the Free University of Bozen-Bolzano, Italy and Martin Homola from the Faculty of Mathematics, Physics and Informatics, Comenius University Bratislava, Slovakia for their exceptional presentations. Their insights were enlightening and deeply resonated with our participants, making their contributions one of the event's highlights.

We hope you find these proceedings informative and inspiring, and we look forward to the future innovations that this work will undoubtedly spark.

December 2024

Pari Delir Haghighi
Solomiia Fedushko
Gabriele Kotsis
Ismail Khalil

Organization

Program Committee Chairs

Pari Delir Haghighi — Monash University, Australia
Solomiia Fedushko — Lviv Polytechnic National University, Ukraine & Comenius University Bratislava, Slovakia

Steering Committee

Gabriele Kotsis — Johannes Kepler University Linz, Austria
Ismail Khalil — Johannes Kepler University Linz, Austria
Natalia Kryvinska — Comenius University Bratislava, Slovakia
Syopiansyah Jaya Putra — Universitas Islam Negeri, Indonesia

Program Committee Members

Andreas Schrader — University of Lübeck, Germany
Andrzej Romanowski — Lodz University of Technology, Poland
Antonio Liotta — Free University of Bozen-Bolzano, Italy
Carlos Calafate — Universitat Politècnica de València, Spain
Chang Wu Yu — Chung Hua University, Taiwan
Chow-Sing Lin — National University of Tainan, Taiwan
Dmytro Chumachenko — National Aerospace University "Kharkiv Aviation Institute", Ukraine
Federico Montori — University of Bologna, Italy
Hong Va Leong — Hong Kong Polytechnic University, China
Irina N. Roddvik — Østfold University College, Norway
Luca Davoli — University of Parma, Italy
Marco Martalò — University of Cagliari, Italy
Markku Turunen — University of Tampere, Finland
Oleksandr Markovets — Lviv Polytechnic National University, Ukraine
Panayotis Fouliras — University of Macedonia, Greece
Paolo Bellavista — University of Bologna, Italy
Ruslan Kravets — Lviv Polytechnic National University, Ukraine
Sami Habib — Kuwait University, Kuwait
Sara Comai — Politecnico di Milano, Italy

Srikanth Thudumu	Deakin University, Australia
Svetlana Boudko	Norsk Regnesentral (Norwegian Computing Center), Norway
Tetiana Klynina	University of Texas at Austin, USA
Tommi Mikkonen	University of Helsinki, Finland
Tsutomu Terada	Kobe University, Japan
Tzung-Pei Hong	National University of Kaohsiung, Taiwan
Tzung-Shi Chen	National University of Tainan, Taiwan
Vitaliy Yakovyna	University of Warmia and Mazury in Olsztyn, Poland
Wen-Yang Lin	National University of Kaohsiung, Taiwan
Wolfgang Schreiner	Johannes Kepler University Linz, Austria
You-Chiun Wang	National Sun Yat-sen University, Taiwan
Yuriy Syerov	Lviv Polytechnic National University, Ukraine
Yusuke Gotoh	Okayama University, Japan
Yuxin Zhang	Monash University, Australia

External Reviewers

Andrzej Romanowski	University of Oldenburg, Germany
Jacek Gwizdka	University of Texas at Austin, USA

Organizers

Contents

Wearable and Sensor-Based Data for Human Performance and Interaction

Investigating Choking Under Pressure in Dance Performance with Motion and Physiological Information Analysis 3
  Shuhei Tsuchida, Ayumi Ohnishi, Kae Mukai, Ken Watanabe, Katsumi Watanabe, Tsutomu Terada, and Masahiko Tsukamoto

A Method for Estimating the Force Applied on the Forearm Using PPG Sensors 18
  Ryo Watabe and Kazuya Murao

Good Vibes! Towards Phone-to-User Authentication Through Wristwatch Vibrations 24
  Jakob Dittrich and Rainhard Dieter Findling

A Method for Embedding Information Into Acceleration Data Using Resonant Frequency Sound to Capacitive Accelerometers 31
  Takeru Yokoyama and Kazuya Murao

Mobile User Experience, Motivation, and Behavior

MEUSec – Method for Enhancing User Experience and Information Security 39
  Max Sauer, Christoph Becker, Andreas Oberweis, Simon Pfeifer, and Jan Sürmeli

Correlation Between Gamification and Intrinsic Motivation with a Mobile Job-Market Application 54
  Niklas Grossmann and Helmut Hlavacs

Query by Trash: Encouraging Green Attitudes and Behavior Through Eco-News Retrieval in Smart Trash Bins 70
  Momo Takeuchi, Yoshiyuki Shoji, and Yusuke Yamamoto

Evaluating the Impact of Color and Sound Combinations on Cognitive Performance in Virtual Reality 86
  Ryoma Nakao and Tatsuo Nakajima

Medical and Cognitive Health Applications

Mild Cognitive Impairment Prediction Using Facial and Speech Data 95
    Chien-Cheng Lee, Wei-Chieh Huang, and Yi-Fang Chuang

Comparing Training of Sparse to Classic Neural Networks for Binary
Classification in Medical Data 101
    Laura Erhan, Antonio Liotta, and Lucia Cavallaro

A Genetic Algorithm-Based Scheduling Method Considering Working
Hours for Medical Doctors 107
    Subaru Narahashi, Eiji Hirakawa, Akira Uchiyama, and Yusuke Gotoh

Image, Video, and Multimedia Processing

Application of Benford's Law to the Identification of Non-authentic
Digital Images 115
    Jaroslaw Kobiela and Piotr Dzierwa

Efficient Moving Object Detection from Ultra-High Resolution
Omnidirectional Video 130
    Takuro Ohashi and Shohei Yokoyama

Evaluation of the Clustering Method Used to Analyze the Proximity
of Mobile Devices Using Indirect Geolocation Indicators 145
    Jaroslaw Kobiela and Piotr Urbaniec

Software and System Intelligence

Cross-Project Software Defect Prediction Using Ensemble Model
with Individual Data Balancing and Feature Selection 161
    Vitaliy Yakovyna and Oleh Nesterchuk

AUTO-DataGenCARS+: An Advanced User-Oriented Tool to Generate
Data for the Evaluation of Recommender Systems 176
    María del Carmen Rodríguez-Hernández, Sergio Ilarri,
    Marcos Caballero, Raquel Trillo-Lado, Ramón Hermoso,
    and Rafael del-Hoyo-Alonso

A Method for Eliminating False Positives of Acceleration-Based Gesture
Recognition Using Eye Tracking 192
    Hinase Kawano and Kazuya Murao

Toward the Implementation of a Cooking Support System Complementing
Nonexistent Objects with Virtual Objects 208
   Taiki Nihanda and Shoji Sano

Author Index 215

Wearable and Sensor-Based Data for Human Performance and Interaction

Investigating Choking Under Pressure in Dance Performance with Motion and Physiological Information Analysis

Shuhei Tsuchida[1], Ayumi Ohnishi[2], Kae Mukai[3], Ken Watanabe[3], Katsumi Watanabe[3], Tsutomu Terada[2], and Masahiko Tsukamoto[2]

[1] Ochanomizu University, 2-1-1 Otsuka, Bunkyo-ku, Tokyo 112-8610, Japan
tsuchida.shuhei@ocha.ac.jp
[2] Kobe University, 1-1 Rokkodai-cho, Nada-ku, Kobe 657-8501, Japan
[3] Waseda University, 3-4-1 Okubo, Shinjuku-ku, Tokyo 169-8555, Japan

Abstract. This study is the initial phase in developing coping mechanisms for individuals who struggle with 'choking under pressure' due to stress. We focus on examining the motion and physiological information of dancers in high-pressure performance and low-pressure practice environments. Our primary objective is to identify key differences in stress responses between individuals who manage pressure well and those who do not. Through a comparative analysis of the motion and physiological information, we seek to identify the disparities between those who are adept at handling choking under pressure and those who are not. To simulate a high-pressure performance environment, a dance audition will be conducted and the physical and mental state of the auditionees during the evaluation process will be monitored and analyzed. The results indicated that auditionees who were unable to cope with choking under pressure showed significantly reduced physical movements compared to those who were able to handle it.

Keywords: choking under pressure · stress management · dance · motion analysis

1 Background

Ideally, we aim to perform as well under pressure as we do in a practice environment. This desire is pervasive in various domains of real-time performance, including sports, public speaking, theatrical arts, and other performance-based activities. However, some researchers suggest that performance under pressure in a live environment often deteriorates as compared to performance in a practice environment, making it challenging to attain the same level of proficiency [19]. This phenomenon, in which one's performance is diminished by pressure despite their best efforts, is commonly referred to as *"choking under pressure"* [1]. Many changes in motor behavior, such as movement instability [20] and changes in movement duration and timing [13], have been reported as consequences of the choking under pressure, leading to a decline in performance quality. It is therefore imperative to effectively manage pressure in order to achieve performance levels in the live environment that are comparable to those in a practice environment.

Many strategies for coping with the choking under pressure have been proposed. Hill et al. [7] found, through interviews with elite golfers and experienced golf coaches, that task-focused (rather than outcome-focused) approach, cognitive restructuring, mental imagery, practicing under pressure, and pre-performance and post-performance routines were interventions that could reduce anxiety. Pre-performance [9] and post-performance [11] routines, such as pre-shot and post-shot routines, have been found to be particularly effective.

However, not everyone can benefit from pre-performance routines and other methods of coping with pressure, as the importance of personalized pre-performance routines has indicated [12]. Some individuals are able to effectively cope with the stress, while others are not. Thus, it is important to develop a system that can provide support to those who struggle with their emotions, taking into account the unique characteristics of each individual. To achieve this, it is necessary to identify the differences between those who can handle the pressure of the live environment and those who cannot, both in high-pressure and low-pressure performance environments.

In this study, we therefore analyze dancers' motion and physiological information both in a high-pressure performance environment and in a low-pressure performance environment with the aim of developing a support system for coping with the choking under pressure in dance performance. To achieve this, we conduct a dance audition and collect and analyze various physical and psychological states of the participants during the audition process. To induce pressure on the participants, we designed the audition to consider the participants, the judges, and the incentives. Based on the results of the experiment, we examine the differences between those who perform well and those who do not perform well under pressure, and we discuss support methods for coping with the pressure based on these differences. By considering various information presentation methods that could help to cope with the pressure, we hope that the performers will be able to maintain consistent high performance in high-pressure situations.

2 Related Work

Many studies [10] investigated the relationship between physiological states and performance in both live and practice environments, with a particular focus on "choking under pressure," freezing up and underperforming when performing under pressure. We outline the physiological and movement changes that occur under pressure and highlight the key areas of focus of our study. We then introduce methods for improving performance through information presentation. We consider the potential for improved performance in the live environment through information presentation that considers the state in the practice environment.

2.1 Choking Under Pressure

One physiological change that occurs under pressure is an increased heart rate. This has been observed in a variety of domains, including freestyle snowboard jumping competitions, rifle shooting competitions, e-sports competitions, piano competitions, and others. In this study, we aim to compare average heart rates between live(audition) and practice environments, considering the intense physical activity involved and the limited measurement time of the live environment (audition environment).

Numerous studies have reported changes in motor function when an individual is under pressure. Yoshie et al. [20] found that motor performance becomes less stable when a task is performed under observation than when it is not. Higuchi et al. [6] reported delayed onset of movement and reduced amplitude of movement as hallmarks of movement under pressure.

As mentioned above, it has been reported that movement becomes unstable under pressure and that the timing of movement changes, under pressure, leading to a deterioration in competition scores and other relevant metrics. This research seeks to understand the physiological and movement characteristics of individuals who perform well in a high-pressure performance environment and those who do not, and to investigate information presentation methods to assist individuals who underperform in high-pressure performance environments.

2.2 Information Presentation Method to Improve Performance

Several strategies have been proposed to improve performance through information presentation. Futami et al. [3] proposed a system that induces a positive mindset and enhances performance by repeatedly presenting stimuli only when the user succeeds in hitting a target while throwing darts. Focusing on golf putting, Tagami et al. [15] developed *"Routine++"*, a virtual golf simulator that provides users with feedback on the successful entry of the ball into the hole without causing discomfort. Studies have shown that Routine++ improves the performance of novice golfers under pressure. These studies primarily focus on information presentation systems designed for general users who are going to perform, rather than for a specific user, such as one who struggles with pressure in high-pressure performance environments. This study aims to discuss information presentation methods to users who are unable to perform well in high-pressure performance environments due to the choking under pressure, with the aim of eliciting the same or better performance in a high-pressure performance environment as compared to a low-pressure performance environment.

3 Experiment

We conducted the experiment to determine the differences between individuals who are able to effectively cope with the choking under pressure and those who are not. The participants were 20 students (4 males and 16 females) from the TOKYO SCHOOL OF MUSIC & DANCE[1], with dance experiences ranging from Punking, Hip-Hop, R&B, Breaking, Girls Hip-Hop, Swag, New Jack Swing, Locking, Cheerleading, Jazz, House, Jazz Funk, Pop, and so on. This experiment was conducted with the approval of the Research Ethics Review Committee of the author's institution.

3.1 Experiment Condition

To clarify the differences between individuals who have the ability to effectively cope with the choking under pressure and those who do not, it is necessary to collect data on each type of motion and physiological data within high-pressure and low-pressure performance contexts, and to construct a performance setting that is under higher pressure than typical practice conditions. Therefore, we conduct a dance audition, in which rehearsals served as the practice environment (low-pressure performance context) and evaluation served as the audition environment (high-pressure performance context). During the dance audition, two judges sit in front of the auditionees and the auditionees danced a choreography of approximately 38 s. The audition was then followed by a five-minute interview with the judges. There were 28 auditionees for the dance audition, from which the final six were chosen. The practice and audition environment are described below.

Practice Environment. The rehearsal was held three days before the audition day. If the rehearsal date was too close to the audition day, the auditionees might become nervous. Conversely, if the date was too distant from the audition day, differences in choreography proficiency could affect the results. To enable the auditionees to approach the dance performance in as relaxed a state as possible, one of the two judges was the primary author, and the other was a student from the TOKYO SCHOOL OF MUSIC & DANCE. It was clarified that the dance performance during the rehearsal day had no influence on the outcome of the judging.

Audition Environment. To put pressure on the auditionees, we created a performance environment that considers the judges and the benefits that could be gained from a successful audition. We first sought the participation of two renowned judges, Mr Akihiko Hashimoto [5] and Mr Minoru Fujimoto [2]. Mr Hashimoto has a noteworthy portfolio, having won several competitions including the "MOST CREATIVE DIRECTOR" award in D-League, a professional dance league established in Japan in August 2020. He has received numerous awards throughout his career. Therefore, we expected that performing in front of him would result in a high level of pressure on the auditionees. Mr Fujimoto has extensive experience in various aspects of live entertainment, including providing light production for popular Japanese artists on their dome

---

[1] https://www.tsm.ac.jp/.

tours and the closing ceremony of the 2020 Tokyo Paralympics. This environment is expected to bring a similar level of pressure to the auditionees as experienced by Mr Hashimoto.

The successful auditionees are given the opportunity to perform in a privileged slot at the TOKYO SCHOOL OF MUSIC & DANCE's graduation performance stage "We are TSM! 2022[2]." The special performance features choreography by Mr Hashimoto and lighting by MPLUSPLUS Co. of which Mr Fujimoto is the CEO. Additionally, the graduation performance stage attracts many directors and producers in the live entertainment industry, presenting a valuable platform for auditionees to showcase their dance skills. Thus, being selected to perform in this coveted slot could potentially lead to future employment opportunities, but also comes with a considerable amount of pressure. It is noted that the audition itself is a highly competitive process, with only a limited number of candidates being chosen. The dance performances of the selected auditionees can be viewed on YouTube[3].

3.2 Experimental Setup

We conducted the experiment on the fifth floor of the TOKYO SCHOOL OF MUSIC & DANCE, which consists of three $65\,m^2$ rooms and a single room with linoleum flooring of $125\,m^2$ (see Fig. 1). The details of the experimental methodology are described in Sect. 3.3, but a brief explanation of the purpose of the rooms is given here. In the Changing room, auditionees are instructed to wear a garment and to attach a heart rate sensor. In the Before room, the auditionees' physiological state prior to the evaluation is measured. In the After room, the auditionees' physiological state is once again measured after the audition.

In this experiment, we measured the psychological state of the participants in both audition and practice environments using a variety of sensors. These sensors included the Polar H10 heart rate sensor, the SR Soft Vision body pressure distribution sensor from Sumitomo Science & Engineering, and the VO2 Master wearable exhaled gas analyzer from Health Sensors. The SR Soft Vision can measure the pressure distribution on the seat surface while sitting in a chair. The VO2 Master can analyze the components of exhaled air. We also used the Azure Kinect DK, a depth sensor from Microsoft that can capture 3D skeletal information, and the 9-axis motion sensor "TSND151" by ATR-Promotions that can measure acceleration and angular velocity of the body movement. The FlexiForce sensor by Nitta Corporation, a pressure sensor capable of measuring foot pressure, was also used in the experiment. In addition, we used eight video cameras, including the HC-W850M-W, HDR-XC470, HC-VX992M, and FDR-AX45.

The sensors used in each room are listed in Table 1 and marked with a checkmark. The placement of the sensors is shown in Fig. 2. The 9-axis motion sensors were attached to five key points: head, neck, waist, right leg, and left leg.

---

[2] https://www.tsm.ac.jp/weare2022/.
[3] https://youtu.be/PUAu7-ikpsk.

Table 1. Locations where sensors are used.

	Room		
	Before	Audition	After
Heart rate sensor (H10)	✓	✓	✓
Body pressure distribution sensor (SR Soft Vision)	✓		✓
Exhaled gas analyzer (VO2Master)	✓		✓
Depth sensor (Azure Kinect DK)		✓	
9-axis motion sensor (TSND151)		✓	
Pressure sensor		✓	
Camera	✓	✓	✓

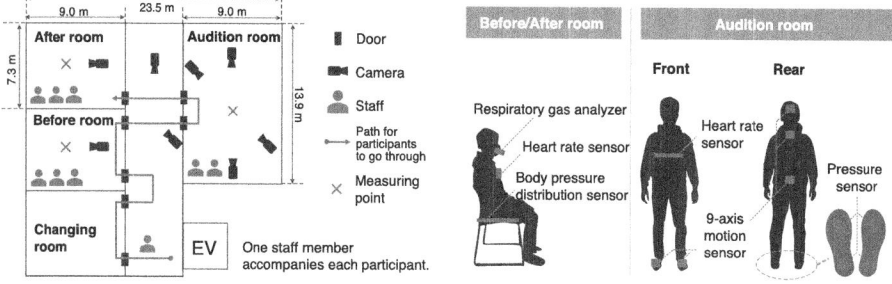

Fig. 1. 5th floor map. **Fig. 2.** Sensor position

Professional dancers (a male and a female) were asked to experience sensor measurements as a preliminary investigation and to perform a dance while wearing multiple sensors used in each of the Before, Audition, and After rooms. The effect of the sensor measurements on the dancers' performance was subsequently evaluated through their interviews. Based on the feedback received, the sensor placement was adjusted to ensure that it did not negatively affect the dancers' performance. Moreover, the two dancers requested that the costumes not be restricted due to the wearing of the sensors, so the auditionees' costumes were not limited.

The auditionees were instructed to learn a single choreography and to participate in a dance audition. The choreography has a duration of approximately 38 s. The used musical piece, with a tempo of 112 BPM, has a length of approximately 42 s, and the choreography begins approximately 4 s after the onset of the musical piece.

On October 6, 2021, a call for auditions and experiments was issued to the professional students of the TOKYO SCHOOL OF MUSIC & DANCE. A total of 28 students applied for the audition, from which 20 participants were selected through a preliminary screening conducted by professional dancers from MPLUSPLUS Co. Due to the time constraints for the judges and the logistical difficulties of conducting auditions for 20 auditionees in a single day, the auditionees were divided into two groups of 10 individuals each. The first group had a rehearsal (practice environment) on October 30 and an audition (audition environment) on November 2, while the second group had a rehearsal on November 3 and an audition on November 6.

3.3 Experimental Procedure

We show the experimental procedure for the rehearsal (practice environment) and the evaluation (audition environment). Auditionees begin the experiment by going to the second-floor reception desk, where they receive an overview of the protocol and relevant measurement details. If they are satisfied with the explanation, they sign a consent form for participation in the experiment and the utilization of their measurement data. They are then asked to fill out a questionnaire about their personal characteristics and their level of psychological tension and confidence regarding their performance on the day of the experiment. To avoid conflicting measurement times, the participants' schedules are adjusted as required. They are then taken to the 5th floor.

Upon reaching the 5th floor, auditionees receive instruction from the measurement staff regarding the correct use of the heart rate sensor. They then enter the changing room, put on the sensor, and change into their costumes. The auditionees are then instructed to proceed to the Before room, where they sit in a chair equipped with a pressure distribution sensor, and attach an exhaled gas analyzer, a 9-axis motion sensor, and shoes with a flexible pressure sensor. For a period of 5 min, participants are instructed to sit quietly with their hands on their knees, while various sensors collect data. After the 5-minute resting phase, the auditionee removes the exhaled gas analyzer, leaves the Before room, and stands still for 10 s in front of a video camera, looking at the lens for capturing their face. They then enter the audition room, where the 9-axis motion sensor begins to take measurements. After the performance, in the audition environment, the auditionee is interviewed by the judges for 5 min. In the rehearsal phase (practice environment), the measurement staff acting as judges briefly outline the flow of the day, and the auditionees are asked to remain seated in a resting state. After the interview, auditionees move to the After room, where they sit again in a chair equipped with a body pressure distribution sensor and attach the exhaled gas analyzer. The same procedures as in the Before room are followed, and measurements are taken for another 5-minute resting phase. The auditionees then remove all sensors and proceed to the reception desk, where they fill out a final questionnaire to complete the experiment. The entire experiment takes approximately 40 min per participant from start to finish.

3.4 Performance Score

To assess the quality of the auditionees' dance performance, we asked three experienced dancers (evaluators) to rate it. The assessment was quantified as a performance score. All of the dancers who were asked to participate in the evaluation had more than 10 years of dance experience and had won or placed in major international and national dance competitions. They also have experience teaching dance as dance instructors.

The evaluation of the dance performance was conducted via the online experimental platform, Gorilla Experiment Builder[4]. The evaluators viewed 40 dance videos (20 auditionees x 2 days [practice and audition environments]), and then rated their performance on a 10-point scale. To reduce the impact of order effects, the presentation order of the 40 dance videos was randomized, both between evaluators and between environments.

If the performance score is observed to decline in a high-pressure audition environment compared to a low-pressure practice environment, it is likely to be due to choking under pressure. In this study, we attribute the decrease in the performance score in the audition environment to the effect of choking under pressure. Based on the obtained performance scores, the auditionees were divided into two groups as follows: Individuals whose performance scores in the audition environment exceeded those in the practice environment were classified as the "**good group**." Conversely, individuals whose performance scores in the audition environment either remained the same or decreased compared to the practice environment were classified as the "**bad group**."

3.5 Data Analysis

In this study, we focused our analysis on the following points among the obtained data.

Physiological Data. To objectively assess the level of psychological tension in both the practice and audition environments, the physiological state was monitored before the audition (Before room) and after the audition (After room). To reduce the effect of physical exertion on the physiological state, the measurements were taken in a sedentary resting position. Heart rate was calculated from the ECG waveforms obtained from the measurements using the following analyses.

First, a bandpass filter with a frequency range of 5–20 Hz was applied to the electrocardiogram waveform, followed by visual elimination of body motion artifacts. The R-wave was then detected and the RR interval (sec) was calculated. This was used to determine the heart rate (BPM: beats per minute) using the 60/RR interval calculation. The mean heart rate (BPM) was calculated as the average heart rate during a 5-min rest period.

Motion Data. To distinguish the movements in the practice environment from those in the audition environment, we collected the skeletal information from the depth sensor was analyzed as follows: Firstly, the skeletal information was synchronised with the video footage captured by the camera during the judging of the jumps performed by the auditionees, and the timing of the skeletal information was standardised for each auditionee. Subsequently, the cross-correlation

---

[4] https://gorilla.sc/.

function was calculated between the audio contained in the video recorded during the judging and the used musical piece, and the moment with the highest value was established as the choreography's starting point, from which data covering 42 s of musical duration was extracted. Considering the variations in the auditionees' physical structure, the 32 feature points (x, y, z coordinates in 3D) acquired by the depth sensor were transformed into unit vectors, each representing 20 skeletal bones ranging from the waist to the head, wrists, and toes. A 60-dimensional unit vector was calculated for each frame, and the distances between unit vectors for all frames were calculated. The average change between frames was determined by calculating the mean value of the unit vector distances for all participants, both in the practice and audition environments.

The acceleration data obtained from the 9-axis motion sensor was analyzed as follows. First, the acceleration data of each auditionee was synchronised with the foot pressure data using the same timestamp as the acceleration data and the video footage captured by the camera at the moment of landing for the jumps performed during the judging. The five 9-axis motion sensors were also synchronised as they were recorded in software using the same timestamp. As with the depth sensor, the acceleration data for the length of the musical piece was extracted from the start timing of the musical piece. The three-axis composite value of acceleration per sample was calculated for each of the five 9-axis motion sensors, and the average value was determined. This calculation was performed for all samples, and the variance of the calculated data was computed. The variance value was calculated for all participants and was used as the variance value of the three-axis composite acceleration data.

To examine the timing of movements, a cross-correlation function was obtained by shifting the acceleration data collected in the practice environment and the acceleration data collected in the audition environment by one sample in a window of 4,000 microseconds. The variance value of the resulting cross-correlation function (representing the deviation in movement timing) was calculated.

Questionnaire. In the pre-experiment questionnaire, auditionees responded to questions regarding their level of psychological tension and confidence via a visual analogue scale (VAS). In the post-experiment questionnaire, participants were asked to provide their perceptions of their performance, psychological tension, and self-confidence through the VAS. In addition to these items, the post-experiment questionnaire also included open-ended questions regarding their dance performance. The content of both the pre-experiment and post-experiment questionnaires was consistent across both the practice and audition environments.

4 Result

The experimental setup is shown in Fig. 3. The left figure shows the auditionee in a seated resting state in a room designated as the Before/After room. The right figure illustrates the auditionee's dance performance at the time of assessment.

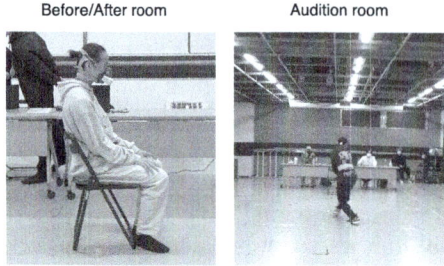

Fig. 3. Measurement and examination in progress

Table 2. Performance score of each auditionee.

	Practice environment				Audition environment			
ID	Evaluator 1	Evaluator 2	Evaluator 3	Ave.	Evaluator 1	Evaluator 2	Evaluator 3	Ave.
1	6	6	9	7.00	9	6	8	7.67
2	**7**	**6**	**6**	**6.33**	**7**	**6**	**3**	**5.33**
3	8	6	9	7.67	9	8	7	8.00
4	**7**	**5**	**5**	**5.67**	**5**	**4**	**6**	**5.00**
5	9	6	7	7.33	9	7	9	8.33
6	5	3	3	3.67	7	2	5	4.67
7	**4**	**2**	**3**	**3.00**	**4**	**2**	**3**	**3.00**
8	4	3	3	3.33	6	4	5	5.00
9	7	3	3	4.33	6	3	5	4.67
10	6	4	3	4.33	8	4	4	5.33
11	**4**	**3**	**4**	**3.67**	**5**	**3**	**3**	**3.67**
12	5	2	6	4.33	6	3	6	5.00
13	4	2	3	3.00	5	3	4	4.00
14	8	5	6	6.33	8	6	8	7.33
15	3	1	2	2.00	7	3	2	4.00
16	5	4	6	5.00	7	4	8	6.33
17	6	4	4	4.67	7	5	4	5.33
18	6	4	7	5.67	7	4	7	6.00
19	**7**	**5**	**7**	**6.33**	**7**	**5**	**7**	**6.33**
20	**8**	**4**	**6**	**6.00**	**7**	**4**	**7**	**6.00**

Note: The bad groups whose performance scores are the same or decreased from the practice environment to the audition environment are shown in bold.

4.1 Performance Score Results

The results of the dance performance evaluation are shown in Table 2. The participants were divided into two groups based on their performance scores: a bad group of six individuals whose scores either remained unchanged or decreased from the practice environment to the audition environment, indicating individuals who have difficulty coping with choking under pressure, and a good group of 14 individuals whose scores improved from the practice environment to the audition environment, indicating individuals who can effectively cope with choking

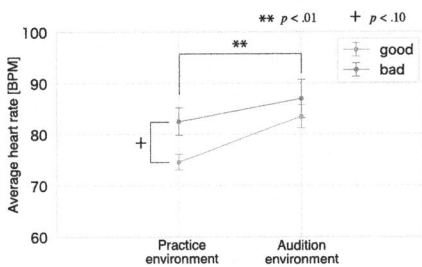
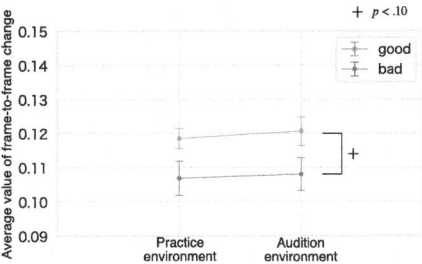

Fig. 4. Average heart rate in Before room

Fig. 5. Average inter-frame change in depth sensor

under pressure. We calculated the correlation coefficients between the performance scores were calculated by the raters and found them to be 0.78, 0.61, and 0.67, respectively.

4.2 Analysis of Physiological Data

The average heart rate in the Before room in both the practice and audition environments is shown in Fig. 4. To assess the psychological state prior to performance, we focused on the measurement results obtained from the Before room, where the effect of exercise was minimal. In the good group, the average heart rate in the practice environment was $74.6\,BPM(SE = 1.5)$, and the average heart rate in the production environment was $83.5\,BPM(SE = 2.3)$. In the bad group, the average heart rate in the practice environment was $82.5\,BPM(SE = 2.7)$, and the average heart rate in the production environment was $87.0\,BPM(SE = 3.7)$. A two-way mixed-design analysis of variance was performed with experimental environment (practice environment, audition environment) and auditionee group (good, bad) as factors, which revealed a significant trend in the difference between auditionee groups ($F(1, 18) = 3.75, p < 0.10$). There was also a significant difference between the experimental settings ($F(1, 18) = 9.83, p < 0.01$).

4.3 Results of Motion Data Analysis

The average value of frame-to-frame change of the depth sensor is shown in Fig. 5. The good group had an average of $0.118(SE = 0.003)$ in the practice environment and $0.120(SE = 0.004)$ in the audition environment. The bad group had an average of $0.107(SE = 0.005)$ in the practice environment and $0.108(SE = 0.005)$ in the audition environment. A two-way mixed-design analysis of variance was performed with the experimental environment (practice environment, audition environment) and auditionee group (good, bad) as factors, which revealed a significant trend in the difference between participant groups ($F(1, 18) = 3.83, p < 0.10$). There was no significant difference among the experimental settings.

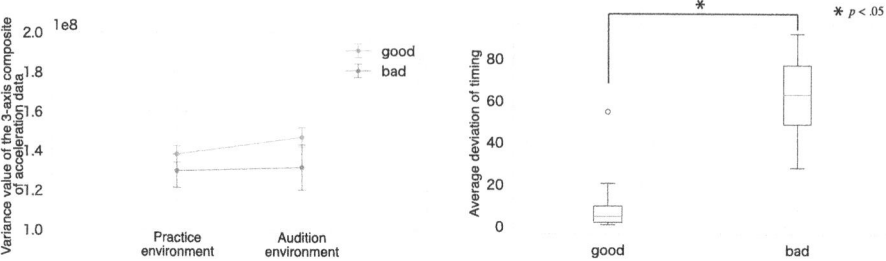

Fig. 6. Variance value of 3-axis composite value of acceleration data

Fig. 7. Variance value of movement timing deviation

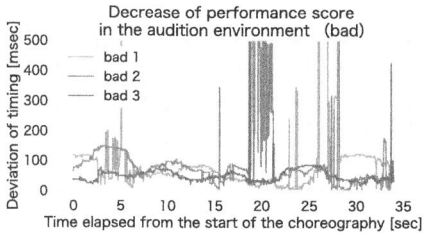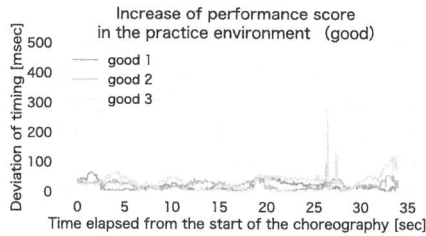

Fig. 8. Timing deviations in the good/bad group (3 people each)

The variance values of the 3-axis composite of the acceleration data are shown in Fig. 6. In the practice environment, the average was $1.38 \times 10^8 (SE = 4.14 \times 10^6)$, and in the audition environment, the average was $1.47 \times 10^8 (SE = 4.83 \times 10^6)$. The bad group had an average of $1.30 \times 10^8 (SE = 8.40 \times 10^6)$ in the practice environment and $1.32 \times 10^8 (SE = 1.14 \times 10^7)$ in the audition environment. A two-way mixed-design analysis of variance was performed with experimental environment (practice environment, audition environment) and participant group (good, bad) as factors. which showed no significant differences in either factor ($p > 0.05$).

The variance values of the movement timing deviations are shown in Fig. 7. The good group showed an average deviation of $10.1 (SE = 4.39)$. The bad group showed an average deviation of $57.4 (SE = 23.00)$. Mann-Whitney's U test results showed significant differences between the auditionee groups ($p < 0.05$). For the good/bad group, three auditionees were selected from each group, and their respective movement timing deviations are shown as line graphs in Fig. 8.

4.4 Questionnaire Results

The average scores for psychological tension on the pre-experimental questionnaire were $4.65 (SE = 0.50)$ for the practice environment and $5.83 (SE = 0.39)$ for the audition environment. The average scores of confidence were $5.06 (SE = 0.39)$ in the practice environment and $5.37 (SE = 2.66)$ in the audition environment.

Moreover, the average scores for performance on the post-experimental questionnaire were $4.65(SE = 0.37)$ for the practice environment and $5.48(SE = 0.44)$ for the audition environment. The average scores for psychological tension were $3.81(SE = 0.44)$ for the practice environment and $5.36(SE = 0.47)$ for the audition environment. The average score of confidence was $4.18(SE = 0.40)$ in the practice environment and $5.41(SE = 0.35)$ in the audition.

A corresponding t-test on each score of the pre-experimental questionnaire showed a significant difference $(t(19) = 2.87, p < 0.05)$ in the psychological tension level. A corresponding t-test on each score of the post-experimental questionnaire showed a significant difference $(t(19) = 2.89, p < 0.05)$ in the psychological tension level. There were also significant differences for self-confidence $(t(19) = 2.89, p < 0.05)$. For performance, the difference between practice and audition tended to be significant $(t(19) = 1.78, p < 0.10)$.

5 Discussion

The results of the experiment indicated that there were significant differences in the average heart rate and responses to the psychological tension questionnaire between the practice and audition environments, respectively. Related to this, the variability of the movement of the bad group is significantly greater than that of the good group (see Fig. 7). This aligns with the reported effect of ascent on movement timing variability [4,6,13,16]. These results indicate that a pressure-inducing audition environment was successfully created.

Next, when looking at the average frame-to-frame changes in the depth sensor data, we observed that the good group that showed improved performance in the audition environment tended to show significantly larger movements compared to the bad group that shows inadequate performance. Therefore, encouraging large physical movements during rehearsal may help prevent choking under pressure and improve performance. It may be effective to develop a system that encourages users to move their bodies more than usual during practice sessions. For example, a related study [17] suggests that presenting a sample video of oneself dancing can contribute to choreography mastery. In addition, Regulating the bass drum's sound pressure [18] may encourage larger movements. By integrating the above techniques, it may be possible to stimulate greater physical movement and optimize dance performance in an audition environment.

When looking at the average heart rate, we observed that the good group tended to have a significantly lower heart rate compared to the bad group (see Fig. 4). This finding suggests that reducing the average heart rate during rehearsal may improve the success of dance performances in an audition environment. For example, Suzuki et al. [14] have made attempts to regulate the tempo of musical performances by providing heartbeat information. The implementation of such technology should be considered in terms of coping with choking under pressure.

From a creative perspective, it is possible that dancers can be empowered to express themselves through the application utilizing pressure. The ability to control pressure not only facilitates agility but also the modulation of physical expression influenced by it, leading to an expansion of the range of physical expression. In the future, we plan to investigate the correlation between body movements and choking under pressure, potentially leading to the emergence of novel forms of expression. Also, It may be possible to develop a system that predicts pressure based on motion and physiological data, thus facilitating the estimation of performance, and ultimately, improving declining performance quality. For example, even if performance quality is reduced due to pressure, the utilization of exoskeletal robots [8] or mobile robots, may harmonize the appearance of movement and thereby maintain or augment performance quality[5]. We expect that the harmonization of movement appearance through exoskeletal robots will maintain or augment performance quality in terms of appearance.

6 Conclusion

In this paper, in an attempt to differentiate between individuals who effectively coped with pressure-induced "choking under pressure" and those who do not, we collected and analyzed the motion and physiological data of auditionees during the dance audition judging process. The analysis results indicated that auditionees who struggled to manage choking under pressure showed significantly smaller physical movements in the practice environment compared to those who effectively cope with the choking under pressure. These results provide essential insights into the behavioral and physiological aspects of performance under pressure, setting the stage for future research directed at developing targeted support methods to aid individuals in managing stress-related performance challenges.

Acknowledgements. This work was supported by JSPS KAKENHI Grant Number JP23K17022, JP22H00090, JP24K21505, and JST-Moonshot R&D Grant JPMJMS2012. We would like to express our deep appreciation to Mr. Akihiko Hashimoto, Mr. Minoru Fujimoto, the staff and students of Tokyo School of MUSIC & DANCE, and the members of MPLUSPLUS Co., Ltd. for their invaluable assistance in conducting the experiments.

References

1. Baumeister, R.F.: Choking under pressure: self-consciousness and paradoxical effects of incentives on skillful performance. J. Pers. Soc. Psychol. **6**(3), 610–620 (1984)
2. Fujimoto, M.: Mplusplus co.,ltd. (2015). http://www.minorufujimoto.com/
3. Futami, K., Terada, T., Tsukamoto, M.: Success imprinter: a method for controlling mental preparedness using psychological conditioned information. In: Proceedings of the 7th Augmented Human International Conference 2016, AH 2016. pp. 1–8 (2016)
4. Gray, R.: Attending to the execution of a complex sensorimotor skill: expertise differences, choking, and slumps. J. Exp. Psychol. **10**(1), 42–54 (2004)

---

[5] https://jizai-arms.com/.

5. Hashimoto, A.: Splendid entity co., ltd. (2021). https://www.splendid-entity.com/
6. Higuchi, T., Imanaka, K., Hatayama, T.: Freezing degrees of freedom under stress: kinematic evidence of constrained movement strategies. J. Human Mov. Sci. **21**(5), 831–846 (2002)
7. Hill, D.M., Hanton, S., Matthews, N., Fleming, S.: A qualitative exploration of choking in elite golf. J. Clin. Sport Psychol. **4**(3), 221–240 (2010)
8. Ladenheim, K., McNish, R., Rizvi, W., LaViers, A.: Live dance performance investigating the feminine cyborg metaphor with a motion-activated wearable robot. In: Proceedings of the 2020 ACM/IEEE International Conference on Human-Robot Interaction, HRI 2020, p. 243-251 (2020)
9. Lautenbach, F., Laborde, S., Mesagno, C., Lobinger, B.H., Achtzehn, S., Arimond, F.: Nonautomated pre-performance routine in tennis: an intervention study. J. Appl. Sport Psychol. **27**(2), 123–131 (2015)
10. Matsumura, S., Watanabe, K., Saijo, N., Ooishi, Y., Kimura, T., Kashino, M.: Positive relationship between precompetitive sympathetic predominance and competitive performance in elite extreme sports athletes. Front. Sports Active Living **3** (2021)
11. Mesagno, C., Hill, D.M., Larkin, P.: Examining the accuracy and in-game performance effects between pre- and post-performance routines: a mixed methods study. J. Psychol. Sport Exerc. **19**, 85–94 (2015)
12. Mesagno, C., Marchant, D., Morris, T.: A pre-performance routine to alleviate choking in "choking-susceptible" athletes. J. Sport Psychol. **22**(4), 439–457 (2008)
13. Sekiya, H., Tanaka, Y.: Movement modifications related to psychological pressure in a table tennis forehand task. J. Percept. Motor Skills **126**(1), 143–156 (2019)
14. Suzuki, D., Takegawa, Y., Terada, T., Tsukamoto, M.: A heart rate presentation system for keeping music tempo in live performance. In: Proceedings of 2013 IEEE 2nd Global Conference on Consumer Electronics, GCCE 2013, pp. 177–181 (2013). https://doi.org/10.1109/GCCE.2013.6664791
15. Tagami, S., Yoshida, S., Ogawa, N., Narumi, T., Tanikawa, T., Hirose, M.: Routine++: implementing pre-performance routine in a short time with an artificial success simulator. In: Proceedings of the 8th Augmented Human International Conference, AH 2017, pp. 1–9 (2017)
16. Tanaka, Y., Sekiya, H.: The influence of monetary reward and punishment on psychological, physiological, behavioral and performance aspects of a golf putting task. J. Human Mov. Sci. **30**(6), 1115–1128 (2011)
17. Tsuchida, S., et al.: Dance practice system that shows what you would look like if you could master the dance. In: Proceedings of the 8th International Conference on Movement and Computing, MOCO 2022, pp. 1–8 (2022)
18. Van Dyck, E., Moelants, D., Demey, M., Deweppe, A., Coussement, P., Leman, M.: The impact of the bass drum on human dance movement. J. Music Percept. **30**(4), 349–359 (2013)
19. Yoshie, M., Kudo, K., Murakoshi, T., Ohtsuki, T.: Music performance anxiety in skilled pianists: effects of social-evaluative performance situation on subjective, autonomic, and electromyographic reactions. J. Exp. Brain Res. **199**(2), 117 (2009)
20. Yoshie, M., Nagai, Y., Critchley, H.D., Harrison, N.A.: Why i tense up when you watch me: inferior parietal cortex mediates an audience's influence on motor performance. J. Scientific Rep. **6**(1), 19305 (2016)

A Method for Estimating the Force Applied on the Forearm Using PPG Sensors

Ryo Watabe and Kazuya Murao(✉)

Ritsumeikan University, Osaka, Japan
`ryo.watabe@iis.ise.ritsumei.ac.jp, murao@fc.ritsumei.ac.jp`

Abstract. This study proposes estimating forearm pressure using a PPG sensor in a smartwatch or activity meter. The method involves creating a regression model that estimates the applied pressure by analyzing changes in the local maximum values of pulse waves before and after the pressure is applied. Experiments with five subjects evaluated the method. The individual evaluation model, using only the user's data, had an average coefficient of determination of 0.57 and an MAE of 1.60 Kg. The total evaluation model, using all subjects' data, had a coefficient of determination of 0.53 and an MAE of 1.97 Kg.

Keywords: Wearable device · Pulse wave · Force estimation

1 Introduction

Wearable devices can be worn on the body, allowing for hands-free use while collecting biometric data through sensors like pulse wave. Suppose that human tactile information can be obtained, the sensations the human body receives can be recorded and communicated to others via robots and actuators, enabling the sharing of sensations and experiences that are difficult to express in language. This study proposes a method to estimate the magnitude of pressure applied to the forearm using a PPG sensor attached to the fingertip. Using the proposed method, the user only needs to wear a wearable device equipped with a PPG sensor to obtain tactile information. This reduces motion restrictions and discomfort compared to conventional methods that require the user to wrap a cloth or other material around the arm to measure pressure.

2 Related Work

Ham et al. [2] proposed a wristwatch-type device as an input device for smart glasses. The device is equipped with a touch panel and an inertial measurement unit. Matsumoto et al. [3] proposed a grip strength measurement method using a softball and a monocular camera. This system estimates grip strength from finger angles with a monocular camera. Funato et al. [1] propose a method for measuring grip strength using bone-conducted sound sensing. A wearable device with a vibration-generating actuator and a contact microphone is used.

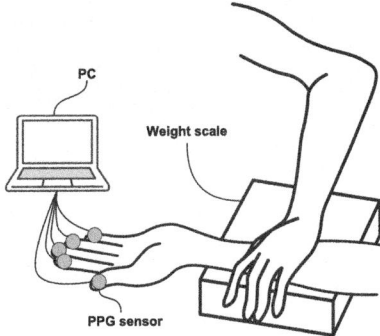

Fig. 1. Preliminary experiment environment to investigate the relationship between pulse waves and pressure.

3 Proposed Method

This section describes a method for estimating the magnitude of pressure applied to the forearm from a PPG sensor attached to the finger.

3.1 Preliminary Experiment

A preliminary experiment was conducted to confirm the calculation between PPG sensor values and the magnitude of pressure applied to the forearm. One subject (male, 22 years old) joined the experiment. He placed his forearm on the scale as shown in Fig. 1, and one of the authors pressed down on the subject's forearm with the palm of the author's hand. The amount of pressure applied was 1, 2, 5, 8, 11, 13 [kg], and the pulse wave was measured three times for 10 s at each pressure. The correlation coefficient is –0.9436, indicating a strong negative correlation between the pulse wave sensor value and the force applied to the forearm.

3.2 Pulse Wave Sensing

The proposed method estimates pressure using pulse wave data obtained from the fingers at a certain time. Let $p(t)$ be the pulse wave measurement at time t obtained by the PPG sensor.

3.3 Local Maximum Detection

The local maximum value is detected for $p(i)$ when i varies from 0 to T. T is the length of the pulse wave measurement. An example of the result of the local maximum detection for $p(t)$ of the pulse wave measurement when the forearm is pressured after the normal condition without pressurization is shown in Fig. 2. The detected local maximum values are stored in array V. Then, let $\text{len}(V)$

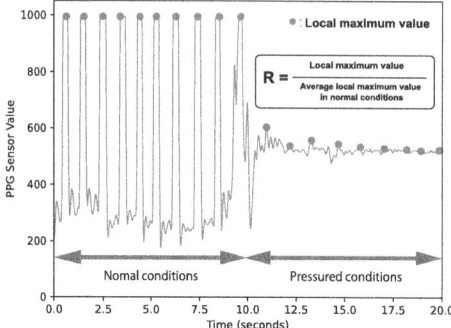

Fig. 2. Pulse wave during normal and pressured conditions.

denote the number of elements in V. In addition, as a calibration process, no force is applied to the forearm for 10 s after the start of pulse wave detection. The average m of the local maximum values of the pulse wave in normal conditions is calculated by $m = \frac{1}{\text{len}(M)} \sum_{t=0}^{\text{len}(M)} M[t]$. The m is used as the reference value for calculating the rate of change of the pulse wave, as described in the next section.

3.4 Local Maximum Value Change Rate Calculation

The rate of change in the local maximum values changed by forearm pressure is calculated. Let r be the rate at the local maximum value at any element $V[j]$ of V has changed due to forearm pressure. Using the average of the local maximum value m in normal conditions and setting $\text{len}(V)$ as the number of elements in V, r can be calculated by $r[j] = \frac{V[j]}{m}, \quad 0 \leq j \leq \text{len}(V)$.

3.5 Model Construction

Training data were first obtained to construct the regression model. The training data consisted of the magnitude of pressure applied to the forearm and the rate of change of the pulse wave. PPG sensors were attached to all fingers, and pulse waves were measured by applying pressure to the forearm at four different intensities. The pulse waves measured from all fingers were summed to create a composite pulse wave. The pressure stages were 2, 5, 8, and 11 [kg], and pulse wave data were obtained at each pressure stage. For calibration, pulse wave measurement was conducted with no force applied to the forearm for 10 s after the start of pulse wave data acquisition, and the average of the local maximum values of the composite pulse wave during the 10 s was m_S. In the next 10 s, the forearm is pressured with n kg in order to check the pulse wave change when the forearm is pressured. Let M_n be the local maximum value of the composite pulse wave obtained at any time during pulse wave measurement, and let R_n be the ratio of the local maximum value changed by the pressure. R_n

is calculated by $R_n = \frac{M_n}{m}$. Since the obtained data include outliers, the top 10% and bottom 10% of R_n when pressurized by n kg are excluded, and the ratio after exclusion is R'_n. Using R'_n, the rate of change of the local maximum value of the composite pulse wave and the pressure applied to the forearm is estimated using a single regression analysis. The rate of change of the local maximum value is the explanatory variable, and the magnitude of the pressure is the objective variable.

3.6 Pressure Estimation

The proposed method is assumed to be used when the forearm is placed on a hard floor or table with the palm facing upwards, as shown in Fig. 1. In that situation, the pressure applied to the forearm by the palm can be estimated. The estimation is conducted by using the rate of change between the local maximum value of the pulse wave when the forearm is not pressured and the local maximum value of the pulse wave in the pressured state and applying it to the learning model that has been constructed previously.

4 Evaluation

This section describes an experiment to evaluate the effectiveness of the proposed method.

4.1 Setup

Five subjects (A~E, all male, mean age 22.8 years) joined an experiment to estimate the pressure applied to the forearm. As shown in Fig. 1, the subjects wore a PPG sensor on each of the five fingers of their left hand, placed their left arm on a weight scale (Tanita Corporation, THA-528)[1] with the palm facing upward, and a third person applied pressure by pressing down on the subjects' forearm. Two training models were created: a model learned pulse wave data obtained from five fingers ("five-finger data"), and a model learned pulse wave data obtained only from the index finger ("index finger data"). Each data was evaluated using an individual evaluation model created for each subject, and a total evaluation model was created using the training data of all subjects. In the five-finger data, pulse wave data of all fingers were added together to obtain a one-dimensional time series waveform. For the five-finger data, pulse wave measurements were taken three times at each of four levels of pressure applied to the forearm, each time for 20 s. For the test data, pulse waves were measured twice at each of the four levels of pressure applied to the forearm for 20 s each time. The coefficient of determination and Mean Absolute Error (MAE) were used as evaluation indices.

---

[1] https://www.tanita.co.jp/product/bathroomscale-babyscale/3064/.

Table 1. Pressure estimation results (five-finger data).

	Subjects	A	B	C	D	E	Ave.
Individual model	R^2	0.73	0.70	0.29	0.35	0.79	0.57
	MAE[kg]	1.38	1.46	2.18	2.01	0.96	1.60
Total model	R^2	0.63	0.76	0.26	0.35	0.63	0.53
	MAE[kg]	2.11	1.41	2.28	2.19	1.86	1.97

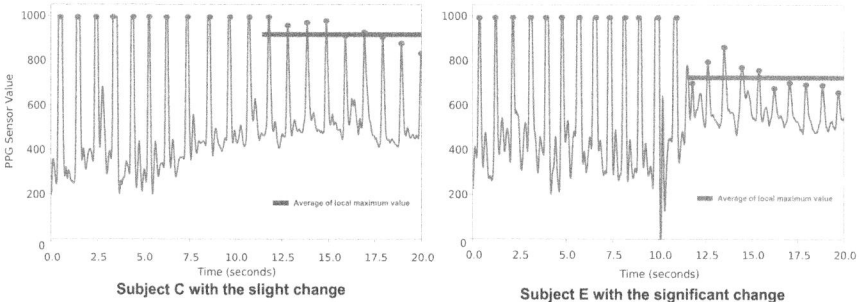

Fig. 3. Pulse wave of two subjects when the same magnitude of pressure is applied

4.2 Five-Finger Data Results

The coefficient of determination and MAE of the pressure estimation results for the individual evaluation model, in which a model was created for each subject using five-finger pulse wave data, and for the total evaluation model, in which a model was created using the data of all subjects, are shown in Table 1. In the individual evaluation model, the average coefficient of determination was 0.57, and the average MAE was 1.60 Kg. In the total evaluation model, the average coefficient of determination was 0.53, and the average MAE was 1.97 Kg. Figure 3 shows the pulse wave of subjects C and E when the same magnitude of pressure was applied to them. As can be seen from the figure, subject C had a slight change in pulse wave when the same amount of pressure was used, while subject E had a significant change.

4.3 Index Finger Data Results

The coefficient of determination and MAE of the pressure estimation results for the individual evaluation model, in which a model was created for each subject using the index finger pulse wave data, and for the total evaluation model, in which a model was created using data from all subjects, are shown in Table 2. In the individual evaluation model, the average coefficient of determination was 0.46, and the average MAE was 1.76 Kg. In the total evaluation model, the mean coefficient of determination was 0.49, and the mean MAE was 1.66 Kg. Like the five-finger data, the individual evaluation model had a more significant average

Table 2. Pressure estimation results (index finger data).

	Subjects	A	B	C	D	E	Ave.
Individual model	R^2	0.53	0.63	0.10	0.45	0.57	0.46
	MAE[kg]	1.83	1.71	1.83	1.68	1.75	1.76
Total model	R^2	0.66	0.50	0.19	0.48	0.63	0.49
	MAE[kg]	1.41	1.83	1.85	1.86	1.38	1.66

coefficient of determination and a smaller mean MAE than the total evaluation model for the index-finger data. Subjects B and E had higher coefficients of determination and smaller MAE. This is because the forearm pressure position might have been located in the vessels that easily affected the index finger vessels. On the other hand, subjects C and D showed low accuracy. This might be because the forearm pressure position set in the evaluation experiment had little effect on the index finger blood vessels. However, MAE was not significantly higher than that of the other subjects. This is because the variance of the total data was small, which may have resulted in a more minor difference between the predicted and measured values throughout the total data.

5 Conclusion

This paper proposed a method to estimate tactile measurement using changes in pulse waves caused by pressure applied to the forearm. As a result of the experiment, the average coefficient of determination was 0.57, the average MAE was 1.60 Kg for the individual evaluation model using five-finger pulse wave data, and the average coefficient of determination was 0.53. The average MAE was 1.97 Kg for the total evaluation model.

References

1. Funato, N., Takemura, K.: Grip force estimation by emitting vibration. In: UIST 2017 Adjunct, pp. 141–142 (2017). https://doi.org/10.1145/3131785.3131829
2. Ham, J., Hong, J., Jang, Y., Ko, S.H., Woo, W.: Smart wristband: touch-and-motion-tracking wearable 3d input device for smart glasses. In: Distributed, Ambient, and Pervasive Interactions, pp. 109–118 (2014). https://doi.org/10.1007/978-3-319-07788-8_11
3. Matsumoto, N., Fujita, K., Sugiura, Y.: Estimation of grip strength using monocular camera for home-based hand rehabilitation. SICE J. Control Meas. Syst. Integrat. **14**(1), 1–11 (2021). https://doi.org/10.1080/18824889.2020.1863612

Good Vibes! Towards Phone-to-User Authentication Through Wristwatch Vibrations

Jakob Dittrich[1,2](✉) and Rainhard Dieter Findling[1,3](✉)

[1] SAIL Department, University of Applied Sciences Upper Austria, Wels, Austria
S2210455017@fhooe.at, rainhard.findling@fh-hagenberg.at
[2] Ventopay GmbH, Hagenberg im Mühlkreis, Austria
[3] Google LLC, Menlo Park, USA

Abstract. While mobile devices frequently require users to authenticate to prevent unauthorized access, mobile devices typically do not authenticate to their users. This leaves room for users to unwittingly interact with different mobile devices. We present GoodVibes authentication, a variant of mobile device-to-user authentication, where the user's phone authenticates to the user through their wristwatch vibrating in their pre-selected authentication vibration pattern. We implement GoodVibes authentication as an Android prototype, evaluate different authentication scenarios with 30 participants, and find users to be able to well recognize and distinguish their authentication vibration pattern from different patters, from unrelated vibrations, and from the pattern being absent.

Keywords: Mobile device-to-user authentication · vibration pattern · hardware phishing attack · phone · wristwatch

1 Introduction

Authentication with mobile devices is usually done from users towards devices (user-to-device authentication), using methods such as PINs, passwords, unlock patterns, or biometrics. That devices typically do not authenticate towards their users leaves room for accidentally interacting with other devices, as well as for targeted hardware phishing attacks [1]. Device-to-user authentication [2], through which users can verify the authenticity of their device, is one way to reduce the risk of such errors and attacks.

In this paper we present GoodVibes authentication, which is a variant of device-to-user authentication with multiple mobile devices. When users start to interact with their phone, thereby wake the device screen, the phone authenticates to them by making the paired wristwatch vibrate in their pre-selected authentication vibration pattern. We implement GoodVibes authentication as an Android prototype and evaluate it with 30 participants to answer the following research questions: RQ1: How well can users recognize when a phone authenticates to them through a wristwatch vibration pattern, and when this vibration pattern is absent, incorrect, or occurs without them interacting with the phone? RQ2: How do users perceive the usability of a phone authenticating to them through a wristwatch vibration pattern?

2 Related Work

Much prior work focuses on mobile user-to-device authentication through knowledge, tokens, or biometrics [3,4]. Such work does not address devices authenticating to users, hence leaves room for users to accidentally interact with other devices, and for targeted hardware phishing attacks [1]. Similar to website-based phishing, hardware phishing attacks try to trick users to interact with phishing devices that appear identical to the user owned devices. When users attempt to unlock such a device with their PIN, password, unlock pattern, or biometrics, they unwittingly disclose this authentication secret to the attackers. As attackers are already in possession of the user device from previously replacing it with the phishing device, they can immediately use that secret to access the user device and the private data on it.

Device-to-user authentication [2] aims to make it easier for users to recognize if they would interact with another device than their own. Prior research investigates phones authenticating to their users through the phone itself vibrating in an authentication pattern when the user wakes the device screen [1]. Findings indicate that users can recognize and distinguish such vibrations (median success rate of 97.5%). However, physical access to the user phone also gives attackers access to the vibration pattern. This allows them to configure the phishing device with the same vibration. GoodVibes authentication addresses this shortcoming, as attackers in control of the locked user phone have no access to the authentication vibration pattern.

Other vibration-based authentication includes Vibrate-to-Unlock [5], which uses vibration patterns on mobile phones to authenticate users to RFID tags. While this approach uses vibrations, it does so to perform user-to-device authentication, hence does not address the need for device-to-user authentication. Prior work on website-to-user authentication investigates watermarking [6] and embedding secrets in website content [7], which aims to make it challenging for attackers to correctly mimic a legitimate website. This requires users to visually inspect the website for the watermark or embedded secret in order to detect phishing attempts.

3 GoodVibes Authentication

To enroll, the user installs the GoodVibes application on their paired phone and wristwatch, and in the application selects the authentication vibration pattern in which the wristwatch should vibrate to indicate that their phone is authenticating to them.

The GoodVibes authentication process works as follows (Fig. 1): when the user starts to interact with their phone, thereby wakes the device screen (1), the

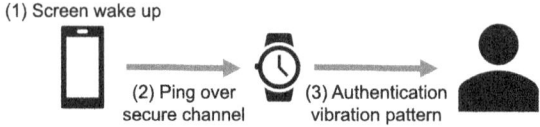

Fig. 1. Overview of the GoodVibes authentication process.

phone sends a ping to the paired wristwatch over the secure channel that exists as a result of the devices being paired (2). The wristwatch receives the ping and vibrates in the user-chosen authentication vibration pattern (3). The user feels the wristwatch vibrating in their authentication vibration pattern, which informs them that they are interacting with their phone.

If the wristwatch would not vibrate, or vibrate in a different pattern, then this would indicate to the user that they might be interacting with a phone that is not theirs. Also, if the user would feel their authentication vibration pattern without interacting with their phone, then this would indicate to them that someone else might be interacting with their phone.

4 Evaluation

We implement GoodVibes authentication as a two-part prototype app[1] for a paired Android phone and Android wristwatch, which can communicate securely with each other over their paired Bluetooth channel. The prototype app can also be controlled remotely by the study supervisor to inject or suppress vibrations, to simulate and evaluate different situational authentication scenarios (Sect. 4.2). As authentication vibration patterns we use the "2" and the "1 3" patterns from [1], with vibration bursts of 60 ms, vibration pauses between bursts of 200 ms, and a total duration of 180 ms and 560 ms, respectively.

4.1 Evaluation Procedure

A supervisor provided instructions and monitored the session. Participants answered demographic and technical knowledge questions. They then took a seat at a desk in an empty office room where only supervisor and participant were present, with the phone on the desk in front of them, and attached the wristwatch to their preferred hand. 50% of participants then chose their preferred authentication vibration pattern in the GoodVibes app, while the other 50% were randomly assigned an authentication vibration pattern. They were instructed to indicate any case of the wristwatch not vibrating in their personal authentication vibration pattern when they started to interact with the phone, and of the wristwatch vibrating in their personal authentication pattern without them having started to interact with the phone. They were then engaged in

---

[1] The GoodVibes authentication prototype app is publicly available at https://github.com/Jakob-Dittrich/GoodVibesAuth.

various tasks and objectives, such as browsing a news website, playing a game, reading a page from a book, or writing a message. This simulated situations of concentration and exposure to distraction, and included points of purposefully starting and stopping to interact with the phone. Participants did those tasks for roughly 35 min, during which they were exposed to 5 different situational authentication scenarios (Sect. 4.2), 24 times in total (9, 6, 3, 3, and 3 times each), in a fixed order. They then completed a questionnaire with 5 Likert-scale questions to evaluate the usability of GoodVibes authentication. Participants were recruited for our evaluation study through word of mouth among students of the University of Applied Sciences Upper Austria and their relatives and friends. Participants received no compensation for their participation. 30 participants (mean age 34.1 years, age std 12.3; 17 female, 13 male, 0 other) completed the study, resulting in 720 authentication results and 60 questionnaire answers.

4.2 Evaluation Scenarios

We evaluate GoodVibes authentication in 5 scenarios that cover different cases where users could incorrectly identify authentication vibration patterns or their absence.

In scenario 1, when the user starts to interact with their phone, the wristwatch vibrates in their personal authentication vibration pattern. We measure how often users incorrectly recognize this as the vibration being absent or as not being theirs.

In scenario 2, without the user starting to interact with their phone, the wristwatch vibrates in a pattern that is not their personal authentication vibration pattern, simulating unrelated notifications, alerts, or alike. We measure how often users incorrectly recognize this as their personal authentication vibration pattern.

In scenario 3, without the user starting to interact with their phone, the wristwatch vibrates in their personal authentication vibration pattern. We measure how often users correctly identify this as their personal authentication vibration pattern.

In scenario 4, when the user starts to interact with their phone, the wristwatch does not vibrate. We measure how often users correctly identify this lack of vibration.

In scenario 5, when the user starts to interact with their phone, the wristwatch vibrates in a different pattern than their personal authentication vibration pattern. We measure how often users correctly identify this mismatch.

5 Results and Discussion

Overall, participants recognized vibrations and their absence well. In scenario 1, participants incorrectly thought the vibration was absent or not their authentication vibration pattern 1% of the time. This indicates that users can reasonably well recognize their authentication vibration pattern in normal authentication situations, and that GoodVibes authentication seems to cause a reasonably low false alert rate.

In scenario 2, participants recognized 97% of the time that the vibration was unrelated to their personal authentication vibration pattern. Similar to the results of scenario 1, this too indicates that users can reasonably well distinguish between GoodVibes authentication vibrations and unrelated vibrations. In the remaining cases (3%) users could easily quickly check their phone's status to ensure that it is actually secure. This seems a sufficiently low false alert rate to not overly annoy GoodVibes authentication users, which questionnaire findings seem to confirm (see below).

In scenario 3, participants recognized 98% of the time that the vibration was their personal authentication pattern without them having started to interact with their phone. This indicates that GoodVibes authentication would likely help users to recognize that someone else started to use their phone, e.g. another person mistaking the phone for theirs, or someone having stolen the phone – and in turn help the user to take timely countermeasures.

In scenario 4 and 5, participants recognized 91% of the time if their wristwatch did not vibrate, and 94% of the time if their wristwatch vibrated in a pattern that was not their personal authentication vibration pattern. Though those error rates are slightly higher than in the scenarios above, this indicates that GoodVibes authentication would likely also help users to recognize cases of them mistaking another phone as theirs, cases of hardware phishing attacks, and cases of their wristwatch coincidentally vibrating for a different reason at the same time. This indicates that GoodVibes authentication could help users to not continue their user-to-device authentication in those moments, thereby protecting their authentication secret towards their phone.

Participants with prior smartwatch experience more often correctly recognized vibrations or their absence than participants without prior smartwatch experience. Over all scenarios combined, 9 participants who use a smartwatch daily achieved 97% correct vibration recognition, and 8 participants who had sometimes used a smartwatch achieved 99% – while 13 participants without prior smartwatch experience achieved 89%. This indicates that users seem able to learn to recognize and distinguish wristwatch vibrations, which in turn indicates that GoodVibes authentication users without prior smartwatch experience should be able to over time learn to distinguish their authentication vibration pattern from other vibrations. Also, over all scenarios combined, participants who could choose their personal authentication vibration pattern achieved better results over participants who were assigned a pattern (2% and 5% overall error rate, respectively). This indicates that it is beneficial to let users choose which vibration pattern they prefer to use with their GoodVibes authentication.

Questionnaire results indicate that participants found GoodVibes authentication easy to use (mean 4.9, std 0.3, from 1 "very difficult" to 5 "very easy"), fast to use (mean 5, std 0, from 1 "very slow" to 5 "very fast"), and easy to adapt to (mean 4.9, std 0.3, from 1 "very hard" to 5 "very easy"). Slightly more users considered it likely than unlikely that they would use GoodVibes authentication if it were available today (mean 3.4, std 0.9, from 1 "very unlikely" to 5 "very likely").

In summary we can answer the posed research questions as follows: RQ1: users seem to well recognize wristwatch vibration patterns through which their phone would authenticate to them (99%), and also to well distinguish them from unrelated vibrations (97%). Users furthermore seem to recognize well if their authentication vibration pattern occurs without them interacting with their phone (98%), as well as when they expect the pattern to occur but it instead is absent (91%) or different (94%). RQ2: users seem to find their phone authenticating to them through wristwatch vibrations easy to use (4.9/5), fast to use (5/5), easy to adapt to (4.9/5), and slightly more users considered it likely than unlikely that they would use such an approach (3.4/5).

6 Conclusion

We presented GoodVibes authentication, where phones authenticate to their users through vibrations of their paired wristwatch. We evaluated how well users can recognize and distinguish such authentication vibration patterns, or their absence, in 5 different authentication scenarios, and how users perceive the usability of such authentication vibrations. Findings include that users seem to be able to well recognize and distinguish their authentication vibration pattern from other vibrations, their pattern occurring without them interacting with their phone, as well as the pattern being absent or different. Users seem to perceive the usability of their phone authenticating to them over vibrations of their wristwatch as good.

Our work is limited by accounting only for a limited threat model without sophisticated attackers, and by assessing vibration pattern recognizably and usability only in a lab study environment with sitting users and short total usage duration. Future research could expand our work by considering a wider threat model with different attackers, and by assessing outside-lab vibration pattern recognizably and usability in a long-term real-world study where a larger number of participants is exposed to diverse distractions and environmental factors that occur in their everyday lives.

References

1. Findling, R.D., Mayrhofer, R.: Towards device-to-user authentication: protecting against phishing hardware by ensuring mobile device authenticity using vibration patterns. In: MUM 2015, pp. 131–135. ACM, New York (2015). https://doi.org/10.1145/2836041.2836053
2. Mayrhofer, R., Sigg, S.: Adversary models for mobile device authentication. ACM Comput. Surv. **54**(9) (2021). https://doi.org/10.1145/3477601
3. Meng, W., Wong, D.S., Furnell, S., Zhou, J.: Surveying the development of biometric user authentication on mobile phones. IEEE Commun. Surv. Tutor. **17**(3), 1268–1293 (2015). https://doi.org/10.1109/COMST.2014.2386915

4. Shah, S.W., Kanhere, S.S.: Recent trends in user authentication - a survey. IEEE Access **7**, 112505–112519 (2019). https://doi.org/10.1109/ACCESS.2019.2932400
5. Saxena, N., Uddin, M.B., Voris, J., Asokan, N.: Vibrate-to-unlock: mobile phone assisted user authentication to multiple personal RFID tags. In: PerCom 2011, pp. 181–188 (2011). https://doi.org/10.1109/PERCOM.2011.5767583
6. Singh, A.P., Kumar, V., Sengar, S.S., Wairiya, M.: Detection and prevention of phishing attack using dynamic watermarking. In: Das, V.V., Thomas, G., Lumban Gaol, F. (eds.) AIM 2011. CCIS, vol. 147, pp. 132–137. Springer, Heidelberg (2011). https://doi.org/10.1007/978-3-642-20573-6_21
7. Varshney, G., Joshi, R.C., Sardana, A.: Personal secret information based authentication towards preventing phishing attacks. In: ACITY 2012, pp. 31–42. Springer, Heidelberg (2012). https://doi.org/10.1007/978-3-642-31513-8_4

A Method for Embedding Information Into Acceleration Data Using Resonant Frequency Sound to Capacitive Accelerometers

Takeru Yokoyama[ID] and Kazuya Murao[✉][ID]

Ritsumeikan University, Osaka, Japan
takeru.yokoyama@iis.ise.ritsumei.ac.jp, murao@fc.ritsumei.ac.jp

Abstract. This paper presents a method to embed arbitrary bit sequences into acceleration data by attacking capacitive accelerometers with sound. Using a loudspeaker, sound data representing bit sequences is irradiated to the device, manipulating the acceleration data instantly and continuously. Evaluation experiments showed that the extraction accuracy of 10-bit binary information is 100% from multifunctional sensors placed on the table, 99.7% from a smartphone placed on the table, 100% from multifunctional sensors worn at the wrist, and 98% from a smartphone held in the hand.

Keywords: Accelerometer · Smartphone · Data embedding

1 Introduction

An attack has been proposed to manipulate the measured acceleration values of capacitive accelerometers by irradiating them with sound [2]. In this study, a method is proposed for embedding specific bit sequences in acceleration data by continuously exposing the accelerometer to the presence or absence of sound. The sound data is transmitted to the accelerometer via a loudspeaker, causing a change in the acceleration data, which is then analyzed to extract the bit string. The duration of the sound used to represent a bit is minimized to maximize throughput while still ensuring that it is long enough for the accelerometer to measure it accurately. The optimal duration is determined through preliminary experiments. The experiment evaluates the accuracy of extracting the embedded information from the device.

2 Related Work

This section introduces research using sound waves, the resonance frequency of capacitive accelerometers, to modify accelerometer data. Trippel et al. [2] introduce an attack on accelerometers by irradiating sound waves to induce changes

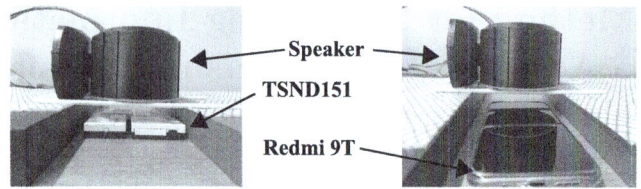

Fig. 1. Sensors and speaker settings in the preliminary experiment.

in the sensor data. Lee et al. [1] proposed an individual sensor authentication method that takes advantage of the slight individual differences in the changes induced in accelerometers by irradiating them with sound waves. There has been research on making accelerometers and angular velocity sensors resonant with sound waves to modify their values. To our knowledge, there is no technology for embedding arbitrary information using resonant frequency sound.

3 Preliminary Experiments

This section describes preliminary experiments conducted to investigate the environment and conditions of sound wave irradiation for altering the acceleration values. The accelerometers used are the MPU-9250 manufactured by InvenSense built into the TSND151 multifunctional sensor manufactured by ATR-Promotions[1] and an accelerometer built into the Redmi 9T smartphone manufactured by Xiaomi[2]. The sound wave irradiation setup used the Pyramid TW28 tweeter loudspeaker[3] and the YAMAHA A-S301 amplifier[4] based on the paper [2]. The loudspeaker was placed 3 cm away from the table surface, facing downwards, with the sensors positioned between the loudspeaker and the ground (Fig. 1). The sounds used for irradiation were created using the sound editing software Audacity[5] and played on a PC. The frequency of sound, sound pressure, and sound length are investigated in the preliminary experiment.

From the experiment, it was found that the acceleration data can be significantly changed when the multifunctional sensors are irradiated with sound at a frequency of 5,200 Hz, a sound pressure of 126 dB or higher, and an irradiation time of 10 ms or longer, and when the smartphone is irradiated with sound at a frequency of 3,240 Hz, a sound pressure of 115 dB or higher, and an irradiation time of 50 ms or longer. The interval length before the effects of irradiating converged was the same as the shortest irradiating time affecting the sensor.

---

[1] https://www.atr-p.com/products/TSND121_151.html.
[2] https://www.mi.com/jp/product/redmi-9t.
[3] https://www.carid.com/pyramid/3-75-600w-4-ohm-aluminum-bullet-tweeters-mpn-tw28.html.
[4] https://jp.yamaha.com/products/audio_visual/hifi_components/a-s301/index.html.
[5] https://www.audacityteam.org/.

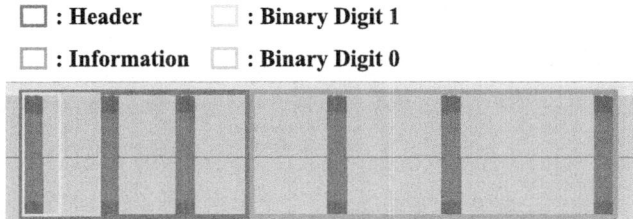

Fig. 2. Sound data representing a 6-bit header [101010] and a 10-bit information part [0010010001].

4 Proposed Method

This section explains a proposed method for embedding bit sequences in accelerometer data through sound wave irradiation. The method comprises three processes: sound data creation, sound irradiation, and information extraction.

4.1 Sound Data Creation

The sound data is created using binary information that needs to be encoded. Each 1-bit sound consists of an acoustic segment, which produces sound if the bit is 1 and remains silent if the bit is 0, and an interval segment, which remains silent regardless of the bit value. The interval segment comes after the acoustic segment because preliminary experiments have shown that it takes a few milliseconds for the reverberation to fade away. The reverberation of sound should not affect the following bit. The sound duration is set to 10 ms for multifunctional sensors and 100 ms for smartphones.

The sound data for a bit sequence comprises two parts: a header, which is a fixed pattern for identification, and an information part, which represents the binary information. The header is a fixed 6-bit pattern and is positioned before the information part. The sound is created from the most significant bit (MSB). Figure 2 illustrates the sound data representing a 6-bit header [101010] and a 10-bit information part [0010010001] with both the acoustic and interval segments set to 10 ms. The header is enclosed in a red frame, and the information is enclosed in a green frame. The most significant bit of the header is 1, creating sound data with sound and a silent interval segment. The following bit is 0, creating sound data with no sound and a silent interval segment, i.e., complete silence.

4.2 Sound Irradiation

The generated sound data is played from a loudspeaker based on the frequency and duration of irradiation determined in the preliminary experiment. As shown in Fig. 3, the acceleration data changes significantly during the sound wave irradiating time and returns to the original state during the interval time.

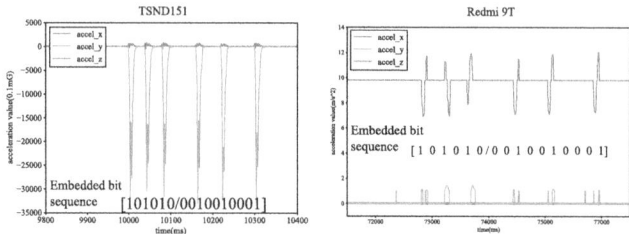

Fig. 3. Examples of acceleration values of multifunctional sensors and smartphone when the information part is [0010010001].

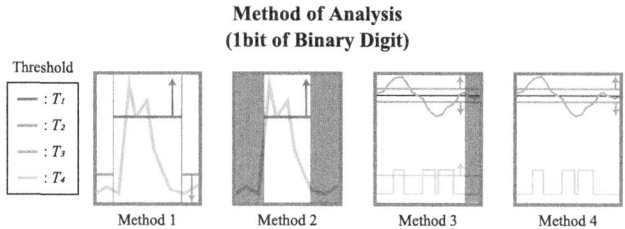

Fig. 4. Bit decoding method.

4.3 Information Extraction

The header is identified, and the information is extracted.

Bit Decording. The change in acceleration is completed within the time period of the sound wave irradiation time plus the interval time. Therefore, if the acceleration value in the extracted data reaches the range indicated by the arrows in Fig. 4, it is set to 1. Otherwise, it is set to 0. When dealing with multifunctional sensors, method 1 is used to decode the header. Method 2 is used to decode the information part. In the case of a smartphone, method 3 is used to decode the header. Method 4 is used to decode the information part.

Bit Sequence Extraction. Initially, the header is searched from the start of the accelerometer data. If the header is found, the section following the header is regarded as the information part from which the embedded bit sequence is extracted. A blank time is inserted after the header to mark the start of the information part. The optimal insertion time is evaluated in the Evaluation section.

5 Evaluation

We conducted the experiment to assess the effectiveness of information embedding using the proposed method. We measure the accuracy of information extraction in two scenarios: when the multifunctional sensors and the smartphone

Table 1. Information extraction accuracy in stationary scenario of multifunctional sensors.

Sensor	Blank time					
	0 ms	1 ms	2 ms	3 ms	4 ms	5 ms
1	1.000	1.000	1.000	1.000	1.000	1.000
2	1.000	1.000	1.000	1.000	1.000	1.000
3	1.000	1.000	1.000	1.000	1.000	1.000
4	1.000	1.000	1.000	1.000	1.000	1.000

Table 2. Information extraction accuracy in stationary scenario of smartphone.

Blank time	0 ms	10 ms	20 ms	30 ms	40 ms	50 ms
Accuracy	0.915	0.976	0.991	0.995	0.997	0.997

are stationary (stationary scenario), when the multifunctional sensors are being worn, and when the smartphone is being grasped (wearing and grasping scenario). The header and information parts of the embedded data are set to a fixed 6 bits and 10 bits, respectively. We tested the information parts in two ways: (data 1) 1023 patterns from 0 to 2024 and (data 2) randomly selected ten patterns between 0 and 1023. For the multifunctional sensors, sound data is used with a 10 ms sound part and a 10 ms interval part per bit. The blank time is set in 6 patterns from 0 to 5 [ms] in 1 ms increments. On the other hand, for the smartphone, sound data is used with a 100 ms sound part and a 100 ms interval part per bit. The blank time is set in 6 patterns from 0 to 50 [ms] in 10 ms increments.

5.1 Stationary Scenario

In this scenario, data 1 is irradiated once. Table 1 shows the accuracy of information extraction using the proposed extraction algorithm for multifunctional sensors. All four sensors were able to extract information with 100% accuracy regardless of the length of the blank time. Table 2 shows the accuracy for the smartphone. With a blank time of 40 and 50 ms after header detection, information was extracted with an accuracy of 99.7%.

5.2 Wearing and Grasping Scenarios

The multifunctional sensors are worn on the wrist and the smartphone is grasped. The devices are put close to the loudspeaker as in Fig. 5. In wearing and grasping scenarios, data 2 is irradiated ten times. Table 3 shows the accuracy of worn sensors. Three of four sensors were able to extract the information with 100% accuracy when a blank time was set from 3 to 5 ms. On the other hand, the accuracy decreased when the blank time was short. This decrease was due to a larger discrepancy between the actual irradiated area and the referenced area.

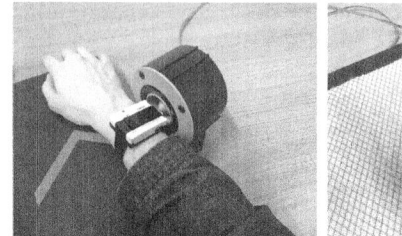

Fig. 5. Sensors in wearing (left) and grasping (right) scenarios.

Table 3. Information extraction accuracy in wearing scenario.

Sensor	Blank time					
	0 ms	1 ms	2 ms	3 ms	4 ms	5 ms
1	0.98	0.99	1.00	1.00	1.00	1.00
2	0.39	0.85	0.98	0.98	0.98	0.98
3	1.00	1.00	1.00	1.00	1.00	1.00
4	0.56	0.85	0.98	1.00	1.00	1.00

Table 4. Information extraction accuracy in grasped scenario.

Blank time	0 ms	10 ms	20 ms	30 ms	40 ms	50 ms
Accuracy	0.87	0.94	0.97	0.97	0.98	0.98

Table 4 shows the accuracy of the grasped smartphone. With a blank time of 40 and 50 [ms] after header detection, information was extracted with an accuracy of 98%.

6 Conclusion

This paper proposed a method to embed arbitrary bit sequences in acceleration data using the sound irradiation attack instantly and continuously. The preliminary experiments examined the best frequency, volume, and sound length. Evaluation experiments showed that the extraction accuracy of 10-bit binary information is 100% from multifunctional sensors placed on the table, 99.7% from a smartphone placed on the table, 100% from multifunctional sensors worn at the wrist, and 98% from a smartphone held in the hand.

References

1. Lee, S., et al.: From attack to identification: mems sensor fingerprinting using acoustic signals. IEEE Internet Things J. **10**, 5447–5460 (2022). https://doi.org/10.1109/JIOT.2022.3221930
2. Trippel, T., et al.: Walnut: waging doubt on the integrity of mems accelerometers with acoustic injection attacks. In: 2017 IEEE European Symposium on Security and Privacy (EuroS&P), pp. 3–18. IEEE (2017). https://doi.org/10.1109/EuroSP.2017.42

Mobile User Experience, Motivation, and Behavior

MEUSec – Method for Enhancing User Experience and Information Security

Max Sauer[✉][iD], Christoph Becker[iD], Andreas Oberweis[iD], Simon Pfeifer[iD], and Jan Sürmeli[iD]

FZI Research Center for Information Technology, 76131 Karlsruhe, Germany
{sauer,christoph.becker,oberweis,pfeifer,suermeli}@fzi.de

Abstract. Digital identity wallets enable the management of digital identities and verification documents such as ID cards and driving licences. This data can be stored efficiently in one place on user devices. Research shows that some of the existing digital identity wallets have user experience and information security deficits. Users struggle to understand the concept of digital identity wallets, personal information is often inadequately secured or released to untrusted parties. Moreover, user experience and information security might influence each other negatively. Hence, it is necessary to consider user experience and information security simultaneously, and to evaluate and improve them together. However, existing methods focus on either aspect and do not consider their interplay. In this paper, we present the MEUSec method to facilitate an analysis and improvement of user experience and information security of digital identity wallets.

Keywords: User Experience · UX · Information Security · Evaluation · Digital Identity Wallets

1 Introduction

Secure digital identity solutions for people, organizations and objects are a key success factor for the digital transformation in areas such as healthcare, mobility or e-government. A particular, user-centric approach is to transfer the idea of a physical wallet into the digital world: A *digital identity wallet* (short: *wallet*) is a software component to manage credentials. In essence, a *credential* is a data record of a claim made about one entity (the holder) by another entity (the issuer), where claims describe properties of the holder (e.g., eye color or serial number) or relationships of the holder with other entities (e.g., parentage or membership). Basic wallet functionality comprises the reception of credentials from issuers and the presentation of credentials to third parties called *verifiers*. Holders retain control over their credentials by deciding which credentials are presented to whom [12].

Successful adoption and wide usage of a wallet require two important properties. First, good user experience (UX) to reduce user errors or simplify operation. Secondly, the wallet should offer a sufficient level of information security

(InfoSec), because credentials may contain personal data that must be protected against misuse. However, high UX and InfoSec for wallets are still the subject of research and are not satisfactory in some of the currently available solutions and therefore need to be improved [5]. An important observation is that UX and InfoSec features can influence each other [1,25].

In this paper, we present our proposed MEUSec method (see Sect. 4), a comprehensive method that facilitates analysis and improvement of UX and InfoSec of wallets. The MEUSec method addresses the interactions of UX and InfoSec and in particular, avoids improving one property at the expense of the other.

The MEUSec method was evaluated on a small scale, that is, by consulting experts from research and industry, especially in the areas of UX, InfoSec and identity management/wallets. Furthermore, the MEUSec method was applied to a rudimentary wallet prototype, i.e. small number of evaluated wallet functions, potential attackers and security relevant components. The lessons learned of this initial evaluation are also described in this paper.

A more thorough, systematic evaluation on an existing wallet is currently conducted, results pending. The MEUSec method has emerged from the context of studying UX and InfoSec of wallets. However, in retrospect it appears feasible to apply the MEUSec method to other software systems – a respective evaluation and the investigation of boundaries are subject of future work.

The paper is structured as follows: After the problem statement in context of related work in Sect. 2 and an introduction to the methodological foundation in Sect. 3, the MEUSec method is presented in Sect. 4. Preliminary evaluation results and design decisions are discussed in Sect. 5, and the paper concludes in Sect. 6.

2 Problem Definition and Related Work

Studies found that state of the art wallets have various UX and InfoSec problems.

- Inexperienced users do not understand how to set up and operate wallets [5]. This can frustrate users or lead to InfoSec problems, such as unwanted sharing of credentials.
- The test subjects of Khayretdinova et al. [5] did not realise where their credentials or data were stored. In some cases, test subjects tried to delete data from the server, even though the data were only stored locally on the smartphone.
- Users have problems with the technical terminology used in wallets, e.g., "Credentials" or "DID" [15], which "ultimately form a barrier to the system's learnability and limit users' confidence to persevere and resolve problems" [6].
- Some wallets also lack help options, such as a tutorial when setting up the wallet that explains the basic functions or FAQs [15,22].
- Users requested a backup and recovery as well as "search" and "sort" functions for their credentials [15].

– Sellung and Kubach [22] did not identify any wallet which would allow to transfer the account and its credentials to another wallet (neither to the same wallet on other smartphones nor to wallets from other providers). This results in a lock-in effect, as switching to another wallet is cumbersome and contradicts the concept of self-sovereign identities (SSI) [12].
– Satybaldy [16] found that some wallets do not have secure authentication procedures to protect the sensitive data in the wallet. In one of the analysed wallets, biometric authentication did not work correctly. In addition, users had problems finding the recovery code and understanding how it works and its benefits.

Therefore, it is important that UX and InfoSec of wallets are increased in order to mitigate aforementioned deficiencies. For that, UX and InfoSec should not be considered separately, as both aspects can influence each other: On the one hand, InfoSec mechanisms can be misused or ignored due to inadequate UX [25]. On the other hand, InfoSec mechanisms can also lead to an inadequate UX, e.g., if they are too difficult [1]. Hence, UX and InfoSec should be evaluated and improved together.

Sauer et al. [17] state the absence of a comprehensive method to evaluate the interactions between UX and InfoSec, but outline promising methods that could be adapted, in particular heuristic walkthrough [21], heuristic evaluation [11], cognitive walkthrough [24] and thinking aloud [9]. Thus, the MEUSec method was developed that adapts those proposed methods.

3 Background

This section explains methods relevant to the MEUSec method. For developing the MEUSec method, the methods compared and proposed by Sauer et al. [17] were adapted:

Thinking aloud is a user-based evaluation method in which test subjects test a software system and continuously express their thoughts. This provides a direct understanding of which UX weaknesses the test subjects encounter during the user test [9].

Cognitive walkthrough is an expert-based evaluation method in which reviewers test a software system and identify UX weaknesses. The reviewers go through typical predefined user tasks and check whether the steps are understandable and intuitive. The reviewers can thereby use four questions for the evaluation: "Will the user try to achieve the right effect? Will the user notice that the correct action is available? Will the user associate the correct action with the effect they are trying to achieve? If the correct action is performed, will the user see that progress is being made toward solution of their task?" [24].

Heuristic evaluation is an expert-based evaluation method in which reviewers evaluate a software system with so-called heuristics [11]. Heuristics provide quality guidelines that address different quality criteria (e.g. UX and InfoSec). Software systems can fulfil heuristics to varying degrees. Yáñez Gómez et al. [26] describe a heuristic as a guideline whose fulfilment is evaluated when the UX of a real system or prototype is evaluated and improved. Well-known UX heuristics were developed by Nielsen [10], e.g., the user's memory load should be minimized by making elements, actions, and options visible. Furthermore, heuristics have been developed for other quality criteria than UX, such as InfoSec: Realpe et al. [13] developed InfoSec heuristics, e.g., a software system should report the possible security consequences of their actions appropriately. Moreover, Sauer et al. [18] developed UX and InfoSec heuristics for wallets. After extending the definition of Yáñez Gómez et al. [26] to include InfoSec heuristics, a heuristic can be defined as a guideline for evaluating and improving the UX or InfoSec of a real system or prototype. These heuristics are valuable in requirements engineering for specifying or assessing the fulfilment of requirements in systems under development, as well as for evaluating and comparing existing systems. These heuristics are then used in a heuristic evaluation by the reviewers to identify weaknesses in the software system so that they can determine a fulfilment score for each [11].

Heuristic walkthrough is an expert-based evaluation method. It combines parts of cognitive walkthrough [24] and heuristic evaluation [11]: Reviewers test a software system in two runs, the 'walkthroughs'. In the first walkthrough, the cognitive walkthrough [24] is applied with predefined tasks. In the second walkthrough, the heuristic evaluation [11] is applied as a free-form evaluation without predefined tasks. This should ensure that no important click paths are forgotten. The advantages of both methods are thus combined [21].

4 The MEUSec Method

The <u>m</u>ethod for <u>e</u>nhancing <u>u</u>ser experience and information <u>sec</u>urity (in short: MEUSec method) can be used to evaluate the interactions between UX and InfoSec of wallets and to find improvement suggestions. The MEUSec method adapts procedures as proposed by literature [17], and, at its core, combines a user-based evaluation with an expert-based evaluation, as the views of users and experts can differ [4]. The input of the MEUSec method is a wallet whose UX and InfoSec are to be evaluated and improved. The output are scores for UX and InfoSec, the evaluation of interactions between UX and InfoSec and finally improvement suggestions. It consists of 8 steps (see Fig. 1). In short, the MEUsec method begins with a definition step (Step 1), continues with a user-based evaluation (Steps 2–4) and an expert-based evaluation (Steps 5–7), and closes with a final step to enhance UX and InfoSec (Step 8). The 8 steps are sketched and justified in the remainder of this section. Additional justifications for design decisions result from the lessons learned (see Sect. 5). A more detailed process model can be found at [19].

4.1 Step 1: Definition of Evaluation Object

Figure 2 presents the sequence of activities that are conducted in Step 1, and that are now explained in written form:

Fig. 1. Simplified steps of the MEUSec method

The *method user* (MU) selects the wallet functionality to be evaluated, e.g., from the wallet functionality list of Krauß et al. [7] or Podgorelec et al. [12]. Wallet functions according to [7] include a detailed view of stored credentials, a search function or functions for backing up, resetting or restoring the wallet. Wallet functions also include the storage of identity-related data, the management of identity-related data and the sharing of identity-related data [12].

Then, the MU and the *InfoSec expert* (ISE) elaborate security relevant components and potential attackers of the defined wallet functionality. This can be done through discussion between MU, ISE and the wallet developers or by viewing relevant documentations, such as the source code or the architecture models. After identifying the potential attackers and security relevant components, their scope must be determined. The scope of the potential attackers and security relevant components is determined by the ISE in consultation/discussion with the ISE. The result of Step 1 is the defined evaluation object.

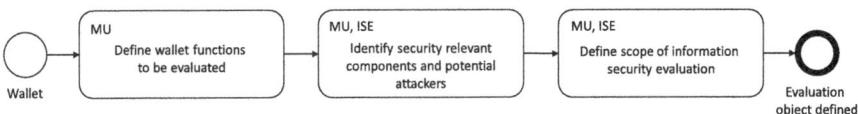

Fig. 2. Step 1 of MEUSec method as BPMN process model

4.2 Step 2: Preparation of User-Based Evaluation

Figure 3 presents the sequence of activities that are conducted in Step 2 as a part of the entire user-based evaluation:

The MEUSec method adapted the heuristic walkthrough procedure [21] (see Sect. 3), in which a cognitive walkthrough [24] is carried out first followed by a heuristic evaluation [11]. In cognitive walkthrough, *UX experts* (UXE) first put themselves in the shoes of potential end users and collect UX weaknesses based on prescribed tasks. This is followed by a free-form evaluation, without prescribed tasks, but using heuristics in which the UX experts check the degree of fulfilment.

The opinions of experts and end users may differ [4]. It is therefore important not only to consider the opinions of experts who put themselves in the shoes of potential end users (as in the cognitive walkthrough), but also to include actual end users. Therefore, a user-based evaluation with the help of thinking aloud [9] (instead of cognitive walkthrough) follows first in the MEUSec method and later an expert-based evaluation with heuristic evaluation. In this step, thinking aloud is prepared with *wallet users* (WU) as test subjects. To this end, UXE, ISE and ISE define user requirements that reflect typical end users. To do this, it is necessary to consider which dimensions such as age, IT-affinity or occupation and which area of the dimensions should be covered by the WU. Then UXE, ISE and ISE define test scenarios based on wallet functionality from Step 1. The ISE sets up the test devices on which the test cases will be executed and runs pretests.

The result of Step 2 is the prepared user-based evaluation.

4.3 Step 3: Execution of User-Based Evaluation

Figure 3 presents the sequence of activities that are conducted in Step 3 as a part of the entire user-based evaluation:

Thinking aloud [9] (see Sect. 3) is carried out. First, the ISE explains the tasks to the WU. Before starting the thinking aloud the ISE has to start the lab recording. The recording should include the screen which the WU are working on, the reaction of the WU as well as the audio of the lab. While the WU perform the test tasks, they should express their thoughts freely. The ISE should only intervene if the WU ask for help. After completing the thinking aloud, the ISE ends the recording and archives it for the following evaluation.

The results of Step 3 are thinking aloud recordings of the WU.

4.4 Step 4: Evaluation of User-Based Evaluation Results

Figure 3 presents the sequence of activities that are conducted in Step 4 as a part of the entire user-based evaluation:

The ISE, UXE and ISE analyse the recordings and document the strengths and weaknesses. A template was developed for this purpose, in which the strengths and weaknesses are documented. This template contains the following data: Unique id, name, detailed description, whether it is a strength or a weakness, whether it affects UX or InfoSec and the affected wallet function(s). The template also notes which UX or InfoSec attribute(s) are affected. For this purpose, the UX attributes of [23] and the InfoSec attributes of [3] can be assigned, e.g., satisfaction (UX attribute), effectiveness (UX attribute), confidentiality (InfoSec attribute) or integrity (InfoSec attribute).

The attributes become important again in Step 7, as the evaluated scores of the heuristics are first aggregated at attribute level. It is clear that detailed InfoSec weaknesses of the wallet cannot be identified by the WU, but only later during the expert-based evaluation. Nevertheless, UX weaknesses that have an impact on InfoSec, such as unclear security notices, can already be identified. UX and InfoSec *heuristics* (see Sect. 3) are then derived from the strengths and weaknesses. Heuristics provide quality guidelines (as for UX or InfoSec), which can be fulfilled to certain degrees by different systems [13,26]. Well-known heuristics were developed by Nielsen [10], e.g., that a software system contains familiar terms and natural language. These heuristics are discussed and documented in the *heuristics catalogue*. To define the heuristics in the heuristics catalogue, the template from the strengths/weaknesses can be used (except for the strengths/weaknesses column).

The results of Step 4 are UX and InfoSec heuristics of the defined wallet functions.

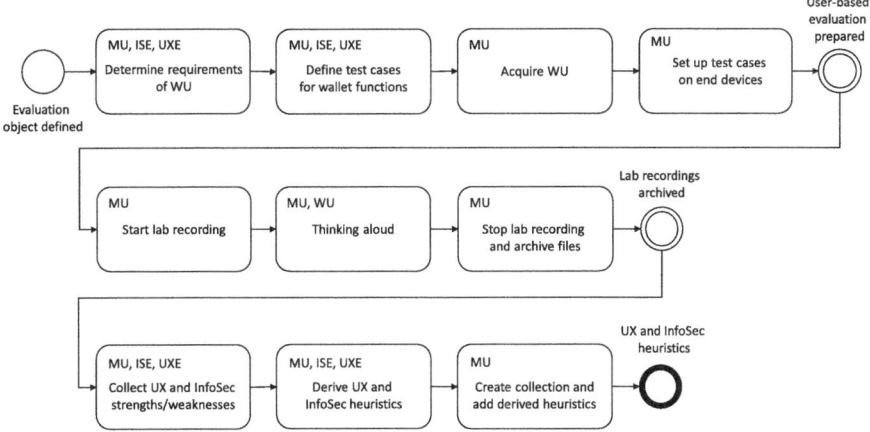

Fig. 3. Step 2–4 of MEUSec method as BPMN process model

4.5 Step 5: Preparation of Expert-Based Evaluation

Figure 4 presents the sequence of activities that are conducted in Step 5 as a part of the entire expert-based evaluation:

As mentioned in Step 2, the user-based evaluation is followed by an expert-based evaluation, because it is important to consider the experts' point of view in addition to that of real users, as their views may differ [4]. In this step, ISE, UXE and ISE prepare an expert-based evaluation by (1) expanding the heuristics catalogue, and (2) weighting each heuristic. In addition to heuristics from Sauer et al. [18] for wallets or from previous method applications, heuristics can be extracted from literature by UXE and ISE. We note that heuristics are not necessarily available in the required form, and might require further development before adding them to the heuristics catalogue. If new heuristics are added, the ISE updates the list of security relevant components, potential attackers and in total the scope of InfoSec evaluation and heuristics. Finally, ISE, ISE and UXE assign weights to the heuristics according to their relevance with a value from 1 (low) to 5 (high), and document those weights in the heuristics catalogue.

The results of Step 5 are weighted heuristics of UX and InfoSec of the defined wallet functions.

4.6 Step 6: Execution of Expert-Based Evaluation

Figure 4 presents the sequence of activities that are conducted in Step 6 as a part of the entire expert-based evaluation:

The UXE and ISE conduct a free-form heuristic evaluation [11] with the weighted heuristics of Step 5, as in a heuristic walkthrough [21]. This enables the discovery of new aspects not considered in the task-based user evaluation (Step 2–4). For this purpose, the UXE and ISE rate the extent to which each heuristic of the catalogue is fulfilled with a score from 1 (not fulfilled) to 5 (completely fulfilled), and document the score and reasoning in a *score sheet*. In a heuristic evaluation, the interactions between UX and InfoSec heuristics are not yet identified. Therefore, the interactions between the heuristics – and therefore between UX and InfoSec of the defined wallet functions – are evaluated using an interaction matrix [8]. The interactions between the heuristics – *complementary*, *conflicting* and *neutral* [2] – are found through discussion between the ISE, UXE and ISE. The interactions of the heuristics are included in the heuristics catalogue by adding another column with the respective interactions to other heuristics.

The results of Step 6 are the scored heuristics and the interaction matrix of the defined heuristics.

4.7 Step 7: Evaluation and Validation of Expert-Based Evaluation Results

Figure 4 presents the sequence of activities that are conducted in Step 7 as a part of the entire expert-based evaluation:

Based on the score sheet and the assignment of each heuristic to UX or InfoSec attributes, the scores of the heuristics can be aggregated on an attribute and category level. For this purpose, the ISE multiplies the weight of each heuristic by its score and calculates the average for each UX and InfoSec attribute. Now, the scores of the UX and InfoSec attributes can be aggregated to a final average score for UX and InfoSec respectively. The scores can be used to compare different wallet versions after applying the MEUSec method, e.g. whether the improvement suggestion of Step 8 have led to an improvement. Then, ISE, UXE and ISE discuss whether problems occurred during the heuristic evaluation, e.g., missing or inaccurate heuristics. If problems occurred, the heuristics must be corrected accordingly, and Step 6 might have to be repeated. The results of Step 7 are the final UX and InfoSec scores of the defined wallet functions on different levels of aggregation.

4.8 Step 8: Enhancement of UX and InfoSec

Figure 5 presents the sequence of activities that are conducted in Step 8:

The interaction matrix (see Step 6) is used as input for improving the UX and InfoSec of the defined wallet functions. First, ISE, UXE and ISE try to resolve

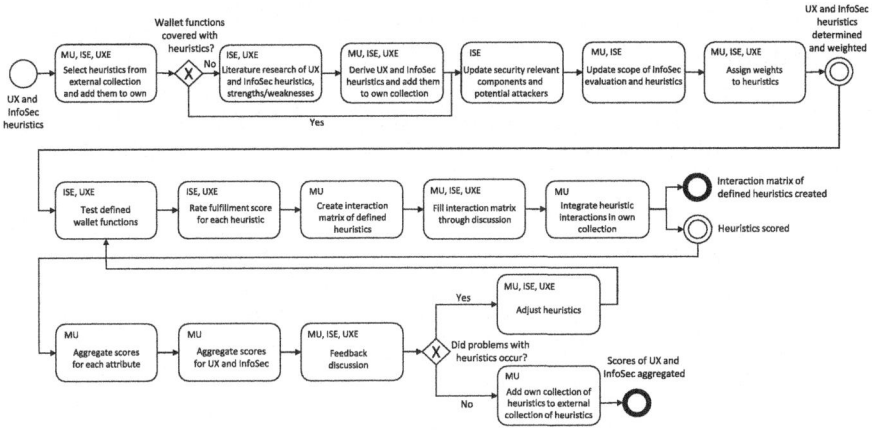

Fig. 4. Step 5–7 of MEUSec method as BPMN process model

conflicts between conflicting heuristics. If no solution can be found for a conflicting pair, either the UX or InfoSec heuristic must be prioritized by ISE in discussion with UXE and ISE. For this purpose, the corresponding heuristics from either prioritised UX or InfoSec are used to improve the wallet. For example, consider that the following UX and InfoSec heuristic to be in conflict: The wallet pin may be a maximum of 4 characters long, otherwise it is unusable (UX heuristic). The wallet pin must be at least 6 characters long (InfoSec heuristic). Further assume that InfoSec is prioritised. As a consequence, the wallet has to be adapted according to the InfoSec heuristic, i.e. the wallet should use the 6-digit pin. The UX heuristic, however, is not deleted from the collection to be used in further iterations of the method and to produce comparable results. Then ISE, UXE and ISE discuss the complementary and neutral heuristics and collect improvement suggestions. Complementary and neutral heuristics have no negative influence, so that the heuristics themselves usually already specify the improvement suggestions.

The results of Step 8 are improvement suggestions for conflicting, complementary and neutral heuristics.

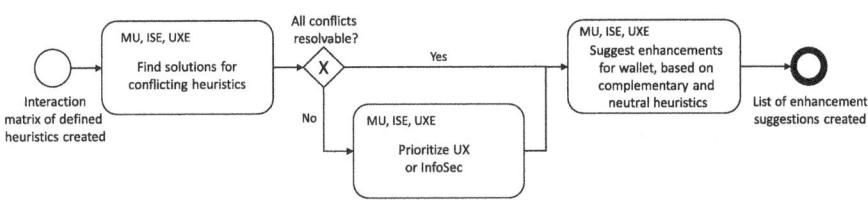

Fig. 5. Step 8 of MEUSec method as BPMN process model

5 Lessons Learned, Design Decisions and Future Evaluation

Table 1 provides a summary of design decisions and lessons learned which are described in more detail in this section.

The MEUSec method was developed iteratively. To this end, the creators of the MEUSec method discussed the MEUSec method with UX, InfoSec and wallet experts from academia and industry. The MEUSec method was also applied to a wallet prototype on a small scale, applying restrictions such as only considering a small number of wallet functions, potential attackers and security components. Parts of the method (e.g., thinking aloud, cognitive walkthrough and heuristic evaluation) were applied separately to wallets to gain important insights for the MEUSec method, e.g. [20]. In the following, the iterative development process is sketched and selected lessons learned (including justifications for design decisions) are described. Finally, plans for a more detailed evaluation are outlined.

Initially, the method of Rusu et al. [14] was considered to develop UX and InfoSec heuristics for wallets with the goal of evaluating and improving the UX and InfoSec of wallets. However, since UX and InfoSec can influence each other, it is not enough to develop UX and InfoSec heuristics for wallets separately. The evaluation of the mutual influence of UX and InfoSec (i.e., between heuristics) was missing. While literature yields no complete method, Sauer et al. [17] state the relevance of such an integrated approach and propose starting points. Thus, the heuristic walkthrough [21] (consisting first of cognitive walkthrough [24] and then heuristic evaluation [11]) was used as a basis.

One challenge is that perspectives of experts and users can differ [4]. Thus, it was decided to complement the purely expert-based method of heuristic walkthrough with a user-based method. The different perspectives of UXE/ISE and WU showed when thinking aloud and heuristic evaluation were applied to a wallet prototype during method development. An experiment [20] showed that 22 of the 24 WU did not notice a security warning – which was not predicted by all of the involved UXE. Therefore, the first part of heuristic walkthrough, cognitive walkthrough, was replaced by thinking aloud (see Step 3) to involve WU and not just UXE/ISE who put themselves in the WU' shoes.

In the second part of heuristic walkthrough, heuristic evaluation, the software system is evaluated using heuristics, analyzing their respective degree of fulfillment by the system (see Step 6). This requires a set of sophisticated heuristics. The results of thinking aloud can be used to formulate UX and potentially InfoSec heuristics, e.g., strengths and weaknesses of UX and the implications thereof for InfoSec. Hence, the development of heuristics was integrated into the MEUSec method (see Step 4). However, it is not sufficient to create InfoSec heuristics based solely on user statements, as, for example, the software components still need to be considered. Therefore, an activity was integrated into the MEUSec method where ISE identify the security relevant components and define the InfoSec assessment scope in order to formulate InfoSec heuristics (see Step

1). This is also important, as the attacker model and the security-relevant components can differ depending on the requirements and use cases. Furthermore, a template was developed for defining the heuristics in the heuristics catalogue (see Step 4). Here, it is particularly important to define the relevant attributes of UX and InfoSec for each heuristic. This enables aggregation of scores over multiple heuristics – first at attribute level and then for UX and InfoSec overall (see Step 7). This means that the MEUSec method promises to be useful for improving early-stage research prototypes, so that the scores can be compared with the scores of a further iteration after the improvement suggestions from Step 8 have been incorporated – right up to the finished product.

Since heuristics have already been developed (e.g., by Nielsen [10], Realpe et al. [13] or Sauer et al. [18]) and can potentially be included in the individual assessment of the wallet, an activity was integrated into the MEUSec method to adapt existing heuristics (see Step 5).

It was found that heuristics can turn out incomprehensible or too abstract during the evaluation itself. Thus, a validation activity was added, to be executed after the heuristic evaluation, triggering another round of heuristic evaluation but with the improved heuristics (see Step 7). Heuristics developed during the implementation of the MEUSec method are specific to wallets and can be reused in subsequent runs. In addition, they can be used for comparison, i.e. whether the improvement suggestions have actually led to improvements.

In order to evaluate the interactions between UX and InfoSec, the definition of an interaction matrix [8] was integrated into the MEUSec method, allowing different interaction properties (complementary, conflicting and neutral) to be assigned to the heuristics (see Step 6). This is particularly important for the final improvement of UX and InfoSec, as a different approach should be taken for each interaction property. For complementary and neutral heuristics, improvements can simply be made with regard to the respective heuristic. For conflicting heuristics, a conflict solution should be sought after first. If none is found, either UX or InfoSec must be prioritized (see Step 8).

We included the ISE in the phase of reviewing the thinking aloud recordings of the test subjects (see Step 4), as the application of the MEUSec method has shown that InfoSec implications also arise from UX aspects. For example, incomprehensible security messages that can lead to InfoSec weaknesses.

For the near future, it is planned to evaluate the MEUSec method in detail. To this end, the MEUSec method is planned to be applied to an existing wallet on the market called Hidy[1]. In particular, the focus will be on the feasibility of the MEUSec method (effectiveness, efficiency and acceptance) and the quality of the results (completeness, correctness, relevance, consistency, comprehensibility and clarity). This promises to trigger another iteration of method development, incorporating the evaluation results into the MEUSec method and thus improving it. Another source of expected feedback are workshops in academia and industry.

---

[1] https://hidy.eu/de.

Table 1. Lessons learned

Nr	Observation	Action
1	Implications of UX and InfoSec cannot be evaluated by merely evaluating heuristics. For conflicting heuristics for which no solution can be found, it must be determined whether UX or InfoSec should be prioritised	The heuristics are included in an interaction matrix during MEUSec and each evaluated with the interaction properties *complementary*, *conflicting* and *neutral* [2]
2	Opinions of experts and actual end users differ as shown by literature and experiments	Heuristic walkthrough was adapted by replacing the first run (cognitive walkthrough) with thinking aloud. In this way, actual end users are involved and not just experts who put themselves in the end user's shoes
3	Results obtained from the user-based evaluation can serve as valuable input for expert-based evaluation, e.g. for formulating heuristics. Combining runs with prescribed user tasks and free-form evaluation reduces the risk of overlooking relevant user tasks	User-based evaluation is carried out first with thinking aloud, and then the expert-based evaluation with the heuristic evaluation
4	In-depth InfoSec evaluation on user interfaces alone is inherently infeasible, nevertheless, thinking aloud may reveal UX weaknesses that negatively impact InfoSec	ISE is involved in Step 4, when collecting the strengths and weaknesses of UX and InfoSec
5	Different attributes of UX (e.g. satisfaction and effectiveness) and InfoSec (e.g. integrity and confidentiality) should be considered and results mapped accordingly, to enable aggregation	A template was created for the formulation of the heuristics so that the heuristics can be included in the heuristic catalogue in a standardised way
6	Identified heuristics should be reusable for subsequent runs, adding to the comparability of results and the assessment of improvements. Heuristics from literature should be adaptable	A step was integrated into MEUSec to adapt existing heuristics
7	Heuristics can prove to be incomprehensible or overly abstract during the evaluation	A validation activity and possible reiteration was introduced to be performed after the heuristic evaluation

6 Conclusion and Future Work

UX and InfoSec are succes factors of wallets that need to be improved. For that, UX and InfoSec should be considered together as the two aspects can influence each other. As no applicable method was found in literature, the MEUSec method was developed together with UX and InfoSec experts from academia and industry.

This paper presents the MEUSec method, which adapts previously identified methods with the goal to evaluate the interactions between UX and InfoSec of wallets and to find improvement suggestions. The MEUSec method is a work in progress, nevertheless it has already been evaluated on a small scale: It was discussed and improved with experts in the fields of UX, InfoSec and identity management/wallets. It was also applied on a small scale to a wallet prototype.

It is planned to further evaluate and improve the method, as outlined in this paper. Other interesting directions of research include investigating whether the improved MEUSec method can also be applied to other software systems, and which steps could be supported – or even fully automated – by software.

Acknowledgements. This paper is a result of the project Showcase Secure Digital Identities Karlsruhe (SDIKA) (https://www.sdika.de/en). The goal of the project is to use digital identities to connect people, organizations, and processes. The values of digital sovereignty, fairness, and interoperability are guiding principles of the project and for the regional showcase. This project is supported by the Federal Ministry for Economic Affairs and Climate Action (BMWK) on the basis of a decision by the German Bundestag.

References

1. Distler, V., Lenzini, G., Lallemand, C., Koenig, V.: The Framework of security-enhancing friction: how UX can help users behave more securely. In: New Security Paradigms Workshop 2020 (NSPW 2020), pp. 45–58. ACM (2020). DOI: https://doi.org/10.1145/3442167.3442173
2. Hintz, A.: Erfolgreiche Mitarbeiterführung durch soziale Kompetenz: Eine praxisbezogene Anleitung. Gabler Verlag, Wiesbaden (2013). https://doi.org/10.1007/978-3-8349-4545-7
3. ISO: ISO/IEC 27000:2018(en) Information technology - Security techniques - Information security management systems - Overview and vocabulary (2018)
4. Jaspers, M.W.: A comparison of usability methods for testing interactive health technologies: methodological aspects and empirical evidence. Int. J. Med. Inf. **78**(5), 340–353 (2009). https://doi.org/10.1016/j.ijmedinf.2008.10.002
5. Khayretdinova, A., Kubach, M., Sellung, R., Roßnagel, H.: Conducting a usability evaluation of decentralized identity management solutions. In: Friedewald, M., Kreutzer, M., Hansen, M. (eds.) Selbstbestimmung, Privatheit und Datenschutz. D, pp. 389–406. Springer, Wiesbaden (2022). https://doi.org/10.1007/978-3-658-33306-5_19
6. Korir, M., Parkin, S., Dunphy, P.: An empirical study of a decentralized identity wallet: usability, security, and perspectives on user control. In: Proceedings of the 18th Symposium on Usable Privacy and Security (SOUPS 2022), pp. 195–211 (2022)
7. Krauß, A.M., Sellung, R.A., Kostic, S.: Ist das die Wallet der Zukunft?: Ein Blick durch die Nutzendenbrille beim Einsatz von digitalen Identitäten. HMD Praxis der Wirtschaftsinformatik **60**(2), 344–365 (2023). https://doi.org/10.1365/s40702-023-00952-6

8. Nechansky, H.: The interaction matrix: from individual goal-setting to the four modes of coexistence. Kybernetes **45**, 87–106 (2016). https://doi.org/10.1108/K-09-2014-0192
9. Nielsen, J.: Usability Engineering. Academic Press, Boston (1993)
10. Nielsen, J.: Enhancing the explanatory power of usability heuristics. In: Proceedings of the SIGCHI Conference on Human Factors in Computing Systems Celebrating Interdependence (CHI 1994), pp. 152–158. ACM Press, Boston (1994). https://doi.org/10.1145/191666.191729
11. Nielsen, J., Molich, R.: Heuristic evaluation of user interfaces. In: Proceedings of the SIGCHI Conference on Human Factors in Computing Systems Empowering People (CHI 1990), pp. 249–256. ACM Press, Seattle (1990). https://doi.org/10.1145/97243.97281
12. Podgorelec, B., Alber, L., Zefferer, T.: What is a (Digital) identity wallet? a systematic literature review. In: Proceedings of the 46th Annual Computers, Software, and Applications Conference (COMPSAC 2022), pp. 809–818. IEEE (2022). https://doi.org/10.1109/COMPSAC54236.2022.00131
13. Realpe, P.C., Collazos, C.A., Hurtado, J., Granollers, A.: A set of heuristics for usable security and user authentication. In: Proceedings of the 17th International Conference on Human Computer Interaction, pp. 1–8. ACM, Salamanca (2016). https://doi.org/10.1145/2998626.2998662
14. Rusu, C., Roncagliolo, S., Rusu, V., Collazos, C.: A Methodology to establish usability heuristics. In: Proceedings of the 4th International Conference on Advances in Com-puter-Human Interactions (ACHI 2011) (2011)
15. Sartor, S., Sedlmeir, J., Rieger, A., Roth, T.: Love at first sight? a user experience study of self-sovereign identity Wallets. In: Proceedings of the 30th European Conference on Information Systems (ECIS 2022) (2022)
16. Satybaldy, A.: Usability evaluation of SSI digital wallets. In: Bieker, F., Meyer, J., Pape, S., Schiering, I., Weich, A. (eds.) Privacy and Identity Management, vol. 671, pp. 101–117. Springer, Switzerland (2023). https://doi.org/10.1007/978-3-031-31971-6_9
17. Sauer, M., Alpers, S., Becker, C.: Comparison of methods for analyzing the correlation of user experience and information security. In: Proceedings of the 5th International Conference on Software Engineering and Development (ICSED 2023). ACM, New York (2024). https://doi.org/10.1145/3637792.3637794
18. Sauer, M., Becker, C., Oberweis, A., Schork, S., Sürmeli, J.: User experience and information security heuristics for digital identity wallets. In: Proceedings of the 8th International Conference on Computer-Human Interaction Research and Applications (CHIRA 2024), Porto, Portugal (2024)
19. Sauer, M., Pfeifer, S.: MEUSec - Method for enhancing user experience and information security (2024). https://doi.org/10.5281/zenodo.10529247
20. Sauer, M., Pfeifer, S., Sürmeli, J., Siebert, E., Woytal, I.: User-friendly integration of identity wallets and mobility platforms: a user experience study conducted in the SDIKA project (2024). https://doi.org/10.13140/RG.2.2.12412.55682
21. Sears, A.: Heuristic walkthroughs: finding the problems without the noise. Int. J. Hum.-Comput. Interact. **9**(3), 213–234 (1997). https://doi.org/10.1207/s15327590ijhc0903_2
22. Sellung, R., Kubach, M.: Research on User experience for digital identitywallets: state-of-the-art and recommendations. In: Open Identity Summit 2023 (2023). https://doi.org/10.18420/OID2023_03
23. Weichbroth, P.: Usability of mobile applications: a systematic literature study. IEEE Access **8** (2020). https://doi.org/10.1109/ACCESS.2020.2981892

24. Wharton, C., Rieman, J., Lewis, C., Polson, P.: The cognitive walkthrough method: a practitioner's guide. In: Usability Inspection Methods, pp. 105–140. John Wiley & Sons, Inc., Hoboken (1994)
25. Whitten, A., Tygar, J.: Why Johnny can't encrypt: a usability evaluation of PGP 5.0. In: Proceedings of the 8th Conference on USENIX Security Symposium, Washington, D.C. (1999)
26. Yáñez Gómez, R., Cascado Caballero, D., Sevillano, J.L.: Heuristic evaluation on mobile interfaces: a new checklist. Scientific World J., 1–19 (2014). https://doi.org/10.1155/2014/434326

Correlation Between Gamification and Intrinsic Motivation with a Mobile Job-Market Application

Niklas Grossmann and Helmut Hlavacs[✉]

Research Group Education, Didactics and Entertainment Computing, University of Vienna, Vienna, Austria
helmut.hlavacs@univie.ac.at

Abstract. In this paper we study the influence of the degree a mobile app is gamified on the motivation of its users. In particular, we created three versions of the same job application app, one without gamification, one with modest gamification, and one with heavy gamification. We then asked 21 student participants about their motivation to use either of these versions. Statistical analysis shows that gamification indeed increases motivation, but there is no significant difference between modest and heavy gamification.

Keywords: Gamification · Intrinsic Motivation · Mobile Application · Empirical Study · Job-Application Concept

1 Introduction

Gamification has gained significant attention in recent years and has already impacted activities, systems, and organizations by incorporating game-like features into non-game contexts to encourage participation and intrinsic motivation [4,6]. It aims to transform serious or monotonous processes into more entertaining and intuitive ones, enhancing the engagement and intrinsic motivation of participants [5,11,17,24]. Empirical studies indicate that gamification positively influences intrinsic motivation and offers multiple benefits, such as increased customer loyalty, sales, and website visits [1,4,9]. As businesses increasingly integrate gamification into their operations, further research on its impact in serious contexts is essential [24]. To address this, an innovative gamified job-application concept, involving a quiz for each job offer, has been developed to reduce barriers for both employers and job seekers. This concept is implemented in a mobile job-market application named *JobQuiz*, with three versions created to evaluate the potential of gamification in a scientific study including 21 students to collect data on intrinsic motivation. This research aims to deepen the understanding of the relationship between gamification and intrinsic motivation in a serious context.

2 Related Work

Gamification involves integrating elements and mechanics of games to foster individuals' motivation and engagement in activities and tasks that are not inherently related to games [21,22]. Werbach (2014) explains gamification as a "process of making activities more game-like" [22]. The idea behind gamification is to achieve the motivating and positive effects of games by integrating game-like features such as points, leaderboards, levels, and achievements in tasks or activities that are typical of a more serious matter [8,23,25]. By incorporating these elements, gamification aims to leverage the intrinsic motivation of users to increase user engagement, participation, and enjoyment [23]. This is achieved using the motivating effect that game elements trigger, but with no game being played [7]. Therefore, gamification aims to make experiences usually unrelated to games more engaging and motivating by incorporating elements that appeal to the human desire for achievement, competition, and status [21,25]. Thus, it encourages individuals to spend more time on an activity or to improve their performance by completing certain tasks [15,20]. Concepts with underlying gamification should be understandable and intuitively usable. Specifically, the user should get the feeling of being immersed in the task [23]. Therefore, gamification design must also consider good usability and design to keep the user motivated during the task [8,15,21,25].

Karl M. Kapp (2013) identified two general types of gamification - content and structural gamification, with the fusion of both types representing the most effective method for bolstering motivation [12]. **Content gamification** alters the content of the application to be more game-like, integrating elements like feedback loops, storytelling, or challenges to enhance user engagement without turning the task into an actual game [12]. **Structural gamification** modifies the structure around the content, using gamified elements like badges, points, and leaderboards to support user motivation without changing the main content [12].

3 The Innovative Job-Application Concept

The current job application process presents challenges for both job seekers and employers. Job seekers invest significant effort in creating and submitting application documents, often repeating this process for multiple jobs, leading to potential demotivation. Employers, especially in larger companies, may lack the expertise to thoroughly review applications, resulting in the oversight of suitable candidates. Additionally, the common application process tends to prioritize appearance, reputation, education, and experience over crucial values such as talent and job-specific knowledge, potentially leading to the premature elimination of highly qualified candidates.

The innovative job-application concept revolves around a quiz-based application method, where individuals apply for a job by participating in a quiz assessing job-related knowledge. This process is designed to automatically rank applicants based on their job-specific knowledge, eliminating the need for traditional application documents at the beginning of the process. The concept aims to enhance motivation for applicants and simplify the initial application round for both applicants and employers. To further reinforce motivation, the concept is supported by gamification, making the application process more enjoyable, stimulating, and informative. An algorithm is employed to score the application quiz and rank applicants based on their job-specific knowledge, reducing the results to a single value. This ensures that applicants are ranked and found based explicitly on their suitability for a specific job, without prejudice based on factors such as education level, curriculum vitae, or appearance. The concept is not industry-bound, offering a wide range of employment opportunities for various job seekers, and supplementary documents are only required after a mutual interest has been established between the job seeker and the prospective employer.

4 The Job-Market Application

The "JobQuiz" application incorporates a unique feature where each job offer includes a job quiz, allowing users to apply for a position by completing the quiz. To manage the evaluation of potentially thousands of quiz attempts, an algorithm has been developed to automatically calculate the results. This algorithm plays a crucial role in supporting the innovative application process by ensuring that applicants are ranked based solely on their knowledge and suitability for the specific job without any bias or prejudice. It is important to note that the algorithm specifically considers only multiple-choice and true-false questions. While open questions are included in the quiz creation process to provide flexibility in asking questions, they must be evaluated manually, a detail that is communicated to the user. The quiz creation process recommends including a minimum of ten multiple-choice and true-false questions to ensure meaningful results and facilitate comparison between applicants. Additionally, the inclusion of one or more open questions is optional, and answers to these questions are only considered for applicants who achieve adequate scores.

The algorithm automatically calculates the quiz results, ranking applicants based on their job-specific knowledge. The algorithm considers factors such as response time and question value, calculating a total score for each applicant. The process involves a dynamic loop to evaluate each question, with the total score being the sum of all question scores. Additionally, the algorithm awards badges to users based on their quiz performance compared with other users.

In summary, the algorithm is a critical component of the "JobQuiz" application, ensuring that applicants are ranked based explicitly on their knowledge and suitability for the specific job. By prioritizing job-specific knowledge over traditional factors such as educational level, curriculum vitae, or appearance, the algorithm contributes to a fair and unbiased initial application round. This approach aligns with the overarching goal of the application to modernize and simplify the job application process, making it more engaging and motivating for both job seekers and employers [2].

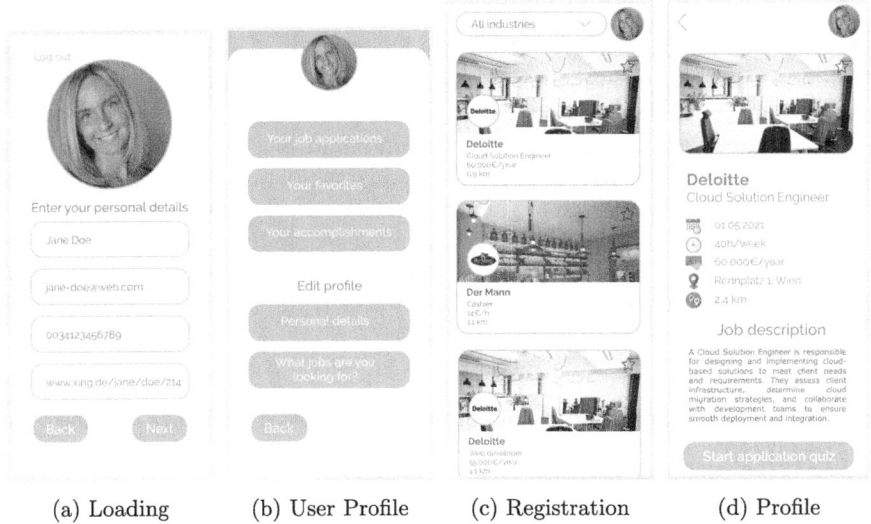

Fig. 1. *JobQuiz* Screens: Loading, User Profile, Job Offers Ovieview and Job Offer Detaild View

In Fig. 1a, a screenshot is presented, where the user can create or manage his profile details. After registration, more information to the profile, like search filters or settings, can optionally be added. The profile of a user can be modified after creation. Figure 1b provides a navigational overview of sub-screens, including job applications and detailed job views. From here, the user can navigate to their fulfilled applications, select favorites, or gain accomplishments. Additionally, the user can edit their personal details or change their job search settings. Figure 1c and Fig. 1d present two essential screens of the *JobQuiz* application. The screens in these figures support scrolling vertically. In particular, in Fig. 1c, an overview of job offers in an infinite scroll view is shown. Thus, the user can scroll down as long as there are job offers in the cloud database. The jobs are sorted by distance and relevance to the user to provide high-potential usefulness. The drop-down menu at the top of the screen allows the user to filter by industry, where the selection "All industries" is used as the default value. Each job is presented in a rounded window, showing the images of the workspace and logo of the employer, in addition to other information about the job. The user can add jobs as favorites at the top-right of each window. The data about the jobs loads automatically while scrolling down or can be manually updated automatically by scrolling up while at the top of the list. These common mobile motions create a smooth and intuitive experience when using the application. If the user clicks on the window, the screen transitions to the job-offer detailed view screen, which is displayed in Fig. 1d. This screen presents a detailed view of a single job offer. The image of the workspace, as well as more information about the job, including current distance and description, can be found on this screen. On the bottom of this screen, a button labeled "Start application quiz" can be found. By clicking this button, a quiz with job-specific questions begins. To prevent cheating during a quiz, it cannot be paused and continued at a later point in time or participated multiple times.

Table 1 presents the implemented elements and mechanics of gamification. As shown in the table, the three different versions of the *JobQuiz* application have integrated different levels of gamification. The names of the versions already indicate the gamified level: Minimally Gamified Version (MGV), Gamified Version (GV) & Highly Gamified Version (HGV). In the following three sections, the different versions of the application are presented, using the example of the job quiz, as it features gamification the most.

Table 1. Integrated Gamification into the *JobQuiz* Versions: Minimally Gamified Version, Gamified Version & Highly Gamified Version

	MGV	GV	HGV
Progress Indicator	✓	✓	✓
Attractive Design	✓	✓	✓
Challenge	✓	✓	✓
Time Challenge	✓	✓	✓
Points		✓	✓
Total Score		✓	✓
Social Impact		✓	✓
Leaderboard		✓	✓
Visual Feedback for Correct Answers			✓
Visual Feedback for Incorrect Answers			✓
Acoustic Feedback for Correct Answers			✓
Acoustic Feedback for Incorrect Answers			✓
Haptic Feedback for Incorrect Answers			✓
Musical Accompaniment of the Quiz			✓
Achievements / Badges			✓

4.1 Minimally Gamified Version

Visualized in Table 1, the *minimally gamified version* integrates four gamification components. The progress indicator, presented as a progress bar, offers information on the user's progress and enhances engagement within the job quiz [10]. *Attractive design* aims to captivate the user's attention and draw them into the application [13]. In the *JobQuiz* application, a *challenge* provides individuals with a sense of purpose and clear objectives, enhancing a sense of accomplishment and personal growth [14,18]. *Time challenges* add urgency to the task, forcing individuals to be more efficient in deciding and influencing the quiz results [16]. This paragraph delves into the significance of these gamification components in this version. The presented elements and mechanics of gamification are the minimum of incorporated gamified elements to ensure meaningful comparisons between the various versions.

4.2 Gamified Version

Referring back to Table 1, the *gamified version* of the *JobQuiz* application extends the *minimally gamified version* with additional gamification elements, including *points, total score, social impact, leaderboard* and *visual feedback for correct answers*. The *visual feedback for correct answers*, is shown to the user, by coloring the selection of the quizquestion green, in case it is correct. The *total score* is the sum of scores from each question, and the *leaderboard* allows users to compare their results with others who applied for the same job. The "Share Results" feature reinforces the *social connection* by allowing users to share their quiz results with others, even if they are not users of the *JobQuiz* application. This enhances motivation and engagement as individuals strive to outperform their competitors [18,19].

4.3 Highly Gamified Version

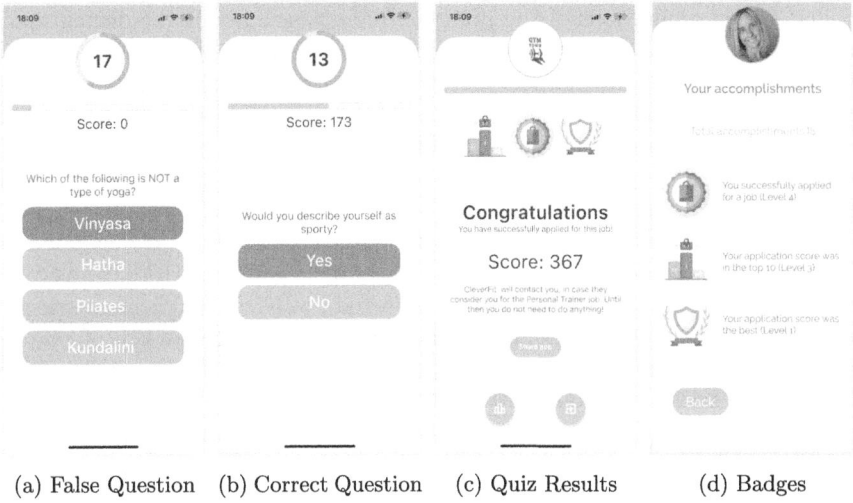

(a) False Question (b) Correct Question (c) Quiz Results (d) Badges

Fig. 2. *Highly gamified version* of *JobQuiz* Application: Implemented Gamification Presented Trough Job Quiz Screens

The *highly gamified version* of the application expands on the *gamified version* by incorporating additional gamification components, including *musical accompaniment of the quiz, visual feedback for incorrect answers, acoustic feedback for incorrect answers, haptic feedback for incorrect answers, acoustic feedback for correct answers,* and *achievements/badges*. This version is the only one to include audio, with tense and exciting music playing quietly in the background during the quiz to captivate the user's attention. However, the study revealed that this musical accompaniment was disturbing to many participants. Additionally, the highly gamified version introduces achievements and badges, allowing users to collect and view their achievements on a separate screen accessible through their profile. By collecting multiple instances of the same achievements, users can reach higher badge levels. These additional gamification elements aim to enhance user engagement and motivation, although the impact of the musical accompaniment on user experience should be carefully considered (Fig. 2).

5 Study on Gamification and Motivation

Similar to [5], this study utilizes the JobQuiz application with three versions: minimally gamified, gamified, and highly gamified. It follows a within-subject design where each participant uses all versions once in a randomized order. Before starting, participants complete an informed consent form and a pre-questionnaire. The informed consent form outlines study details, ethical principles, and data privacy, while the pre-questionnaire collects demographic and personal information. Questions cover demographics, digital affinity, and professional work situation to evaluate study results.

The first two questions of the *pre-questionnaire* ask about the demographic features of the participants. The participants are between 19 and 34 years old. The majority, with almost 62%, are between 19 and 21, with seven 21-year-olds. The median age of the respondents is 21; the average is 23. More women than men participated in the study. From a total of 21 subjects, only eight (38%) selected the "Male" option, and 13 (62%) chose "Female". No participant answered with "No comment".

The *pre-questionnaire* continues with a question about the average amount of time spent on a phone a day. Three participants answered "1h", six answered "2h", and with a majority of 57%, twelve selected ">2h". No participant selected the "<1h" option. Question number 4 asked about the frequency of playing digital games. The results are relatively equally distributed between the different options. Five participants answered "Daily", four picked "Multiple times a week", five chose "Multiple times a month", only three selected "Multiple times a year", and four answered that they "Never" play digital games. As a result, 81% of the participants participate in digital games, and only 19% are not.

The last two questions of the *pre-questionnaire* cover the area of professional work. Question 5 asked about the employment status of the respondents. The majority of 62% answered that they work "Part-time". The remaining eight participants (38%) chose the option "Unemployed". At this point of the study, the question "Which option does being a full-time student belong to?" was raised several times. After clarification, those people selected the "Unemployed" option. The results to the question "Are you currently looking for a job or a different job?" are presented. Five answers were given to "Yes", which is roughly 24%, and around 42% of the participants chose the "Open for offers" option. 1/3 of respondents were not looking for a job or open for job offers when the study was conducted.

5.1 Questionnaire

The participants execute a task on a randomly selected mobile application version and fill out a *questionnaire*. The questionnaire consists of 12 statements covering intrinsic motivation, overall feeling, and engagement, measuring participants' motivation and satisfaction [5].

Table 2. Questionnaire

1	Completing the process was entertaining
2	I feel good after applying for the job
3	I want to apply for other jobs
4	Applying for a job this way was amusing
5	I have never applied for a job so easily
6	I was bored during the process
7	My motivation to answer correctly was high
8	The quiz was exciting
9	I forgot I was applying for a job
10	It felt wrong to apply for a job this way
11	Next time I want to perform better
12	Answering correctly felt good

The *questionnaire* in the study allows participants to rate each statement using a Likert scale with five levels, providing a structured and quantitative method for capturing subjective data. The scale assigns integer values from -2 for "Strongly disagree" to +2 for "Strongly agree" to each level. The polarity of statements can be positive or negative, with negatively formulated questions being inverted at evaluation. Control statements, such as statement 1 and 6 in Table 2, are integrated to improve data quality and identify biases.

The study was conducted with an iPhone 11 Pro and a MacBook Pro, requiring a reliable network connection for real-time data transmission. The duration aimed to be between 15 and 20 min, and the researcher's presence was required to demonstrate the application and answer questions. Participant interaction was allowed, and documentation was crucial for data integrity and traceability.

The study, conducted in May 2023 in Vienna, involved 22 participants, with one excluded due to inconsistent answers in the control statements. Thus, the number of relevant participants decreased to 21. The topic was introduced abstractly to prevent bias. Prospective participants voluntarily chose to take part in a study on user interaction in human-computer interaction. Those who agreed signed the *informed consent form* and received an ID for anonymity and started the study by filling out the *pre-questionnaire* form.

After completing the pre-questionnaire, the main phase of the study began. The researcher introduced the JobQuiz application, demonstrating its navigation and explaining the job market concept. Participants were informed that their quiz participation served as a job application. The application was pre-configured with a user profile, and the JobQuiz cloud database contained relevant data, simulating an actively used application with job offers like "Software Developer" and "Mechanic", along with related information such as job quizzes, badges, and scores. The data presented varied based on the application version's level of gamification. The initial round of the main phase of the study always started by randomly selecting one of the three versions of the application. The participant was told to apply for any job by participating in the quiz of a job offer of their choice. Before the participant started, the researcher underlined that the application was only for fictive jobs. After the respondents finished the quiz connected with the chosen job, they filled out a *questionnaire*.

After completing the initial study round, the second round immediately commenced. Participants were given the test device with another random gamified version of the *JobQuiz* application. In each round, participants had to choose a different job to apply for to prevent familiarity with quiz questions that could bias behavior. The *questionnaire* had to be completed after the application task. This process was repeated to ensure each participant experienced all three application versions in a randomized order, following a within-subjects design.

To calculate the results, the Wilcoxon singed-rank test was calculated with the IBM SPSS statistics tool and manually.

6 Study Results

This empirical study focuses on measuring changes in intrinsic motivation within an application with varying levels of gamification. The two-tailed Wilcoxon

Table 3. Results of Questionnaires: Sum of Scores for Each Statement

Statement	Minimally Gamified Version	Gamified Version	Highly Gamified Version
1	8	22	26
2	3	15	10
3	7	21	20
4	0	23	22
5	24	23	22
6	16	26	27
7	9	27	24
8	7	17	19
9	−4	−1	1
10	5	17	3
11	7	23	22
12	−1	29	28
Sum of Sums	**81**	**242**	**224**

signed-rank test is used for statistical evaluation, comparing paired data samples representing different application versions. Three paired samples are analyzed: minimally gamified vs. gamified version, minimally gamified vs. highly gamified version, and gamified vs. highly gamified version. Data is collected through a questionnaire with 12 statements rated by participants from "Totally disagree" to "Totally agree", converted to numerical values. As shown in Table 3, the sum of values for each statement is calculated, resulting in 12 results for each gamified version. These sums are used for the Wilcoxon signed-rank test.

6.1 Minimally Gamified Version vs. Gamified Version

In this section, the Wilcoxon signed-rank test is applied to compare the collected data through the *questionnaire* between the *minimally gamified version* and the *gamified version*. The test determines whether a significant difference exists in the compared survey results. For this test, another null hypothesis and an alternative hypothesis are defined:

- H_0: The level of gamification does not influence the intrinsic motivation to perform a task in a serious context.
- H_1: Incorporating some gamification elements into a serious context influences the intrinsic motivation to accomplish a task.

Table 4 presents the descriptive statistics of the tested versions. Although the min and max values do not differ much, the average and the sum of sums values already indicate a difference in the results of the two versions (*Minimally Gamified Version* and *Gamified Version*). Still, the question remains if the difference is of a significant size.

Table 4. Descriptive Statistics: *Minimally Gamified Version*, *Gamified Version* and *Highly Gamified Version*

Statistics								
	N	Mean	Median	Min	Max	Variance	SDev	Sum of Sums
MGV	12	6.75	7	−4	24	52.35	7.24	81
GV	12	20.17	22.5	−1	29	56.81	7.54	242
HGV	12	18.66	22	1	28	75.56	8.69	224

For this test, the p-value is $p = 0.003$, and the Z-value is $Z = 2.984$. Since $p \leq \alpha$, H_0 is rejected and the alternative H_1 is accepted. In other words, the test suggests a statistically significant relation between gamification and intrinsic motivation in a serious context.

For a more exhaustive analysis, the effect size of the results is calculated with the formula

$$r = \left| \frac{Z}{\sqrt{N}} \right|$$

The effect size r is calculated with two variables. The standardized test statistic Z determines the statistical significance of the observed differences, and N represents the number of samples used in the test. In this case, $Z = 2.984$, and $N = 24$ since there are two times 12 samples tested. This results in an effect size of

$$r = \left|\frac{2.984}{\sqrt{24}}\right| = 0.6091.$$

To determine the significance of this effect size, it is interpreted with Cohen's effect size table visualized in Table 5, showing that the effect size is large [3]. Thus, utilizing some gamification elements in a serious context motivated the participants a lot more than the version with minimal gamification. Conclusively, the results indicate that the level of gamification influences the intrinsic motivation to accomplish a task in a serious context. Furthermore, the results indicate that gamification has an influence of a positive nature on intrinsic motivation.

Table 5. Cohen's Effect Size Table [3]

Strength of association	Coefficient r
Small	0.1–0.3
Medium	0.3–0.5
Lange	0.5–1.0

6.2 Minimally Gamified Version vs. Highly Gamified Version

The previous section compared the *minimally gamified version* and the *gamified version*. Thereby, the results indicate that the gamified version positively influences the intrinsic motivation of the participant during the quiz conduction. Here, this work compares the *minimally gamified version* with the *highly gamified version* to gain more insights into the changes in motivation. Similar to the Wilcoxon test from the previous section, H_0 and the alternative H_1 are defined:

– H_0: The level of gamification does not influence the intrinsic motivation to perform a task in a serious context.
– H_1: Incorporating many gamification elements into a serious context influences the intrinsic motivation to accomplish a task.

The above Table 4 presents the descriptive statistics of the two tested versions. Being not difficult to detect, the differences are large between the values of mean, median, and, most noticeably, the sum of sums between these two versions. This difference is an indication in favor of the *highly gamified version* and therefore also of H_1. Most ranks are positive, and only 2 of 12 are negative, indicating that the *highly gamified version* performed better than the *minimally gamified version*. This imbalance in positive and negative ranks already indicates a tendency in favor of H_1 - that high gamification influences intrinsic motivation. To empirically demonstrate the significance of the difference, the conduction of the Wilcoxon signed-rank test is pursued. In accordance with the issued results $p = 0.005$ and $Z = 2.826$ suggest that H_0 is rejected. Thus, H_1 is accepted, suggesting that a high level of gamification has an influence on intrinsic motivation to complete a task in a serious context.

In this Wilcoxon signed-rank test, the calculated effect size is $r = 0.5769$, which is categorized as a large effect size. Because the effect size r is less than the one from the first Wilcoxon test, the test between *gamified version* and *highly gamified version* may lead to a decrease in motivation. This is tested in the following section.

6.3 Gamified Version vs. Highly Gamified Version

For the final Wilcoxon signed-rank test, the null hypothesis and its alternative are:

- **H_0**: The motivation to perform a task in a serious context is similar in the *gamified version* and the *highly gamified version*.
- **H_1**: The motivation to perform a task in a serious context is higher (or lower) in the *gamified version* compared to the *highly gamified version*.

In this test, the survey results of the two gamified versions are compared to gain valuable insights regarding changes in intrinsic motivation. As perceived in the previous sections, the *gamified version* performs better than the *highly gamified version*. But the question remains if the measured difference is substantial enough to be deemed statistically significant, which would reject H_0.

The test continues by looking at the descriptive statistics of the two tested versions, shown in Table 4. The median, min, and max values are very similar. Noticeably, the variance and standard deviation values are bigger for the *highly gamified version*. That generally indicates a greater dispersion in the data, meaning that the data points are more spread out from the mean or central tendency. The values for the mean and sum of sums are larger at the *gamified version*, which vaguely indicates that the perceived intrinsic motivation is greater. To find evidence for this statement, the Wilcoxon signed-rank test is performed.

Four ranks favor the *highly gamified version*; the remaining eight are in favor of the *gamified version*. These findings are surprising because one might expect that incorporating more gamification elements and mechanics would further reinforce the intrinsic motivation of the participants. Contrary to expectations, the *gamified version* demonstrated superior performance.

Here $p = 0.404$, and $Z = -0.835$. This leads to the decision to retain H_0 and reject the alternative H_1. In other words, the perceived difference in intrinsic motivation is too small to exceed a threshold, which leads to the statement that the differences in data samples are statistically non-significant. The effect size for this test is

$$r = \left| \frac{-0.835}{\sqrt{24}} \right| = 0.170$$

The effect size r is notably small, further indicating a lack of substantial impact. It can be concluded that participants did not perceive a significant difference in their intrinsic motivation to perform a task in a serious context when it was presented with some or many gamification elements. Therefore, the perceived intrinsic motivation between the *gamified version* and the *highly gamified version* is similar.

7 Discussion

The evaluation in Sect. 6.1 highlights that gamification positively impacts participants' intrinsic motivation in serious tasks. This leads to the rejection of H_0, indicating no influence between gamification and intrinsic motivation, and supports H_1, confirming gamification's impact. The second Wilcoxon test comparing minimally and highly gamified versions reaffirms these findings, strengthening the correlation between gamification and intrinsic motivation. Surprisingly, the highly gamified version did not outperform the gamified version in the last test, leading to the rejection of alternative H_2. This suggests that the level of gamification does not significantly affect intrinsic motivation in a serious context. Overall, the study provides empirical evidence supporting the positive influence of gamification on intrinsic motivation, emphasizing the importance of gamification in enhancing engagement and motivation in serious tasks.

The minimally gamified version of the JobQuiz application performed poorly compared to the gamified and highly gamified versions, with significant effect sizes of 0.6091 and 0.5769, indicating a large negative impact on motivation. Participants expressed dissatisfaction, lack of enjoyment, confusion about correctness, and noted the absence of feedback and scores. Overall, this version lacked gamification elements, leading to the lowest intrinsic motivation for the participants.

The gamified version of the JobQuiz app excelled in intrinsic motivation compared to other versions, although not all participants shared the same positive sentiment, leading to divided opinions due to the lack of integrated negative feedback. Feedback highlighted the absence of feedback for wrong answers and the lack of audio or haptic feedback for correct answers, impacting user satisfaction. Comparisons with the highly gamified version, which includes haptic feedback for incorrect answers, revealed differences in user satisfaction. Participants noted the absence of visual and acoustic feedback compared to the highly gamified version, affecting their satisfaction levels. Overall, while well-received by most, the gamified version faced user experience issues and contrasts with the highly gamified version.

The study found that the highly gamified version ranked well in intrinsic motivation, closely behind the gamified version. However, feedback highlighted issues with the audio component, as participants found the volume disruptive and the music annoying. Some preferred no audio at all. Additionally, dissatisfaction was expressed regarding the lack of haptic feedback for correct answers, with participants emphasizing the importance of tactile feedback. Despite the majority enjoying the highly gamified version, audio-related problems led to a performance decline, with audiologic issues and absence of haptic feedback for positive answers potentially influencing lower ratings in the questionnaire.

8 Future Work and Limitations

The study highlighted the need for improvement as none of the three gamified versions satisfied all participants, emphasizing the importance of exploring diverse combinations of gamification components to enhance intrinsic motivation. Future research should include more gamified versions to deepen the understanding of gamification's impact. Subsequent studies could focus on identifying effective gamification elements for boosting intrinsic motivation in serious contexts, considering feedback for research design. With a small sample size of 21 and some bias of involving mostly students, larger and more diverse participant pools are recommended for broader applicability. Targeted studies with unemployed individuals could provide valuable insights while increasing the number of gamified versions can offer detailed insights into gamification elements. Expanding the serious context of studies beyond job markets could strengthen research validity and enhance understanding of gamification's impact on intrinsic motivation.

9 Conclusions

The study aimed to explore the impact of gamification on intrinsic motivation in a serious context, focusing on an innovative job-application concept designed to enhance motivation among applicants. The research question addressed whether gamification influences intrinsic motivation in performing tasks seriously. The study integrated gamification into a cross-platform mobile application and evaluated different versions to assess intrinsic motivation. Results showed that gamification reinforces intrinsic motivation in serious contexts, particularly in job applications, with no significant difference between gamified versions. The work concludes that implementing gamification substantially influences intrinsic motivation in serious contexts, highlighting that the absence of gamification diminishes motivation. Therefore, utilizing moderate to high levels of gamification enhances intrinsic motivation when performing tasks in a serious context.

References

1. An empirical study on gamification for learning programming language website **81** (02 2019). https://doi.org/10.11113/jt.v81.11133, https://journals.utm.my/jurnalteknologi/article/view/11133
2. Carless, S., Imber, A.: The influence of perceived interviewer and job and organizational characteristics on applicant attraction and job choice intentions: The role of applicant anxiety. Int. J. Sel. Assess. **15** (2007). https://doi.org/10.1111/j.1468-2389.2007.00395.x

3. Cohen, J.: Statistical Power Analysis for the Behavioral Sciences, 2nd edn. Routledge, London (1988)
4. Conaway, R., Garay, M.C.: Gamification and service marketing. SpringerPlus **3**(1), 653 (2014). https://doi.org/10.1186/2193-1801-3-653
5. Cvetkovic, P., Harbord, C., Hlavacs, H.: A study on gamification effectiveness, March 2020 . https://doi.org/10.5220/0009340102360244
6. Deterding, S., Dixon, D., Khaled, R., Nacke, L.: From game design elements to gamefulness: defining gamification, vol. 11, pp. 9–15, August 2011. https://doi.org/10.1145/2181037.2181040
7. Deterding, S., Sicart, M., Nacke, L., O'Hara, K., Dixon, D.: Gamification: using game design elements in non-gaming contexts, vol. 66, pp. 2425–2428, May 2011. https://doi.org/10.1145/1979742.1979575
8. Hamari, J.: Do badges increase user activity? A field experiment on effects of gamification. Comput. Hum. Behav. **71**, 469–478 (2017). https://doi.org/10.1016/j.chb.2015.03.036
9. Hamari, J., Koivisto, J., Sarsa, H.: Does gamification work?– A literature review of empirical studies on gamification, January 2014. https://doi.org/10.1109/HICSS.2014.377
10. Hattie, J., Timperley, H.: The power of feedback. Rev. Educ. Res. **77**(1), 81–112 (2007)
11. Kankanhalli, A., Taher, M., Cavusoglu, H., Kim, S.: Gamification: a new paradigm for online user engagement. In: International Conference on Information Systems, ICIS 2012, pp. 3573–3582. International Conference on Information Systems, ICIS 2012 (2012). international Conference on Information Systems, ICIS 2012 ; Conference date: 16-12-2012 Through 19-12-2012
12. Kapp, K.M.: The Gamification of Learning and Instruction Fieldbook: Ideas into Practice. John Wiley & Sons, Hoboken (2013)
13. Keusch, F., Zhang, C.: A review of issues in gamified surveys. Soc. Sci. Comput. Rev. **35**, 147–166 (2017). https://doi.org/10.1177/0894439315608451
14. Legaki, N.Z., Xi, N., Hamari, J., Karpouzis, K., Assimakopoulos, V.: The effect of challenge-based gamification on learning: an experiment in the context of statistics education. Int. J. Hum. Comput. Stud. **144**, 102496 (2020). https://doi.org/10.1016/j.ijhcs.2020.102496, https://www.sciencedirect.com/science/article/pii/S1071581920300987
15. Mazarakis, A.: Gamification reloaded: current and future trends in gamification science. i-com **20**, 279–294 (2021). https://doi.org/10.1515/icom-2021-0025
16. Moller, A.C., Meier, B.P., Wall, R.D.: Developing an experimental induction of flow: effortless action in the lab. Effortless attention: a new perspective in the cognitive science of attention and action, pp. 191–204 (2010)
17. Park, H., Bae, J.: Study and research of gamification design **8**, 19–28 (2014). https://doi.org/10.14257/ijseia.2014.8.8,03
18. Reeve, J.: A Self-determination Theory Perspective on Student Engagement, pp. 149–172, January 2012. https://doi.org/10.1007/978-1-4614-2018-7_7
19. Schlömmer, M., Spieß, T., Schlögl, S.: Leaderboard positions and stress-experimental investigations into an element of gamification. Sustainability **13**(12), 6608 (2021)
20. Seaborn, K., Fels, D.: Gamification in theory and action: a survey. Int. J. Hum.-Comput. Stud. **74**, 14–31 (2015). https://doi.org/10.1016/j.ijhcs.2014.09.006
21. Strahringer, S., Leyh, C.: Gamification und Serious Games - Grundlagen, Vorgehen und Anwendungen, May 2017. https://doi.org/10.1007/978-3-658-16742-4

22. Werbach, K.: (Re)Defining gamification: a process approach. In: Spagnolli, A., Chittaro, L., Gamberini, L. (eds.) PERSUASIVE 2014. LNCS, vol. 8462, pp. 266–272. Springer, Cham (2014). https://doi.org/10.1007/978-3-319-07127-5_23
23. Xi, N., Hamari, J.: Does gamification satisfy needs? A study on the relationship between gamification features and intrinsic need satisfaction. Int. J. Inf. Manag. **46**, 210–221 (2019). https://doi.org/10.1016/j.ijinfomgt.2018.12.002, https://www.sciencedirect.com/science/article/pii/S0268401218307436
24. Zichermann, G.: Gamification: from buzzword to strategic imperative. Wallstreet J. https://deloitte.wsj.com/articles/gamification-from-buzzword-to-strategic-imperative-01671213686. Accessed 18 May 2023
25. Zichermann, G., Cunningham, C.: Gamification by Design: Implementing Game Mechanics in Web and Mobile Apps, 1st edn. O'Reilly Media, Inc., Sebastopol (2011)

Query by Trash: Encouraging Green Attitudes and Behavior Through Eco-News Retrieval in Smart Trash Bins

Momo Takeuchi[1], Yoshiyuki Shoji[2], and Yusuke Yamamoto[3(✉)]

[1] Kubota Corporation, Naniwa-ku, Osaka, Japan
momo.takeuchi@kubota.com
[2] Shizuoka University, Hamamatsu, Shizuoka, Japan
shojiy@inf.shizuoka.ac.jp
[3] Nagoya City University, Mizuho-ku, Nagoya, Japan
yusuke_yamamoto@acm.org

Abstract. This paper proposes a smart trash bin to promote pro-environmental attitudes and behavior. The proposed system automatically searches for and displays news articles that are relevant to the type of trash discarded. The device ranks news articles in consideration of both the discarded trash type and its potential to evoke a sense of environmental urgency or guilt. To achieve this ranking, we constructed a dataset of news articles annotated for their "crisis/guilt" sentiment and trained a ranking model using a learning-to-rank algorithm. The highest-ranked article is displayed on a screen installed in the device.

The results of a user study demonstrated that a prototype device presented an opportunity for participants to reflect on environmental issues and demonstrated a modest influence on the formation of pro-environmental attitudes.

Keywords: IoT · green technologies · behavior change · human-computer interaction · information retrieval

1 Introduction

More people are paying attention to environmental issues, e.g., global warming and ocean pollution, and mass media (TV and newspapers) frequently feature SDG issues. Thus, many consumers understand the need to take appropriate action to solve environmental issues. According to a public opinion poll conducted in 2020[1] 88.3% of respondents said they are "concerned" about global environmental issues. This suggests that interest in environmental issues is generally high in Japan. However, a 2018 report by the United Nations[2] revealed

---

[1] Cabinet Office of Japan, Public Opinion Survey on Climate Change, 2020; https://survey.gov-online.go.jp/r02/r02-kikohendo/.
[2] United Nations Environment Programme (UNEP), "Single-Use Plastics: A Roadmap for Sustainability," 2018; https://www.unep.org/ietc/ en/node/53.

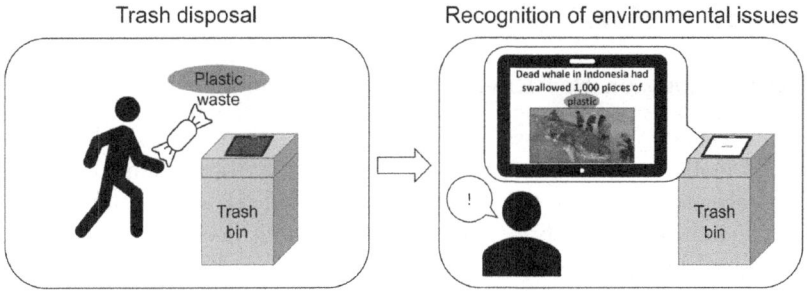

Fig. 1. Proposed smart trash bin device.

that Japan has the second highest per capita consumption of plastic packaging waste in the world, which indicates that although many Japanese people want to be environmentally friendly, few people take appropriate actions.

In environmental psychology, one reason for this discrepancy is that environmental effects are not easily recalled when making decisions or taking action [5]. For example, even if people want to reduce carbon dioxide emissions or reduce ocean pollution, most people do not consider how much carbon dioxide they emit when driving cars or the impact of throwing away plastic bottles.

Therefore, this study attempts to enhance pro-environmental attitudes and behavior by creating opportunities to consider the impact of human actions on environmental problems. This paper proposes a trash bin device that displays news articles about environmental issues, as shown in Fig. 1. The proposed smart trash bin device automatically searches for and displays news articles that are relevant to the discarded trash and ranks news articles considering both the discarded trash type and its potential to evoke a sense of environmental urgency or guilt. Using the proposed device, users can dispose of trash and recognize environmental problems simultaneously, allowing them to feel a connection between their behavior and environmental problems. Thus, it is expected that their willingness to act responsibly will increase.

We conducted a user study to confirm the positive effects on participants' attitudes and behavior when they used the proposed device, and the results revealed the following tendencies.

- The proposed system created opportunities to think about trash and environmental problems without interrupting their trash disposal.
- The proposed system has a certain effect on the formation of pro-environmental attitudes.
- To enhance environmental awareness and behavior, it is necessary to optimize news presentation on the device such that users can easily understand the news articles.

2 Related Works

2.1 Psychology on Pro-Environmental Behavior

According to environmental psychology, the psychological process from "concern about the global environment" to "motive toward pro-environmental actions" requires recognition of both environmental risk and the attribution of responsibility. Nonami et al. analyzed the role of media in decision making for pro-environmental behavior using path analysis [16]. They found that mass media, e.g., TV and newspapers, affect the recognition of environmental risk and the attribution of responsibility, and that they encourage the formation of pro-environmental attitudes. However, they also found that other factors, e.g., closeness to the local community and communication, are required to realize individualized/specific pro-environmental behavior.

This study attempts to promote recognition of environmental risk and attribution of responsibility to form pro-environmental attitudes and influence positive behavior by displaying news articles that give a sense of crisis and guilt.

2.2 Human-Computer Interaction to Promote Pro-Environmental Behavior

Many studies have investigated using information technology to promote pro-environmental behavior, e.g., visualization of carbon emissions from food consumption [12] and visualization of energy consumption [6].

BINCAM is a trash bin device [1] that is similar to the proposed device. BinCam captures images of kitchen garbage automatically and posts them on social networking services (SNS) to provide feedback on users'recycling behavior and leftover food consumption. User experiments demonstrated that feedback on trash disposal increased the awareness of related behavior. However, few users used the SNS application for feedback to check evaluation results. Such feedback may not be suitable for individuals with low awareness of environmental problems because it imposes a large psychological burden. Automatic trash classification [9] can contribute to solving environmental problems independent of the users' environmental awareness; however, it cannot promote the formation of pro-environmental attitudes among those who generate trash.

Unlike BINCAM, the proposed system attempts to form pro-environmental attitudes and promote pro-environmental behavior by presenting information according to the users' trash-disposal behavior.

2.3 News Article Features to Attract People and Change Behaviors

In the web science and natural language processing fields, studies have investigated the characteristics of impressive news articles, e.g., the characteristics of news titles that are likely to be clicked on [15] and the structure and appearance of words in fake news, which has become a problem because false information is spread widely [7]. Several studies have revealed that news articles with high topicality and publicity tend to contain negative topics [17].

In this study, we developed a news article ranking system to generate a sense of crisis and guilt using a learning-to-rank technique.

3 Proposed System

The proposed system attempts to motivate pro-environmental attitudes and behavior by displaying relevant news articles to develop a sense of crisis and guilt. When a user throws away trash, the system recognizes the type of trash using a built-in camera. The system then ranks news articles related to the identified trash according to the degree of sense of crisis and guilt. The top-ranked news article is presented on the device's display.

Two functions are implemented in the proposed system to realize the above scenario. The trash image recognition function identifies relevant news articles, and the news article ranking function selects articles that evoke a sense of crisis and guilt.

3.1 Trash Image Recognition

The proposed system displays relevant news articles by recognizing the trash captured in the acquire images. Highly relevant news articles are more effective in terms of enhancing pro-environmental attitudes and behavior. For example, when a user throws away plastic trash, an article about plastic ocean pollution is more likely to make a stronger impression than an article about global warming.

The proposed system classifies the trash images into trash types using VISION TRANSFORMER, which is a pretrained image recognition model [4]. We fine-tuned the pretrained VISION TRANSFORMER model to perform trash category classification using the TACO [19]trash image dataset. The TACO dataset has 1500 images and 4784 annotations on 28 categories. The results of cross-validations demonstrate that the trained image recognition model performed well for popular trash categories, e.g., "clear plastic bottle" (precision/recall = 0.893/0.781), "drink can" (0.947/0.643), and "plastic bottle cap" (0.714/0.857). However, some categories, e.g., "plastic film," were difficult to recognize (0.442/0.667). Due to page limitations, we show the image classification results on our website[3].

3.2 Ranking News Articles by Sense of Crisis and Guilt

According to Koike et al., motivation to take pro-environmental actions is formed by recognizing environmental risk and attributing responsibility [13]. By applying this finding to the waste disposal behavior context, it is possible to interpret the recognition of environmental risk as a feeling of the seriousness of environmental problems and the recognition of the attribution of responsibility as a

---

[3] Classification performance, https://www.ds.nagoya-cu.ac.jp/~yamamoto/download/goodit2024_supporting_material.pdf.

feeling of responsibility for one's waste disposal. We interpret the recognition of environmental risk as a "sense of crisis" and the recognition of attribution of responsibility as a "sense of guilt," and we construct a machine learning model to rank news articles according to the sense of guilt using learning-to-rank algorithms. There are various types of news articles about environmental problems. Because articles about harms caused by environmental problems may provide a greater sense of guilt, we expect the ranking model will rank such articles higher than articles about companies working to solve environmental problems.

Ranking Model Construction. Ranking models for information retrieval sort a list of documents in terms of their importance for a given query, i.e., a search term. *Learning-to-rank* [2] is a machine learning method that automatically constructs a model to rank documents in order of importance using a set of documents labeled with importance for a given query. Learning-to-rank methods have been widely used in information retrieval and web search tasks. We consider trash categories as queries, news articles as documents, and the degree of sense of guilt as the document importance. We then construct a ranking model using a learning-to-rank method to rank news articles related to a specific trash type in order of the degree of sense of guilt.

We use LAMBDARANK [2], a pairwise learning-to-rank algorithm, to construct the ranking model. The pairwise learning-to-rank algorithm learns a model to rank documents using annotated pairs of documents to determine which document is better in the given pair. We use LGBMRANKER in the LIGHTGBM framework [11] as an implementation of LAMBDARANK.

Learning-To-Rank Features. We use the titles, images, and body of news articles as learning-to-rank features, which are extracted from the *article style*, *emotion*, and *body content*.

Article style The news article style can affect a reader's impression. To attract interest, writers elaborate on the superficial features of articles. Different features, e.g., the length of the title and body, the presence of characteristic words, and the presence of images, influence the reader's impression of the article. Using the Japanese morphological analysis engine MECAB [14], we extract the number of tokens, the number of specific terms (numerals, place names, and question words) in the title and body of the news articles.

Emotion Emotional terms in articles are used as a learning-to-rank feature because they can evoke a sense of guilt. J-LIWC2015 [8], i.e., a dictionary that assigns words to psychological categories, is used for sentiment analysis of the news titles and bodies. J-LIWC2015 is the official Japanese version of the Linguistic Inquiry and Word Count (LIWC2015) [18]. J-LIWC2015 assigns 11,609 words to 69 emotion categories, e.g., *anxiety*, *causation*, and *achievement*. We count how many times the terms in each emotion category appear in the title and body of the articles using the J-LIWC2015 dictionary.

Body content We extract embedding vectors of news articles as the content features using BERT [3], a pretrained model that is effective at understanding

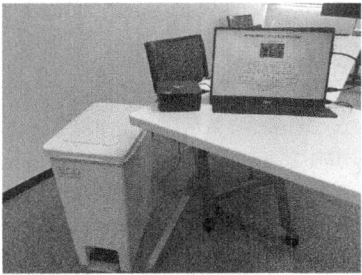

Fig. 2. Prototype system

the context of text. Then, the average vector of tokens in the output final layer of the BERT model is extracted as a feature representing the content of the news articles. Here, we use the pretrained Japanese BERT model[4] to analyze Japanese news articles.

3.3 Prototype System

The prototype system employed in the user study included functions to rank articles for trash and display relevant articles. Here, we fixed the trash type into general trash (wrapping paper for chocolate) to prove that displaying relevant news articles can evoke pro-environmental attitudes after trash is thrown away. Thus, trash classification function was not implemented in the prototype, and we assumed that the trash category was fixed. Before the user study, we crawled news articles from several websites listed in Table 1. The prototype ranked the crawled articles and displayed a top-ranked article. When trash was thrown away, the prototype ranked the crawled articles and randomly displayed an article from among the top-10 ranked news articles.

Figure 2 shows the prototype system. The prototype comprised a trash bin, a mini-PC, a USB-connected enter key, and a display. The system was implemented using the Flask web application framework[5] When the user pressed the trash bin pedal, which was connected via a USB enter key, the system detected that the user was throwing away trash. Then, the system displays a randomly selected news article. The system switches from the standby screen to the news search screen when the enter key is pressed. The 15-inch display switches to the next screen after 3 s on the news search screen and 20 s on the news display screen.

In the news display screen, the title font size is 35px, the image size is 150px high, and the text font size is 16px. Note that the news display screen only shows the first 500 characters of the selected article.

4 Evaluation of News Ranking Model

---

[4] Tohoku University, Inui Lab; https://github.com/cl-tohoku/bert-japanese.
[5] Flask; https://flask.palletsprojects.com/en/3.0.x/.

Table 1. Crawled news articles

Websites	URL	#Article
Rakuten Infoseek	https://news.infoseek.co.jp/g/	400
CNN.co.jp	https://www.cnn.co.jp/topic/environmental-issues/	480
Forbes JAPAN	https://forbesjapan.com/tag/detail/environment_problems	127
Mynavi News	https://news.mynavi.jp/techplus/tag/environment/	399
Green goo	https://www.goo.ne.jp/green/column/tag/environmental_issues	399
Jiji.com	https://www.jiji.com/jc/list?g=dts	11
Asahi Digital	https://www.asahi.com/eco/list/	40
Toyokeizai Online	https://toyokeizai.net/list/	400
Nikkei Shinbun	https://www.nikkei.com/business/energy/	399
Business Insider Japan	https://www.businessinsider.jp/tag/environment/	153

Prior to conducting the user study, we evaluated the performance of the news article ranking models.

4.1 Dataset

We collected news articles from Japanese websites that publish a large number of news articles on environmental issues. Table 1 shows the article sources and the number of articles collected from each source. Using the BeautifulSoup[6] Python library, the title, image, and body data of each article in the list of target articles were extracted. A total of 2,760 news articles were collected (excluding duplicates).

We used a Japanese crowdsourcing site, i.e., Lancers[7], to annotate the degree of the sense of guilt for the crawled news articles. We asked crowd workers to read the news articles and score their sense of crisis and guilt. The crowd workers were then asked the following questions.

- How much of sense of crisis about environmental issues did you feel after reading the news article?
- How much of sense of guilt about environmental issues did you feel after reading the news article?
- Which of the following types of trash do you think the news article is about?

Sense of crisis/guilt were ranked on a five-point Likert scale (1: "did not feel at all" to 5: "felt a lot"), and the trash type was selected from "plastic, burnable trash (general trash), plastic bottles, jars & cans, food waste, and waste paper". Here, 420 workers were recruited to have at least three workers perform the labeling task for each of the 2,760 news articles (20 news articles were assigned to each worker). The maximum time required for each task was 30 min, and the reward was 150 yen.

---

[6] https://www.crummy.com/software/BeautifulSoup/.
[7] https://www.lancers.jp/.

Table 2. Number and percentage of relevant news articles in each trash category

	plastic	burnable trash	plastic bottles	general trash
Number of relevant articles	95	30	30	121
Ratio of relevant articles	48.0%	38.0%	46.2%	45.8%

As a result, 320 valid responses were collected from 420 respondents. Sixty-five of the 2,760 prepared news articles had broken links. Finally, 2,271 news articles labeled by two or more workers were considered as news article data. The average response score of the assigned workers was used as the impression degree label for each news article, and 1,977 of the 2271 articles were judged as irrelevant. Thus, we used the remaining 294 articles to evaluate the learning-to-rank model.

4.2 Procedure

We evaluated the news ranking model using the 294 labeled news articles. We divided the news articles into training, validation, and test sets at a ratio of 5:2:3, holding the percentage of samples for each trash type. Here, we focused on four trash types (plastic, burnable trash, plastic bottles, and general trash) as queries because the other trash types did not have sufficient news articles for the learning-to-rank model (less than 30 articles). The general trash category included articles related to all trash categories, e.g., plastic, burnable trash, or plastic bottles.

We used the normalized discounted cumulative gain (NDCG) [10] and precision as evaluation metrics. For NDCG, a higher value indicates that the article has a higher ranking and its relevance is greater. Let r_i be the score for the degree of sense of crisis and guilt of the i th ranked news article. The DCG for a list of k articles is expressed as follows.

$$DCG@k = r_1 + \sum_{i=2}^{k} \frac{r_i}{log_2 i} \qquad (1)$$

Then, NDCG@k is calculated as follows.

$$NDCG@k = \frac{DCG@k \text{ of the predicted ranking}}{DCG@k \text{ of the correct ranking}} \qquad (2)$$

We also used precision to evaluate the ranking model. Here, if the crowd workers assigned a score greater than 3.0 on average for the sense of guilt to a news article, the article was set as *relevant*; otherwise, the article was *irrelevant*. The precision of the top k articles is expressed as follows.

$$Prec@k = \frac{|\{\text{Articles actually relevant}\} \cap \{\text{Articles predicted to be relevant in top k}\}|}{|\{\text{Articles predicted to be relevant in top k}\}|} \qquad (3)$$

Table 2 shows the number and ratio of relevant articles in each trash category.

Table 3. Precision of ranking models for each feature combination (maximum values are shown in bold)

Features	Precision @5/@10			
	plastic	burnable trash	plastic bottles	general trash
$Model_S$: Article style	0.94/0.90	0.78/0.63	0.82/0.66	0.88/0.84
$Model_E$: Emotion	0.96/0.93	0.82/0.61	0.84/0.71	0.90/0.89
$Model_B$: Body content	**1.00/0.98**	0.84/0.68	0.88/0.71	**1.00**/0.99
$Model_{EB}$: Emotion & Body content	**1.00/0.98**	0.88/0.69	0.90/0.69	**1.00**/0.99
$Model_{SB}$: Article style & Body content	**1.00/0.98**	0.86/0.65	**0.92/0.73**	**1.00**/0.99
$Model_{SE}$: Article style & Emotion	0.98/0.96	**0.92/0.70**	0.88/0.71	0.98/0.95
$Model_{SEB}$: Article style & Emotion & Body content	**1.00/0.98**	0.82/0.68	**0.92**/0.72	**1.00/1.00**
Random	0.48/0.48	0.38/0.38	0.46/0.46	0.46/0.46

Table 4. NDCG of ranking models for each feature combination (maximum values are shown in bold)

Features	NDCG @5/@10			
	plastic	burnable trash	plastic bottles	general trash
$Model_S$: Article style	0.91/0.92	0.91/0.90	0.94/0.94	0.88/0.89
$Model_E$: Emotion	0.96/0.96	0.94/0.90	0.96/0.96	0.94/0.95
$Model_B$: Body content	**0.97/0.97**	0.95/0.93	0.96/0.96	**0.97/0.97**
$Model_{EB}$: Emotion & Body content	**0.97/0.97**	0.96/**0.94**	0.97/0.96	**0.97/0.97**
$Model_{SB}$: Article style & Body content	**0.97/0.97**	0.96/0.93	**0.97/0.97**	**0.97/0.97**
$Model_{SE}$: Article style & Emotion	0.96/0.96	**0.97/0.94**	0.97/0.96	0.96/0.96
$Model_{SEB}$: Article style & Emotion & Body content	**0.97/0.97**	0.95/0.93	**0.97**/0.96	**0.97/0.97**

4.3 Results

To investigate the best ranking model, five ranking models were constructed and evaluated for each combination of feature categories listed in Sect. 3.2: : $Model_B$, $Model_{EB}$, $Model_{SB}$, $Model_{SE}$, and $Model_{SEB}$. Tables 3 and 4 show the focused features on each model, and the precision and NDCG scores, respectively.

Although the precision scores become slightly lower in Precision@5 and @10, the best ranking models in each trash type tended to be almost the same. Furthermore, all ranking models outperformed the baseline method, which guessed relevancy randomly based on the ratio of relevant samples. For the "plastic" and "general trash" types, the precision values of $Model_B$, $Model_{EB}$, $Model_{SB}$, $Model_{SE}$, and $Model_{SEB}$ were greater than 0.95 of Precision@10. For "burnable trash," $Model_{SE}$ obtained high precision, 0.92 for @5, and 0.70 for @10, and for "plastic bottles," $Model_{SB}$ and $Model_{SEB}$ obtained high precision, 0.92 for @5, and approximately 0.73 for @10.

Regarding NDCG, for "plastic" and "general trash", $Model_B$, we observed the same tendency as the precision values on $Model_{EB}$, $Model_{SB}$, and $Model_{SEB}$. For "burnable trash" and "plastic bottles" , $Model_B$, $Model_{EB}$, $Model_{SB}$, $Model_{SE}$, and $Model_{SEB}$, had the maximum NDCG scores, respectively.

We read the top-10 articles ranked by the full model (i.e., $Model_{SEB}$) to assess the articles. Many of the news articles in the "plastic category" contained the word "plastic" in the title, and articles in the "burnable trash" category included various content, e.g., trash, carbon dioxide, and food loss. News articles in the "plastic bottles" category were primarily related to the natural environment, e.g., oceans, rivers, and mountains. For the "general trash" category, the top-ranked news articles were related to the large amount of waste disposal and environmental issues.

5 User Study with Prototype System

A user study with was conducted with the prototype system to survey the participants' impressions about the system and changes in their awareness of environmental issues. We recruited 10 undergraduate and graduate students (four males and six females) from Shizuoka University, Japan. The participants were divided into two groups: five participants for the experimental group and five for the control group. We displayed different news articles to these groups around the trash bin. We also analyzed the results of a postquestionnaire administered to the participants.

5.1 Procedure

The user study was conducted in the following order: (1) a prequestionnaire, (2) the main task, and (3) a postquestionnaire. In the prequestionnaire, we asked the participants to identify their demographics, e.g., gender and age.

In the main task, each participant was asked to eat individually packaged chocolate candies while looking at several images displayed on a screen. These images were not related to global environmental issues and intended to relax each participant for eating chocolate. Once they finished eating chocolate, they were asked to place the candy packaging trash in the proposed trash bin device. Then, they answered questions about the taste of the candy. We asked the participants to perform the above task for two types of chocolate candies. Here, we did not explain the true purpose of the study to avoid satisficing behavior, where participants make favorable assessments with minimal effort.

We conducted a postquestionnaire two hours after the main task. The postquestionnaire asked for impressions about using the trash bin and changes in attitudes and behavioral intentions toward environmental issues before and after using the trash bins, as well as the factors that contributed to these changes.

5.2 Materials

For the user study, we collected 851 new news articles from the websites in Table 1. The collected articles were ranked in order of the impression of a sense of crisis and guilt by the trained learning-to-rank model using the features in Sect. 3.2. For the experimental group, we randomly displayed one of the top five

(a) News article example displayed for **experimental group**   (b) News article example displayed for **control group**

Fig. 3. Displayed articles (excerpts)

news articles with the trash bin device. For the control group, we randomly displayed one news article collected from the top Yahoo! News pages and major Japanese news websites. We confirmed that these articles included sports and political news unrelated to trash or environmental issues. Examples of the displayed news articles are shown in Fig. 3.

5.3 Metrics

In the postquestionnaire, the participants were asked about their daily trash disposal behavior and changes in their pro-environmental attitudes/behavior. The participants were also asked to describe their impressions about the news articles displayed by the trash bin. Table 5 lists the 11 questions which we asked each participants in the postquestionnaire.

To verify whether displaying trash-related news articles was effective at enhancing pro-environmental attitudes and behavior (**H1**), Q1, Q2, Q3, Q4, Q9, and Q10 (Table 5) asked about the connection between the displayed news articles and the trash that was thrown away, as well as the participant's trash disposal awareness. To verify whether displaying news articles that gave a sense of crisis or guilt was effective in terms of enhancing pro-environmental attitudes and behavior, (**H2**), Q5, Q6, Q7, Q8, and Q11 asked about the degree of the sense of crisis and guilt, as well as the level of recognition of environmental risk and responsibility. Regarding the impression of the displayed news articles, we asked the participants to describe their impressions about seeing the news and using the trash bin.

5.4 Results

Table 5 summarizes the means of the experimental and control groups'responses (five-point Likert scale) to the postquestionnaire . A t-test at the 5% significance level revealed that the mean score for Q1 of the experimental group was significantly greater than that of the control group (i.e., whether they wanted to be involved in solving environmental issues (2.8 vs. 1.6)). This result also held for

Table 5. Comparison of postquestionnaire score means (significantly different values are shown in bold)

No.	Question text	Experimental	Control
Q1	Have you become interested in getting involved in solving environmental problems?	**2.8**	**1.6**
Q2	Do you think that regular use of the trash bin will encourage you to take more environmentally conscious actions?	3.0	2.0
Q3	Do you remember what the news articles displayed?	3.0	4.0
Q4	Are you interested in the news articles?	3.6	3.6
Q5	Did you feel a sense of crisis about environmental issues when you saw the news?	**3.4**	**2.0**
Q6	Did you feel sense of guilt about environmental issues when you saw the news?	2.4	2.0
Q7	How serious do you think the environmental issues are?	4.4	4.0
Q8	Do you believe that individual efforts are meaningful in solving issues?	4.2	3.8
Q9	Was the news article displayed relevant to the trash you threw away?	**3.4**	**1.4**
Q10	Did you feel close to the news events when you saw the news articles displayed?	3.8	3.2
Q11	Did you feel that you had damaged the environment by throwing away your trash?	2.4	1.4

Q5 (their sense of the environmental crisis in news articles (3.4 vs. 2.0)) and Q9 (whether the news story was related to the trash they threw away (3.4 vs. 2.0)).

The responses to the free-answer questions are summarized below. When we asked the participants what they were willing to do for the global environment, the experimental group responded with "watching news on environmental issues," "sorting trash," and "using water bottles instead of plastic bottles." In contrast, all control group participants answered "none." When we asked how the participants felt when they viewed the news articles on the trash bin device, the experimental group indicated that "the plastic problem is a major environmental problem," "I felt a connection of news to trash," and "the amount of trash is increasing." These responses indicate their interest in the trash, and one participant in the experimental group answered "I felt a little guilty." In contrast, the control group remembered that the news article was displayed; however, they did not identify any specific impressions. When we asked what the trash bin in the laboratory study would be helpful for, the control group responded that the displayed news would be mainly valuable in providing opportunities to watch the news. In contrast, the experimental group indicated that the news would help "inform people about the reality of trash," "prevent environmental destruction," and "make environmental issues more familiar." For free answers, some participants stated that they "did not have time to read the news during the task" and " could only read the news halfway through, so I was curious about the rest of the story."

6 Discussion

6.1 Ranking of News Articles to Evoke Sense of Crisis and Guilt

The Precision@k and NDCG@k values for news article rankings were sufficiently high for ranking models that included body content features ($Model_B$, $Model_{EB}$,

$Model_{SB}$, and $Model_{SEB}$). The results demonstrated that body content features are important to rank the news articles relative to sense of guilt and crisis.

As an exception, the ranking model that used the article style and emotion features ($Model_{SE}$) obtained the highest precision for "burnable trash," with a Precision@5 value of 0.92 and a Precision@10 value of 0.70. The NDCG values for "burnable trash" for $Model_{SE}$ were also high (NDCG@5 was 0.97 and NDCG@10 was 0.94). For the top-ranked news articles on burnable trash, the article style and emotion features could be more critical than body content features. The top-ranked news articles on "plastic," "plastic bottles," and "general trash" were primarily about plastic-related pollution of the natural environment. In contrast, the top-ranked news articles on "burnable trash" were about various topics, e.g., decarbonization, global warming, and food loss; thus, we assume that features other than body content were more important.

The NDCG@k values of the ranking model using all features ($Model_{SEB}$) were 0.9 or higher for all categories, which means that the full model can predict rankings with higher performance. However, this ranking model was limited to the plastic, burnable trash, and plastic bottles categories. Thus, in the future, we must tune the ranking model to handle other types of trash.

6.2 Design of the Proposed Trash Bin

The results for Q3 and Q4 demonstrate that both the experimental and control groups were interested in the news articles and remembered their content. From these results, we consider that showing news articles during trash disposal is impressive to participants (regardless of the news article's content). In addition, the mean value of the responses to Q1 (whether the participants became more interested in solving environmental problems) was 2.8 for the experimental group and 1.6 for the control group, representing a significant difference. This indicates that the proposed system can affect the formation of pro-environmental attitudes. In summary, the user study demonstrates that the proposed system can affect the formation of pro-environmental attitudes; however, the effect on pro-environmental behavior must be clarified.

The results for Q9 indicate that the participants felt high relevance between the displayed articles and the trash they threw away when using the proposed system. In the free-answer question about the impressions of the news articles, only the experimental group participants referred to "trash" and "environmental problems." These results suggest that displaying trash-related news articles can trigger people to think about trash disposal and environmental problems.

As for **H1**, the results of the user study indicate that the relevance between the displayed articles and trash could enhance pro-environmental attitudes and behavior. However, in this user study, the participants used the trash bin device only twice; thus, long-term user studies are required to verify the effect of the proposed system on the formation and promotion of pro-environmental attitudes and behavior over time. We must also examine the effectiveness of our device for different types of trash.

In the user study, we observed a significant difference in the mean of the responses between the experimental (3.4) and control (2.0) group to Q5 (whether they felt a sense of crisis when they viewed the news article). Although no significant difference in scores was observed for the sense of guilt (Q6), one participant in the experimental group stated they "felt a little guilty" when they saw the news articles. Some participants felt a sense of crisis and guilt when they viewed the news article displayed by the proposed device, while others did not. This could be because the participants did not have sufficient opportunity to read the articles during the study, as indicated by the following free answers.

- *I thought news articles would interfere with the progress of the task. I should have looked at the news a little more.*
- *I did not have time to read the news during the task.*
- *I could only read the news halfway through.*

Regarding **H2**, we partially verified that displaying articles with content that provides a sense crisis and guilt during trash disposal enhances pro-environmental attitudes. The results of Q5 suggest that displaying relevant news articles can make people feel a sense of crisis about environmental issues. However, additional studies are required to verify whether evoking a sense of crisis can promote ongoing pro-environmental behavior. Furthermore, to evoke a sense of crisis and guilt during the brief trash disposal action, it is necessary to devise a mechanism to convey the article content to participants concisely and effectively.

7 Conclusion

This paper has proposed a trash bin type device to enhance pro-environmental attitudes and behavior. The proposed device ranks news articles in order of the impressions of a sense of crisis and guilt regarding the global environment. Then, the proposed device displays the highest ranked article when people use the device in conjunction with throwing away trash. The experimental results show that the ranking model can find impressive news articles by focusing on the emotional, textual, and semantic features of the articles. Furthermore, a user study revealed that the proposed device can trigger users to contemplate environmental problems and trash by displaying news articles that evoke a sense of crisis when they throw trash away. However, our study did not clarify the long-term effects of the proposed system. Thus, further user studies and performance improvements are required to verify the long-term formation and promotion of pro-environmental attitudes and behaviors realized by the proposed system.

References

1. Anja, T., et al.: We've bin watching you: designing for reflection and social persuasion to promote sustainable lifestyles. In: Proceedings of the SIGCHI Conference on Human Factors in Computing Systems, pp. 2337–2346. CHI'12 (2012)
2. Burges, C.J., Ragno, R., VietLe, Q.: Learning to rank with nonsmooth cost functions. In: Advances in Neural Information Processing Systems, vol. 19, pp. 193–200. NIPS706 (2006)
3. Devlin, J., Chang, M.W., Lee, K., Toutanova, K.: Bert: pre-training of deep bidirectional transformers for language understanding. In: Proceedings of Annial Conference of the North American Chapter of the Association for Computational Linguistics, pp. 4171–4186 (2019)
4. Dosovitskiy, A., et al.: An image is worth 16×16 words: transformers for image recognition at scale. In: Proceedings of the 9th International Conference on Learning Representations (2021)
5. Hirose, Y.: In: Kankyo to shouhi no shakaishinrigaku. The University of Nagoya Press (1995)
6. Holmes, T.G.: Eco-visualization: combining art and technology to reduce energy consumption. In: Proceedings of the 6th ACM SIGCHI Conference on Creativity & Cognition, pp. 153–162. C&C '07 (2007)
7. Horne, B.D., Adali, S.: This just in: fake news packs a lot in title, uses simpler, repetitive content in text body, more similar to satire than real news. In: Proceedings of the International AAAI Conference on Web and Social Media, pp. 759–766 (2017). 11(1)
8. Igarashi, T., Okuda, S., Sasahara, K.: Development of the Japanese version of the linguistic inquiry and word count dictionary 2015. Front. Psychol. **13**, 841534 (2022)
9. Jacobsen, R.M., Johansen, P.S., Bysted, L.B.L., Skov, M.B.: Waste wizard: exploring waste sorting using ai in public spaces. In: Proceedings of the 11th Nordic Conference on Human-Computer Interaction: Shaping Experiences, Shaping Society, pp. 1–11. ACM (2020)
10. Jarvelin, K., Kekalainen, J.: Cumulated gain-based evaluation OF IR techniques. ACM Trans. Inf. Syst. **20**(4), 422–446 (2002)
11. Ke, G., et al.: Lightgbm: a highly efficient gradient boosting decision tree. In: Proceedings of the 31st International Conference on Neural Information Processing Systems, pp. 3149–3157. NIPS'17 (2017)
12. Kim, S., Saskia, B., Steven, H.: Econundrum: visualizing the climate impact of dietary choice through a shared data sculpture. In: Proceedings of the 2020 ACM Designing Interactive Systems Conference, pp. 1287–1300. Dis'20 (2020)
13. Koike, T., et al.: Basic study on psychological processes and activities related to environmental problems. Annu. J. Hydraul. Eng. JSCE **47**, 361–366 (2003)
14. Kudo, T., Yamamoto, K., Matsumoto, Y.: Applying conditionalrandom fields to Japanese morphologiaical analysis. IPSJ Techn. Rep. **47**(NL161), 89–96 (2004)
15. Kuiken, J., Schuth, A., Spitters, M., Marx, M.: Effective headlines of newspaper articles in a digital environment. Digit. Journal. **5**(10), 1300–1314 (2017)
16. Nonami, H., Sugiura, J., Ohnuma, S., Yamakawa, H., Hirose, Y.: The roles of various media in the decision making processes for recycling behavior: a path analysis model. Jpn. J. Psychol. **68**(4), 264–271 (1997)

17. Ohata, K., Iyatomi, H., Morita, H., Iizuka, K.: How are negative articles consumed? A quantitative analysis of user behavior in a real news service. In: 2023 IEEE International Conference on Systems, Man, and Cybernetics (SMC), pp. 5311–5316 (2023)
18. Pennebaker, J.W., Boyd, R.L.: A way with words: using language for psychological science in the modern era. In: Consumer Psychology in a Social Media World, pp. 222–236 (2015)
19. Proença, P.F.S.P.: Taco: trash annotations in context for litter detection. In: arXiv preprint arXiv:2003.06975 (2020)

Evaluating the Impact of Color and Sound Combinations on Cognitive Performance in Virtual Reality

Ryoma Nakao[✉] and Tatsuo Nakajima

Waseda University, Tokyo, Japan
{r.takenoko,tatsuo}@dcl.cs.waseda.ac.jp

Abstract. Virtual Reality (VR) has expanded into various fields. This research explores the effects of virtual environments on task performance, with a focus on the combination of environmental elements such as colors and sounds and cognitive tasks. Participants completed tasks in virtual environments with varied auditory and visual stimuli. Findings show natural sound-color combinations enhance concentration and efficiency. This study emphasizes how sensory stimuli in VR can optimize learning and work environments, demonstrating VR's potential as a transformative tool for society.

1 Introduction

The use of Virtual Reality (VR) has been rapidly expanding across various fields, including education, entertainment, and healthcare. This study aims to contribute to this growing body of research by investigating how the combination of auditory and visual elements affects cognitive performance within VR environments. Specifically, the study explores how natural sound and color combinations influence task efficiency and concentration, with an emphasis on their practical applications in educational and workplace settings.

The advent of VR technology has revolutionized how we interact with digital content, providing immersive experiences that go beyond the constraints of the physical world. In educational settings, VR has been recognized for its potential to enhance learning by creating interactive and engaging environments. In workplace contexts, VR is used for training and simulation, where realistic scenarios are crucial for skill development. Despite these advancements, the integration of sensory elements such as sound and color within VR environments has not been thoroughly explored.

Understanding how these elements interact and affect cognitive processes is crucial for optimizing VR applications. By investigating the combined effects of auditory and visual stimuli, this study addresses a significant research gap. The ability to effectively incorporate sensory elements like sound and color into VR environments could lead to substantial improvements in user experience and performance, particularly in settings where cognitive tasks are central.

Existing research underscores the influence of environmental factors on cognitive performance. Studies on context-dependent memory highlight that memory retrieval is more effective when the learning and retrieval contexts are congruent [3,6]. This concept is particularly relevant in VR environments where the ability to match sensory inputs with cognitive tasks could enhance learning and task performance.

The psychological impact of color has been extensively studied, revealing that color can affect cognitive abilities and emotional states. For instance, Jin et al. [2] found that certain color combinations can improve cognitive performance under low cognitive load, while Elliott et al. [1] demonstrated that the color red might reduce intellectual performance in certain contexts. These findings suggest that color plays a significant role in influencing cognitive tasks and emotional responses.

Auditory stimuli are equally important in cognitive processes. Research by Van Hedger et al. [5] indicates that environmental sounds from natural settings can influence relaxation and focus, which are critical for optimal cognitive performance. The interplay between sound and color, including studies on synesthesia, further suggests that specific color-sound combinations can enhance task efficiency. For example, Sun et al. [4] found that matching colors and sounds can lead to improved performance on various tasks.

Despite these insights, there is a notable gap in research focusing on the combined effects of auditory and visual stimuli within VR environments. This study aims to fill this gap by conducting three experiments. The first experiment explores the associations between natural sounds and colors, the second examines how these sound-induced colors affect cognitive task performance, and the third assesses the impact of different sound-color combinations on task efficiency and concentration. By addressing this gap, the study seeks to provide valuable insights into how sensory elements can be optimized in VR environments to enhance user experience and performance.

2 System Design

2.1 System Overview

This system is designed to manipulate color and sound within virtual spaces and to perform computational tasks. The system enables users to create and associate colors with sounds in a virtual environment, enhancing the intuitive association between auditory and visual stimuli. Additionally, the system allows users to perform computational tasks while altering the surrounding colors, aiming to evaluate the impact of these changes on cognitive performance and to improve task efficiency and user concentration.

2.2 Sound Source Evaluation System

The first component of the system allows users to listen to sound sources and generate corresponding colors in the virtual space. Users can adjust the RGB values to create a wide range of colors, which are then displayed to reflect the auditory input. This system helps to explore the relationship between sound and color perception and its potential effects on cognitive tasks.

2.3 Computational System

Evaluation System. The second part of this system is for performing computational tasks within the virtual space. As shown in Fig. 1, the user enters numerical answers to computation problems and presses the "OK" button to submit the answers. If the answer is correct, the count increases, and the input can be reset with the "Clear" button. When the count reaches 30, the elapsed time from pressing the "Start" button is displayed as the score.

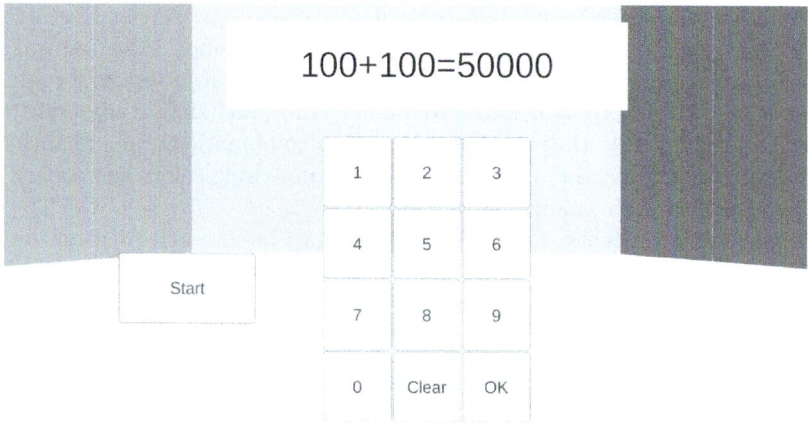

Fig. 1. Calculation System

Surrounding Color Transition System. This system allows users to change the surrounding color within the virtual environment, offering options such as red, blue, or green. By altering the color of the environment, the system aims to investigate how these visual changes impact the user's task performance and concentration during computational activities.

3 Experiment 1

3.1 Purpose of Experiment 1

Experiment 1 explored how natural sounds are associated with colors. By examining these associations, the study aimed to understand their potential impact on task efficiency in later experiments. To minimize participant bias, the sequence of Experiments 1, 2, and 3 was randomized.

3.2 Description of Experiment 1

Participants, aged 19 to 24 (38 males, 7 females), listened to natural sounds such as waves, campfire, and forest. They were asked to create colors using RGB combinations that intuitively matched each sound. The order of sound playback was randomized to avoid bias.

3.3 Results of Experiment 1

The analysis revealed statistically significant associations between the natural sounds and specific colors. Waves were commonly associated with blue, campfire with red, and forest with green. These findings suggest that natural sounds can influence color perception, providing insights into the relationship between sound and color.

4 Experiment 2

4.1 Purpose of Experiment 2

This experiment aimed to explore whether colors perceived from sounds influence task efficiency, building on the associations identified in Experiment 1. The focus was on cognitive tasks, specifically arithmetic problems, to evaluate the potential impact of sound-induced colors on performance.

4.2 Description of Experiment 2

Participants, aged 19 to 24 (38 males, 7 females), performed arithmetic tasks within a virtual environment. Before the main task, they completed a 5-minute practice session to become familiar with the system. During the experiment, one of the natural sounds from Experiment 1 was randomly selected and played. Participants then solved 30 arithmetic problems, with their completion times recorded. Afterward, they rated their concentration on a 10-point Likert scale.

4.3 Results of Experiment 2

The data included completion times for arithmetic tasks and perceived concentration levels. The Kruskal-Wallis test revealed no significant differences in task performance (p-value = $0.893 > 0.05$) or concentration (p-value = $0.339 > 0.05$) across different sound sources. These findings suggest that the colors induced by sounds did not significantly influence task efficiency or concentration.

5 Experiment 3

5.1 Purpose of Experiment 3

Experiment 3 examined how different combinations of sound and color affect task efficiency and concentration. Specifically, it assessed the impact of environmental sound-color combinations on task performance and explored how surrounding colors influenced concentration on the sound sources.

5.2 Description of Experiment 3

Participants, aged 19 to 24 (38 males, 7 females), completed arithmetic tasks in a virtual environment where the background color alternated between red, blue, and green. During each task, a natural sound from Experiment 1 was randomly played. Participants solved 30 arithmetic problems, with the time taken recorded. After each task, they rated their concentration and focus on the sound source using a 10-point Likert scale.

5.3 Results of Experiment 3

In Experiment 1, the colors red, blue, and green were classified based on the perceived intensity for each sound source. Using this data, the most intuitively related and least related combinations were selected, and the time required and perceived concentration data were classified accordingly. T-tests conducted on these datasets showed no significant difference in the required time (p-value $= 0.334 > 0.05$). However, a significant difference was observed in perceived concentration (p-value $= 0.047 < 0.05$). The mean and median values of the same and different color-sound combination data are shown in Table 1. Results of the Friedman test conducted to compare the effects of surrounding colors yielded (p-value $= 0.0064 < 0.05$). Post hoc tests adjusted using the Shaffer method and conducted with the Wilcoxon signed-rank test suggested that blue and green may enhance concentration on the sound source compared to red.

Table 1. Mean and Median Values for Same combination Data and Different combination Data

	Same	Different
Mean Calculation Time	129.51	127.10
Median Calculation Time	125.00	124.00
Mean Perceived Concentration	6.93	6.29
Median Perceived Concentration	7.00	7.00

6 Conclusion

This study examined the effects of natural sound and color combinations on cognitive performance in Virtual Reality (VR) environments, addressing a gap in the current literature. The research aimed to explore how these sensory elements influence task efficiency and concentration.

In Experiment 1, specific color associations with natural sounds were identified: waves were associated with blue, campfire with red, and forest with green. These associations provide a basis for understanding how natural auditory stimuli can affect color perception.

Experiment 2 investigated whether sound-induced colors impact arithmetic task performance. Despite the established color-sound associations, no significant differences were found in task performance or concentration due to these colors. This suggests that while color-sound associations exist, their direct effect on cognitive performance in VR may be minimal.

Experiment 3 explored the impact of various sound-color combinations on cognitive performance and concentration. It was found that certain combinations, particularly involving blue and green, significantly improved task efficiency and concentration compared to red. This highlights the potential of using specific sensory combinations to enhance cognitive performance in VR settings.

Overall, the study indicates that integrating sensory stimuli in VR environments can influence cognitive performance. Although sound-induced colors did not show significant effects in all cases, thoughtful combinations of sound and color can enhance concentration and efficiency. Future research should further explore individual differences, task types, and the long-term effects of sensory integration in VR to fully understand its potential benefits.

This research contributes to the knowledge of VR and sensory integration, offering practical insights for optimizing VR applications in education, work, and beyond.

References

1. Elliot, A., Maier, M.A.: Color and psychological functioning. Curr. Dir. Psychol. Sci. **16**, 250–254 (2007). https://doi.org/10.1111/j.1467-8721.2007.00514.x
2. Jin, T., Zhou, S., Lang, X., He, J., Wang, W.: Combined effect of color and shape on cognitive performance. Math. Probl. Eng. (2022). https://doi.org/10.1155/2022/3284313
3. Smith, S., Vela, E.: Environmental context-dependent memory: a review and meta-analysis. Psychon. Bull. Rev. **8**, 203–20 (2001). https://doi.org/10.3758/BF03196157
4. Sun, X., et al.: An extended research of crossmodal correspondence between color and sound in psychology and cognitive ergonomics. PeerJ **6**, e4443 (2018). https://doi.org/10.7717/peerj.4443
5. Van Hedger, S.C., Nusbaum, H.C., Clohisy, L., Jaeggi, S.M., Buschkuehl, M., Berman, M.G.: Of cricket chirps and car horns: The effect of nature sounds on cognitive performance. Psychonomic Bulletin & Review **26**(2), 522–530 (Apr 2019). https://doi.org/10.3758/s13423-018-1539-1, https://doi.org/10.3758/s13423-018-1539-1
6. Zhang, Y.: Research on the application of computer "virtual reality" technology in physical education of colleges and universities, pp. 1284–1287 (2018). https://doi.org/10.2991/MEICI-18.2018.261

Medical and Cognitive Health Applications

Mild Cognitive Impairment Prediction Using Facial and Speech Data

Chien-Cheng Lee[1](✉) [iD], Wei-Chieh Huang[1], and Yi-Fang Chuang[2,3]

[1] Department of Electrical Engineering, Yuan Ze University, Taoyuan, Taiwan
cclee@saturn.yzu.edu.tw
[2] Institute of Public Health, College of Medicine, National Yang Ming Chiao Tung University, Taipei 112, Taiwan
[3] Department of Psychiatry, Far Eastern Memorial Hospital, New Taipei City 220, Taiwan

Abstract. Mild cognitive impairment (MCI) represents a transitional stage between the cognitive decline associated with normal aging and more severe conditions such as dementia. Early diagnosis of MCI is crucial for effective healthcare intervention. However, current detection methods are often costly and time-consuming. This study introduces a multimodal fusion network (MFN) designed to predict MCI more efficiently. The proposed network utilizes dual-stream ResNets to process both facial and speech features. These features, extracted from the convolutional and subsampling layers of the ResNets, are subsequently fused in a fully connected layer to generate the final prediction. The dataset comprises a total of 52 participant videos, with an equal distribution: 26 videos from participants with normal cognitive function and 26 videos from participants diagnosed with MCI. Experimental results demonstrate the effectiveness of this approach, with an F1 score of 0.89 across test participants.

Keywords: MCI Prediction · Multimodal Fusion Network · Facial and Speech Data · ResNet

1 Introduction

Mild Cognitive Impairment (MCI) is a transition from normal aging to dementia. Once MCI enters the dementia stage, caring for these patients becomes complicated and costly. Early identifying patients with MCI and timely applying treatment can delay the progress of the MCI to Alzheimer's disease (AD). However, the symptom of MCI is often neglected due to inconvenient, expensive, and/or time-consuming methods for its early detection. Therefore, the early diagnosis of MCI plays an important role in human healthcare.

Current methods of MCI detection include cognitive tests to screen for executive function impairments, possibly followed by neuroimaging tests. One of the common cognitive screening tests for MCI is the Mini-Mental State Examination (MMSE) [1]. Cognitive tests are not completely objective and may be influenced by the conducting physician or the patient's age and educational background. Furthermore, neuroimaging methods are expensive and time-consuming, making them unsuitable for screening large populations. Consequently, a non-invasive, cost-effective, and easy-to-use screening method is critical for detecting MCI.

Over the past decade, biomarkers combined with machine learning algorithms have become commonly used to detect MCI. These biomarkers include cognitive tests, electroencephalograms (EEG), speech analysis, facial imaging, and neuroimaging tests. In this study, we propose a multimodal fusion network (MFN) that integrates speech and facial dynamics to predict MCI. The network consists of two convolutional neural networks (CNNs). Log-mel spectrograms generated from speech and the optical flow of facial dynamics are input into the two CNNs to extract latent features. These speech and facial dynamic features are then fused and passed through linear layers to predict MCI.

Experimental results show that this method achieves excellent performance with an F1 score of 0.89. This indicates that an automatic, non-invasive, and inexpensive MCI screening method using speech and facial data is feasible, eliminating the need for highly subjective paper-and-pencil questionnaires.

2 Related Work

Speech reveals multidimensional information about the speaker (e.g., age, gender, sociolinguistic characteristics, physiological condition) and can function as a fingerprint that identifies patients with MCI from healthy controls. Several studies have demonstrated that MCI and dementia can be detected by machine learning technologies from speech data [2, 3]. On the other hand, the use of facial data to detect MCI and dementia has attracted the attention of many researchers because of its easy availability [4, 5]. Most of them use static facial images to extract facial expressions and features such as action units, eye gaze, and lip activity. Tanaka et al. [4] proposed a method to automatically detect dementia from a human face. They identified various contributing features, such as action units, eye gaze, and lip activity.

Facial changes over time contain more information than static images. In other words, more complete facial features include not only spatial features, but also motion features when people respond to certain questions. Wang et al. [5] compared different deep learning methods for assessing facial dynamics such as talking, singing, neutral and smiling in AD-patients. These methods include 3D CNNs, two-stream CNNs, as well as improved dense trajectories.

3 Proposed Method

3.1 Data Collection and Preprocessing

All participants gave their informed consent for inclusion before they participated in the study. There are 52 participants in this study, 26 are cognitively normal (median age: 71 years, IQR: 67–76.75 years, 10 males, 16 females) and 26 are diagnosed with MCI (median age: 73 years, IQR: 69–78 years, 10 males, 16 females). Table 1 shows the gender and age distribution of the participants. In order to collect realistic and reasonable data from participants without stress or embarrassment, participants recorded videos while participating in the MMSE.

Table 1. Gender distribution of participants.

	Female	Male	Total
Normal	16	10	26
MCI	16	10	26
Total	32	20	52

In this study, we utilize speech and facial dynamics to predict MCI. The dataset comprises a total of 52 participant videos, with an equal distribution: 26 videos from participants with normal cognitive function and 26 videos from participants diagnosed with MCI. To reduce spatial and temporal redundancy before processing, the frame resolution was resized to 640 × 480, and the video frame rate was downsampled to 5 fps. Next, the videos were divided into several non-overlapping segments, each with a length of 20 frames. The optical flow technique was then used to capture the facial dynamics from the segment frames. Optical flow, a method used in computer vision, obtains the motion field on an individual pixel basis between two image frames. The stacked optical flow fields in the x and y directions were calculated to represent facial motion information. In this study, we chose the TVL1 optical flow algorithm [6], implemented by OpenCV with CUDA.

To extract the speech data, we calculate the log-mel spectrogram [7] from the audio channel in the video. Since the videos are recorded during the MMSE test, the audio channel contains both the participant's and the conducting physician's voices. We use a speaker diarization technique [8] to automatically identify and segment the audio recording into distinct speech segments. Next, we manually label the participants' speech segments and divide them into several 15-s waveforms. Short-time Fourier transforms (STFTs) are applied to the waveforms to generate spectrograms. Mel filter banks are then applied to the spectrograms, followed by a logarithmic operation to extract the log-mel spectrograms, as shown in Fig. 1.

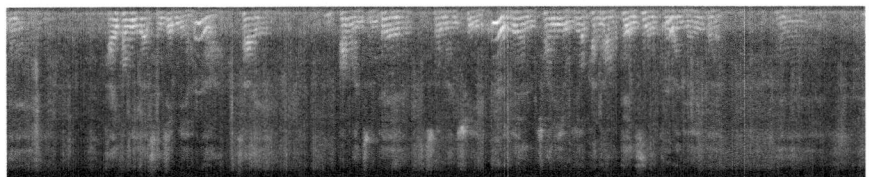

Fig. 1. An example of log-mel spectrogram.

3.2 Multimodal Fusion Network

The proposed MFN consists of three CNNs, a fusion mechanism, and a fully connected layer serving as the classifier, as shown in Fig. 2. The three CNNs are designated for speech, x-motion, and y-motion analysis. The network receives log-mel spectrograms and x, y stacked optical flow fields from a video segment as inputs, and uses the three CNNs to extract speech and motion features. These speech features, x-motion features, and y-motion features are concatenated to form a one-dimensional vector. Finally, the fused feature vector is classified as MCI or normal through a batch normalization (BN) layer and a fully connected (FC) layer.

In this study, a modified ResNet-18 architecture utilizing the Mish activation function serves as the backbone for the CNN in the MFN. To improve the training process, the Ranger optimizer [9] is employed. The model benefits from transfer learning with pretrained weights of ResNet-18. During the fine-tuning phase, the final convolutional layer, BN layers, and FC layers are retrained, while the remaining layers are kept frozen to leverage the pretrained knowledge.

The MFN functions as a segment classifier within the MCI prediction model. For each segment, the MFN classifier produces a unique decision regarding the segment's identity. Finally, a majority voting scheme aggregates these individual decisions to output the final prediction for the participant. It is worth mentioning that since the video segments are not time-aligned with the log-mel spectrograms, we randomly sample a log-mel spectrogram from the same video for each segment.

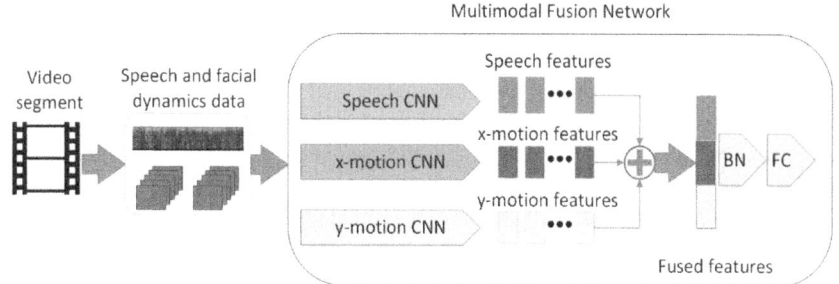

Fig. 2. Architecture of the multimodal fusion network.

4 Experimental Results

We use OpenFace [10] to filter out inappropriate videos, such as those with face masks, extreme face angles, or subjects at too great a distance from the camera. We then randomly select appropriate videos in roughly equal proportions across classes to mitigate the data imbalance problem. Finally, all participants are randomly grouped into training and validation groups in a ratio of approximately 8:2, maintaining the same class proportions as in the original dataset. After grouping participants, all video segments are assigned to the training or validation sets based on their corresponding participant IDs in these groups.

Table 2 shows the numbers of segments in the training and validation sets. The training set comprises 3,842 segments from 42 participant videos, while the validation set contains 990 segments from 10 participant videos. MCI segments are marked as positive, and normal segments are marked as negative. Due to the limited amount of video data, we do not have a separate test set. Instead, the validation set will be used during the model testing phase to evaluate the model's performance.

Table 2. Numbers of training and validation sets.

	Training set		Validation set	
	Videos	Segments	Videos	Segments
Normal	21	1913	5	495
MCI	21	1929	5	495
Total	42	3842	10	990

We conducted all experiments on a computer with Intel(R) Core(TM) i9-12900 2.4 GHz CPU and NVIDIA GeForce RTX 3090 Ti GPU. The PyTorch deep learning framework is used to implement our model. We set the initial learning rate to 0.001, the batch size to 16, and the training epoch to 30, respectively. An exponential learning rate decay is also used in model training. The best mode during the training will be stored and used for testing. Table 3 summarizes the sensitivity, specificity, accuracy, and F1-score results of the models using Swish and Ranger. The proposed model achieved an F1 score of 0.89 at the participant level and an F1 score of 0.83 only at the segment level during the validation phase.

Table 3. MCI prediction results of the best model.

	Training		Validation	
	Participant	Segments	Participant	Segments
sensitivity	1.00	0.98	0.80	0.78
specificity	0.95	0.90	1.00	0.91
Accuracy	0.98	0.94	0.90	0.84
F1	0.98	0.94	0.89	0.83

5 Conclusion

In this study, we propose an MCI prediction method based on a novel MFN. Participant-level evaluations show that the ResNet-18 backbone combined with Swish activation and Ranger optimizer achieves an F1-score of 0.89. However, there is potential for further improving the MFN through refinements such as hyperparameter tuning.

The MFN captures latent speech features and facial dynamic features from videos, providing robust representations without the need for handcrafted features commonly used in traditional machine learning methods. Research indicates that MCI can be detected through speech and facial dynamics, making these features valuable biomarkers for MCI. This approach holds great promise for developing accurate models for MCI screening using facial and speech data. It demonstrates that automated, non-invasive, and cost-effective MCI screening methods are feasible, eliminating the need for highly subjective paper-and-pencil questionnaires.

Acknowledgments. This study was funded by the Ministry of Science and Technology of Taiwan (grant number: MOST 109-2221-E-155-054).

Disclosure of Interests. The authors have no competing interests to declare that are relevant to the content of this article.

References

1. Tombaugh, T.N., McIntyre, N.J.: The mini-mental state examination: a comprehensive review. J. Am. Geriatr. Soc. **40**, 922–935 (1992)
2. Themistocleous, C., Eckerström, M., Kokkinakis, D.: Voice quality and speech fluency distinguish individuals with mild cognitive impairment from healthy controls. PLoS ONE **15**, e0236009 (2020)
3. Yu, B., Williamson, J.R., Mundt, J.C., Quatieri, T.F.: Speech-based automated cognitive impairment detection from remotely-collected cognitive test audio. IEEE Access **6**, 40494–40505 (2018)
4. Tanaka, H., Adachi, H., Kazui, H., Ikeda, M., Kudo, T., Nakamura, S.: Detecting dementia from face in human-agent interaction. In: Adjunct of the 2019 International Conference on Multimodal Interaction, pp. 1–6 (2019)
5. Wang, Y., Dantcheva, A., Broutart, J.C., Robert, P., Bremond, F., Bilinski, P.: Comparing methods for assessment of facial dynamics in patients with major neurocognitive disorders. In: Leal-Taixé, L., Roth, S. (eds.) Computer Vision – ECCV 2018 Workshops. ECCV 2018. LNCS, vol. 11134, pp. 144–157. Springer, Cham (2019). https://doi.org/10.1007/978-3-030-11024-6_10
6. Zach, C., Pock, T., Bischof, H.: A duality based approach for realtime TV-L 1 optical flow. In: Hamprecht, F.A., Schnörr, C., Jähne, B. (eds.) Pattern Recognition. DAGM 2007. LNCS, vol. 4713, pp. 214–223. Springer, Berlin, Heidelberg (2007). https://doi.org/10.1007/978-3-540-74936-3_22
7. Kong, Q., Cao, Y., Iqbal, T., Wang, Y., Wang, W., Plumbley, M.D.: PANNs: large-scale pretrained audio neural networks for audio pattern recognition. IEEE/ACM Trans. Audio Speech Lang. Process. **28**, 2880–2894 (2020)
8. Park, T.J., Koluguri, N.R., Balam, J., Ginsburg, B.: Multi-scale speaker diarization with dynamic scale weighting. arXiv preprint arXiv:2203.15974 (2022)
9. Wright, L.: New deep learning optimizer, ranger: synergistic combination of radam+ lookahead for the best of both (2019). Github https://github.com/lessw2020/Ranger-Deep-Learning-Optimizer
10. Baltrušaitis, T., Robinson, P., Morency, L.-P.: Openface: an open source facial behavior analysis toolkit. In: 2016 IEEE Winter Conference on Applications of Computer Vision (WACV), pp. 1–10. IEEE (2016)

Comparing Training of Sparse to Classic Neural Networks for Binary Classification in Medical Data

Laura Erhan[1], Antonio Liotta[1], and Lucia Cavallaro[2](✉)

[1] Free University of Bozen-Bolzano, Bolzano, Italy
{laura.erhan,antonio.liotta}@unibz.it
[2] Radboud University, Nijmegen, The Netherlands
lucia.cavallaro@ru.nl

Abstract. Sparse Neural Networks are increasing in popularity and provide the opportunity for compact and efficient models for resource-constrained environments which are expanding as the number of IoT devices is increasing and as the Edge Computing and Fog paradigms are gaining traction. We investigate and evaluate sparsifying the training of Convolutional Neural Networks for the task of binary classification on medical datasets. We considered low (*i.e.*, 28×28) grey-scale resolution images that are memory-friendly and suitable for storing and analysing on lightweight devices. We found out that high sparsification strategies (above 75%) can achieve comparable performances with that of the fully connected counterpart while allowing for a reduction in inference time and peak memory usage, beneficial for resource-constrained environments part of Edge Computing. It is important to note that, as might be expected, after 90% sparsity, the performance can oscillate, and the results can vary significantly.

Keywords: Sparse Artificial Neural Networks · Binary Classification · Edge Computing · Medical datasets

1 Introduction

In recent years, machine learning models led to improved performance across different research domains, and has witnessed an entry to the edge, fog and IoT computing paradigms [1].

However, one of the biggest limits in training such models is, apart from being energy and time-consuming processes, to achieve computational efficiency with resource constraints when dealing, for instance, with IoT devices or in a broader context of stand-alone systems [2].

For those reasons, sparse neural networks have emerged as a promising alternative to their dense counterparts, as they are characterized by their reduced number of parameters and connections that can offer potential benefits in terms of lower memory consumption while still preserving accuracy [4,5,9,10]. These attributes are especially critical in medical applications, where large datasets and complex models often pose substantial computational challenges. [7] provides an extensive overview of sparsity in deep learning and its advantages.

Binary classification tasks are commonplace in medical diagnostics, where the goal is to distinguish between two classes, such as the presence or absence of a disease [6,12]. Traditional dense neural networks have demonstrated substantial success in these tasks, benefiting from their ability to model complex relationships within data. However, the computational demands of these networks can be prohibitive, particularly when deployed in resource-limited environments or when handling large-scale medical datasets.

This paper investigates how sparse neural networks compare to classic dense neural networks in the context of binary classification of medical data as a case study. We considered two medical image datasets that are *Malaria dataset* [11], on which we conducted already preliminary analysis in our previous work [3], and *Pneumonia MedMNIST v2* dataset [13]. In both cases, we are looking at low gray-scale resolution images, 28 × 28, that are memory-friendly and suitable for storing and analysing on lightweight devices.

Our aim is to evaluate and compare the performances of those two models in terms of accuracy, inference time and computational resource usage. By examining their relative strengths and limitations, we seek to determine whether the trade-offs associated with sparsity, such as reduced parameter count and potential loss in representational capacity—affect their effectiveness in medical classification tasks.

To do so, we focused on Convolutional Neural Networks (CNNs) as our analyses unveiled that such a model achieved better results in the context of image classification, which is consistent with the literature [8]. We varied the sparsity ratio up to 95% to unveil the best performance trade-off between accuracy and compression.

This study provides insights into the practicality and efficacy of sparse neural networks, comparing them with their classic counterparts. Through this study, we aim to contribute to the ongoing dialogue on optimizing neural network architectures on a wider range of applications, to support not only the development of more efficient and scalable diagnostic tools but to generate a standards pipeline for future developments of edge computing and server-less cloud computing.

2 Methodology

2.1 Malaria Dataset

The Malaria dataset is a publicly available dataset [11], chosen for its curated data, balanced distribution, and representative collection of images suitable for addressing the complexity of our research problem. The dataset comprises 27,558 images, evenly divided into two classes representing infected and uninfected cells. The images were normalised to maintain values within the [0, 1] range. The dataset was partitioned into training, testing, and validation sets respecting the following percentages: 80% of the data for training and 20% for testing; the training data was further split into training and validation sets, maintaining the 80% and 20% split.

2.2 Pneumonia MNIST

MedMNIST v2 is a large-scale MNIST-like dataset collection of standardized biomedical images [13]. Part of it is Pneumonia MNIST, a dataset composed of 5,856 pediatric chest X-Ray image samples out of which 4,708 are used for training, 524 for validation and 624 for testing. The task is to binary classify pneumonia against normal.

2.3 CNN Classification Model

CNNs employ a hierarchical architecture to systematically analyze visual data, an approach that enables CNNs to identify and prioritize relevant features, facilitating heightened precision and efficacy in tasks such as image recognition, classification, and segmentation [8]. The chosen model is a regular CNN, comprising of 3 convolutional layers consisting of 8, 16, and 32 filters, respectively, alternating with 3 max pooling layers. We employ a dropout layer of 0.5, followed by a flattened layer, a dense layer with 64 neurons and ReLU activation, and finally, a single neuron output layer with sigmoid activation.

2.4 Experimental Setup

For the analysis, we used the same image resolution for both datasets, namely 28×28. Furthermore, the images were processed as gray-scale. This translates to a lightweight setup. The model was trained in each case for 30 epochs in total, and we investigated sparsity percentage levels of 0% (fully connected NN), 75%, 80%, and from 85% to 95%, with a step of 1%. If the sparsity level is set to zero, the model progresses without parameter reduction. Otherwise, the model is pruned at every epoch to the desired sparsity level by employing the *tfmot.sparsity.keras.prune_low_magnitude* function. All the processing and experiments have been performed on an NVIDIA A100 GPU.

Further, we offer a brief overview of the **evaluation metrics.**

Accuracy, Precision, and **Recall** represent the model's efficiency as the percentage of accurately classified instances out of the total inferences made, the ratio of truly identified infected cells to the total number of cells predicted as infected and the model's capability to accurately identify infected cells, respectively.

Inference time delineates the temporal interval between tensor allocation and output formulation. A lower inference time aligns with our objective to craft sleek and efficient models.

Training time measures the time needed for training the model by monitoring the execution time for the *model.fit* function.

Peak memory usage provides insight into the peak memory utilised by the model and the resource requirements for optimizing deployment across diverse environments. It is monitored using the *tracemalloc* module.

3 Experimental Results

All the results achieved are summarised in Table 1, in which the accuracy metric refers to the testing dataset.

For the Pneumonia dataset, we can consider that the model experienced a sudden drop in accuracy at a sparsity level of 94%. For the Malaria dataset, the drop is experienced at 93%. However, it is important to note, that during multiple runs, it is consistent that the drop happens after the 90% sparsity level. Another interesting metric to note is the inference time. In all sparse scenarios considered, there is an approximately 15% drop in inference time for the Malaria dataset and one of 30% for the case of the Pneumonia dataset. A drop is experienced also for the peak memory usage metric, namely at least 45% for the Pneumonia dataset, and 35% for the Malaria dataset. For the total execution time associated with the training, the values corresponding to the sparse cases are slightly increased (*i.e.*, of 20%) due to the extra pruning operations associated with sparsifying the network at every epoch.

In Fig. 1, for the sake of visual comparison, the training and validation curves over the 30 epochs for the fully connected network and the corresponding NN with a 75% sparsity level for the two datasets are shown. We can notice the same trend in all 4 cases, namely that the validation curve follows the training curve. Furthermore, the accuracy is comparable in the sparse scenario to that of the fully-connected case.

Table 1. Table summarising main metrics for the Pneumonia (marked by P and the blue color) and Malaria (marked by M and the orange color) datasets

Sparsity (%)	Accuracy (%)		Precision (%)		Recall (%)		Inference time (s)		Training time (s)		Peak memory usage (MB)	
	P	M	P	M	P	M	P	M	P	M	P	M
0	87.02	95.05	84.72	93.58	96.67	96.73	5.76E-05	4.47E-05	188.74	659.34	29.28	35.38
75	83.17	90.48	79.87	89.74	97.69	91.40	3.89E-05	3.79E-05	230.27	798.87	16.59	22.52
80	88.30	91.78	86.27	92.04	96.67	91.47	3.87E-05	3.75E-05	227.82	799.61	14.14	20.36
85	85.74	86.25	82.93	82.56	97.18	91.91	3.89E-05	3.74E-05	230.50	804.88	14.15	20.44
86	87.18	83.62	84.75	82.09	96.92	85.99	3.87E-05	3.75E-05	231.23	798.13	14.18	20.42
87	86.06	83.24	83.30	85.59	97.18	79.93	3.91E-05	3.73E-05	230.19	778.60	14.14	20.41
88	80.77	79.12	77.00	78.45	98.72	80.30	3.76E-05	3.72E-05	229.30	772.45	14.14	20.35
89	86.38	82.93	87.29	86.00	91.54	78.66	3.80E-05	4.62E-05	230.74	783.00	14.18	20.42
90	83.81	80.32	80.94	83.78	96.92	75.18	3.84E-05	3.71E-05	232.13	777.12	14.23	20.38
91	83.97	82.93	81.39	82.38	96.41	83.78	3.83E-05	3.77E-05	232.53	778.51	14.17	20.38
92	86.06	81.02	84.99	82.99	94.36	78.05	3.86E-05	3.74E-05	232.53	775.62	14.22	20.36
93	79.17	50.00	76.53	50.00	96.15	100.00	3.98E-05	3.72E-05	231.12	780.87	14.25	20.47
94	62.50	74.60	62.50	72.48	100.00	79.32	4.25E-05	3.75E-05	230.43	785.19	14.18	20.41
95	68.43	78.83	66.50	75.75	99.74	84.80	3.85E-05	3.73E-05	229.83	780.98	14.17	20.35

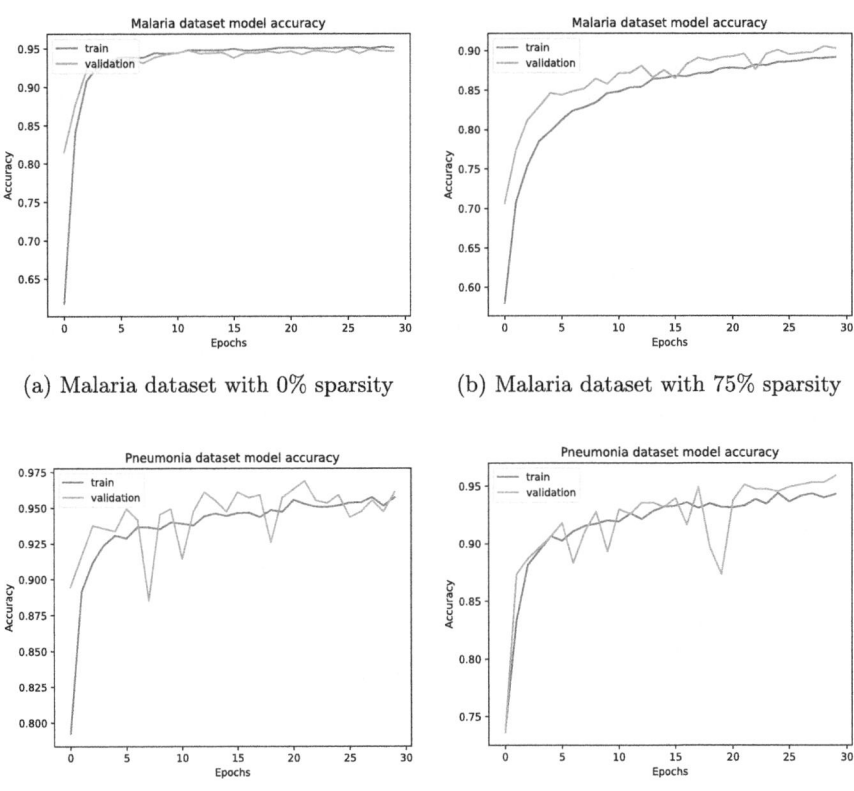

Fig. 1. Training (blue curve) and validation (orange curve) model accuracies plots for the Malaria and the Pneumonia dataset for the fully connected (*i.e.*, 0% sparsity) and the 75% sparsity scenarios (Color figure online)

4 Conclusions and Future Work

In this work, we used sparsification strategies for neural networks to obtain more lightweight models and, therefore, employable in an Edge Computing scenario. The accuracy results are comparable to the case of fully connected neural networks, and metrics such as inference time and peak memory usage are reduced. To demonstrate this, we performed an experimental analysis considering two medical datasets of different sizes, namely the Malaria dataset and the Pneumonia MNIST v2 dataset, with an image resolution of 28×28 in grey-scale, and a variety of sparsity levels to spot the threshold between reliable accuracy and lightweight models. The results achieved so far are promising, so future research directions include a generalization of this approach by considering more configurations of task type and datasets, edge deployment options (testing deployment on a variety of IoT/edge devices), and the expansion of the experimental matrix to include different and more complex sparsification strategies, models and architectures.

Acknowledgements. This work was supported by the PRIN 2020 project COMMON- WEARS (grant number I53C21000210001) and the STEADIER Project (grant num- ber I55F21001900005).

References

1. Ahmad, S., Shakeel, I., Mehfuz, S., Ahmad, J.: Deep learning models for cloud, edge, fog, and IoT computing paradigms: survey, recent advances, and future directions. Comput. Sci. Rev. **49**, 100568 (2023)
2. Ajani, T.S., Imoize, A.L., Atayero, A.A.: An overview of machine learning within embedded and mobile devices-optimizations and applications. Sensors **21**(13), 4412 (2021)
3. Cavallaro, L., Serafin, T., Liotta, A.: Miniaturisation of binary classifiers through sparse neural networks. Numer. Comput. Theory Algorithms NUMTA **2023**, 74 (2023)
4. Changpinyo, S., Sandler, M., Zhmoginov, A.: The power of sparsity in convolutional neural networks. arXiv preprint arXiv:1702.06257 (2017)
5. Gale, T., Elsen, E., Hooker, S.: The state of sparsity in deep neural networks. arXiv preprint arXiv:1902.09574 (2019)
6. Garg, A., Mago, V.: Role of machine learning in medical research: a survey. Comput. Sci. Rev. **40**, 100370 (2021)
7. Hoefler, T., Alistarh, D., Ben-Nun, T., Dryden, N., Peste, A.: Sparsity in deep learning: pruning and growth for efficient inference and training in neural networks. J. Mach. Learn. Res. **22**(1) (2021)
8. Li, Z., Liu, F., Yang, W., Peng, S., Zhou, J.: A survey of convolutional neural networks: analysis, applications, and prospects. IEEE Trans. Neural Netw. Learn. Syst. **33**(12), 6999–7019 (2021)
9. Liu, S., et al.: The unreasonable effectiveness of random pruning: return of the most naive baseline for sparse training. In: International Conference on Learning Representations (2022)
10. Mocanu, D.C., et al.: Sparse training theory for scalable and efficient agents. In: Proceedings of the 20th International Conference on Autonomous Agents and MultiAgent Systems, AAMAS 2021, pp. 34–38. International Foundation for Autonomous Agents and Multiagent Systems, Richland (2021)
11. Rajaraman, S., et al.: Pre-trained convolutional neural networks as feature extractors toward improved malaria parasite detection in thin blood smear images. PeerJ **6**, e4568 (2018)
12. Shehab, M., et al.: Machine learning in medical applications: a review of state-of-the-art methods. Comput. Biol. Med. **145**, 105458 (2022)
13. Yang, J., et al.: MedMNIST v2 - a large-scale lightweight benchmark for 2D and 3D biomedical image classification. Sci. Data **10**(1), 41 (2023)

A Genetic Algorithm-Based Scheduling Method Considering Working Hours for Medical Doctors

Subaru Narahashi[1], Eiji Hirakawa[2], Akira Uchiyama[3], and Yusuke Gotoh[4(✉)]

[1] Graduate School of Natural Science and Technology, Okayama University, Okayama, Japan
narahashi@s.okayama-u.ac.jp
[2] Department of Neonatology, Kagoshima City Hospital, Kagoshima, Japan
[3] Graduate School of Information Science and Technology, Osaka University, Osaka, Japan
[4] Faculty of Environmental, Life, Natural Science and Technology, Institute of Academic and Research, Okayama University, Okayama, Japan
y-gotoh@okayama-u.ac.jp

Abstract. With the diversity of work styles in recent years, we need to solve issues such as the aging of the working-age population and the increasing responsibilities of caregiving. In particular, the medical field requires efficient and appropriate scheduling due to the lengthening of working hours caused by the shortage of human resources. Many researchers have addressed the Nurse Scheduling Problem (NSP). However, the scheduling problem for medical doctors is more difficult than NSP because they have more varied work arrangements and more stringent constraints than those of the NSP. In this paper, we propose a method to automatically generate work scheduling that considers the work hours of medical doctors. The proposed method classifies medical doctors into four types of work arrangements (morning shift, afternoon shift, semi-night shift, and night shift) and constructs rules to generate constraints for each work arrangement. In addition, the proposed method uses a genetic algorithm to generate the optimal work schedules for multiple medical doctors considering computer resources in heuristic search. The evaluation results showed that the proposed method can generate work schedules that satisfy as many contraints as possible.

Keywords: Genetic algorithm (GA) · nurse scheduling problem (NSP) · scheduling for medical doctor · work style reform

1 Introduction

Work styles in Japan have diversified in recent years, and we need to address the issues of an aging population, including a declining working-age population and an increasing burden of caregiving. As a solution to these problems, it is necessary to generate work schedules that fully consider the work-life balance of medical doctors. As a solution to these problems, it is necessary to generate work schedule that fully considers the work-life balance of medical doctors.

In the medical field, many researchers have developed algorithms for generating work schedules, such as the Nurse Scheduling Problem (NSP) [1–3] and Operating Room Scheduling (ORS) [4,5]. In the NSP, nurses mainly work three types of shifts: day shift, semi-night shift, and night shift, and the working hours for each type of work assignment are clearly defined. Since the number of constraints on the work assignments of nurses is smaller than that of medical doctors, a work schedule created based on the conventional NSP cannot be applied to the case of medical doctors.

Our research group proposed a scheduling method to automatically generate work schedules for medical doctors [6]. This scheduling method constructs rules that generate constraints that are added or deleted according to changes in the medical system managed by the hospital and the work-life balance of each individual medical doctor. However, conventional scheduling methods can only assign one work mode, such as day shift or duty shift, for each work day of medical doctors. In this paper, we propose a work scheduling method that considers realistic working hours of medical doctors. The proposed method classifies a day into four types of work arrangements (morning shift, afternoon shift, semi-night shift, and night shift), and it constructs rules to generate constraints for each work assignment based on the working hours of medical doctors. In addition, the proposed method uses genetic algorithms (GAs) [7–9] to generate the optimal work schedules for multiple medical doctors considering computer resources in heuristic search. The main contributions of this paper are that we propose a method to generate a work schedule that divides a working day into four detailed work arrangements, and the evaluation results demonstrate that the proposed method can generate a work schedule that satisfies more constraints than the conventional scheduling methods.

2 Proposed Method

2.1 Outline

We propose a scheduling method considering working hours for medical doctors. The proposed method classifies a day into four types of work arrangements. Based on a GA, the proposed method searches for the optimal solution to the work schedule that satisfies the constraints for all medical doctors. The medical doctor in charge of creating the work schedule can generate a work schedule that satisfies as many constraints as possible.

We interviewed medical doctors who create work schedules at the Department of Neonatology at Kagoshima City Hospital in order to set constraints for creating work schedules that consider the actual working hours of medical doctors. We categorized medical doctors who work at the hospital into four types of work arrangements: morning shift (8:30 to 12:00), afternoon shift (12:00 to 17:15), semi-night shift (17:15 to 24:00), and late-night shift (24:00 to 8:30), based on the work rules specified for each work mode.

Table 1. Work rules for each work mode

Work modes	Work rules
Day shift (D)	(1) Work at affiliated hospital from 8:30 to 17:15
Unauthorized on-duty work (N_1, N_2)	(2) Work at affiliated hospital from 8:30 to 12:00 the next day
On-duty work at home (T)	(3) Work at home from 8:30 to 8:30 the next day
Authorized outside work (O_1, O_2)	(4) After day shift at the hospital, night shift at hospital O_1 or O_2
	(5) After day shift off, night shift at hospital O_1 or O_2
	(6) Work at hospital O_1 or O_2 from 8:30 to 8:29 the next day
Unauthorized outside work (O_3)	(7) Work at the hospital O_3 from Friday 17:00 to Monday 9:00
Authorized outside work (O_4)	(8) Work at the hospital O_4 from Friday 17:00 to Sunday 17:00
Day off (H)	(9) Taking the day off

2.2 Work Mode

There are nine types of work modes (D, T, N_1, N_2, O_1, O_2, O_3, O_4, H) established for medical doctors. Medical doctors work according to the rules defined for each work mode. Table 1 shows the work rules for each work mode where the place of work outside the hospital (outside work) is anonymized.

We set the following eight constraints by considering the work rules in the work style reform for medical doctors and the hospital-specific rules based on our interviews.

c_1: At least 7 medical doctors are assigned to work modes (other than day off) in a day.
c_2: The number of days off in a month is equal to the number of Saturdays and Sundays.
c_3: Each doctor is assigned a work mode based on their skill.
c_4: N_1 is assigned to one medical doctor per day.
c_5: N_2 is assigned to one medical doctor per day.
c_6: Unauthorized night and day shifts require 18 h of uninterrupted rest.
c_7: O_1 is assigned to one or fewer medical doctors per day.
c_8: O_2 is assigned to one or fewer medical doctors per day.

2.3 Algorithm of Proposed Method

Figure 1 shows a flowchart for generating the work schedule by our method, which is based on the constraints $c_1, \cdots, c_8$. The shift s is created by combining seven of the nine work modes (D, T, N_1, N_2, O_1, O_2, H) according to the work rules. The proposed method generates work schedules by assigning O_3 and O_4 to shift s and then assigning the other seven work modes to shift s. In addition, by using four work arrangements while considering the work rules for each work

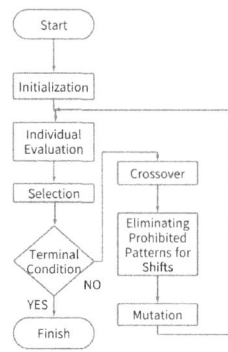

Fig. 1. Flowchart of proposed method

Table 2. Parameters

Item	Initial value
Number of medical doctors	13
Assigned number of days	30
Number of shifts	32
Number of generations	3,000
Number of individuals	1,000
Number of elite individuals	300
Crossover rate	0.90
Mutation rate	0.10

mode, we generated 32 shifts that could be assumed in the work scheduling for medical doctors.

First, the initialization creates initial values of the individuals p for the GA. Each individual is represented by a matrix with rows for medical doctor i and columns for assignment date j. For this matrix, the work schedule is generated using $s_{i,j}$ with shifts s which is randomly assigned. Individual p is generated based on the pre-defined number of individuals and included in the initial generation, $P_{initial}$. In individual evaluation, each individual p is assigned the fitness calculated from the objective function if the constraints are satisfied. The proposed method maximizes this fitness. In selection, the proposed method uses elite selection, where the top few elite individuals with the highest fitness are generated as the population P_{select}. In crossover, we perform a two-point crossover on the individual based on the crossover rate. In two-point crossover, parts of the individuals are replaced based on two crossover points that are randomly selected. In mutation, we perform a general mutation, randomly replacing some of the individuals according to the mutation rate.

2.4 Eliminating Prohibited Patterns for Shifts

In this research, we generated all possible patterns of shifts to be assigned to medical doctor i on their assigned day j. Since we do not assign the semi-night shift or the night shift to the day shift, there is no prohibited shift pattern that does not satisfy the work rule. When shifts are assigned on multiple consecutive assignment days, a prohibited shift pattern that does not satisfy the work rule occurs. In this paper, more essential constraints are satisfied by eliminating the prohibited shift patterns for multiple consecutive assignment days.

3 Evaluation

We evaluate the usefulness of the proposed method using computer simulations. Table 2 shows the parameters used in the evaluation based on interviews. The

Table 3. Skills of medical doctors

	Medical doctor ID												
	1	2	3	4	5	6	7	8	9	10	11	12	13
N_1, N_2	o	o	x	o	o	o	o	o	o	o	o	x	o
O_1	x	x	x	o	x	x	x	x	x	o	o	x	x
O_2	o	x	x	x	o	o	o	x	x	x	x	x	o
O_3	x	o	x	x	x	x	x	o	x	x	x	x	x
O_4	x	x	x	o	x	x	x	x	x	x	x	o	x

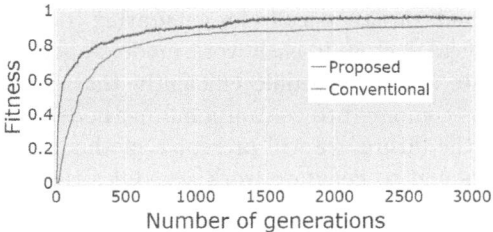

Fig. 2. Fitness according to number of generations

number of allocated days was set to 30, and the termination condition is when the number of generations reaches 3,000 or when all constraints are satisfied. The number of individuals, the number of elite individuals, the crossover rate, and the mutation rate were set based on a prior evaluation.

The skills of each medical doctor are shown in Table 3. The rows indicate shifts and the columns indicate medical doctor IDs. Based on the skills of the 13 medical doctors working in the Department of Neonatology, Kagoshima City Hospital in Japan, we set the availability of work assignments for five different shifts: one duty shift and four shifts of outside work (O_1, O_2, O_3, and O_4).

To confirm the usefulness of the proposed method, we evaluated the fitness with the number of generations. We compared the proposed method with a conventional method that introduces the conventional GA. The proposed method eliminated prohibited shift patterns. On the other hand, the conventional method did not eliminate such prohibited shift patterns. Figure 2 shows the fitness according to the number of generations. The horizontal axis is the number of generations, and the vertical axis indicates fitness. Here, fitness is normalized, and the closer the fitness is to 1, the more constraints are satisfied.

In Fig. 2, the fitness of the proposed method is higher than that of the conventional method. For example, when the number of generations is 3,000, which is the terminal condition, the fitness of the proposed method is about 0.95 and the conventional method is about 0.90. In addition, when the number of generations is between 0 and 500, the fitness of the proposed method increases more rapidly than the conventional method. Our proposed method can also increase fitness by satisfying constraints that occur in shifts with multiple consecutive days, such as N_1. On the other hand, the conventional method generated prohibited patterns in shifts with consecutive multi-day assignments. Therefore, the conventional method satisfies fewer constraints than the proposed method.

4 Conclusion

In this paper, we proposed a method for generating work schedules that consider the working hours of medical doctors. The proposed method classifies a day into four work modes (morning shift, afternoon shift, semi-evening shift, and night shift) and constructs rules for generating constraints based on the working hours of medical doctors in each work mode. A genetic algorithm makes it possible to generate a work schedule efficiently that satisfies the largest number of constraints compared to conventional methods.

In the future, we will present a method to improve the adaptability to constraints and to generate work schedules that satisfy more constraints. We will also develop a method for generating work schedules when only some shifts need to be updated due to sudden changes in a medical doctor's schedule.

Acknowledgment. This work was supported by JSPS KAKENHI Grant Numbers JP23K21660 and JP23K24843.

References

1. Ikegami, A., Niwa, A.: A subproblem-centric model and approach to the nurse scheduling problem. Math. Program. **97**, 517–541 (2003)
2. Duenas, A., Tütüncü, G.Y., Chilcott, J.B.: A genetic algorithm approach to the nurse scheduling problem with fuzzy preferences. IMA J. Manag. Math. **20**(4), 369–383 (2009). https://doi.org/10.1093/imaman/dpn033
3. Ohki, M.: Nurse scheduling by cooperative GA with effective mutation operator. IEICE Trans. Inf. Syst. **E95.D**(7), 1830–1838 (2012). https://doi.org/10.1587/transinf.E95.D.1830
4. Abdelrasol, Z., Harraz, N., Eltawil, A.: Operating room scheduling problems: a survey and a proposed solution framework. In: Kim, H.K., Ao, S.-I., Amouzegar, M.A. (eds.) Transactions on Engineering Technologies, pp. 717–731. Springer, Dordrecht (2014). https://doi.org/10.1007/978-94-017-9115-1_52
5. Lin, Y.-K., Yen, C.-H.: Genetic algorithm for solving the no-wait three-stage surgery scheduling problem. Healthcare **11**(5), 1–14 (2023)
6. Gotoh, Y., et al.: A proposition of physician scheduling method for improving work-life balance. In: Barolli, L., Natwichai, J., Enokido, T. (eds.) EIDWT 2021. LNDECT, vol. 65, pp. 333–343. Springer, Cham (2021). https://doi.org/10.1007/978-3-030-70639-5_31
7. Goldberg, D.E.: Genetic Algorithms in Search, Optimization, and Machine Learning. Addison-Wesley Longman Publishing Co. (1989)
8. Gonçalves, J.F., Mendes, J.J.M., Resende, M.G.C.: A hybrid genetic algorithm for the job shop scheduling problem. Eur. J. Oper. Res. **167**(1), 77–95 (2005). https://doi.org/10.1016/j.ejor.2004.03.012
9. Kim, K.-J., Han, I.: Genetic algorithms approach to feature discretization in artificial neural networks for the prediction of stock price index. Expert Syst. Appl. **19**(2), 125–132 (2000). https://doi.org/10.1016/S0957-4174(00)00027-0

Image, Video, and Multimedia Processing

Application of Benford's Law to the Identification of Non-authentic Digital Images

Jaroslaw Kobiela(✉) ⓘ and Piotr Dzierwa ⓘ

Institute of Computer Science, University of Opole, Opole, Poland
{jaroslaw.kobiela,piotr.dzierwa}@uni.opole.pl

Abstract. This study evaluated Benford's law for detecting non-authentic digital images by analyzing the first digits of pixel values after a discrete cosine transform (DCT). We analyzed 137 pairs of authentic and modified JPEGs using ROC curves, k-means clustering, chi-squared tests, and PCA. The results showed AUC values near 0.5, indicating low classification performance. The k-means algorithm had 49% precision with low completeness, and PCA revealed a significant overlap between the authentic and manipulated images. These findings suggest the limited effectiveness of Benford's law alone, highlighting the need to integrate advanced image-processing methods and explore additional pixel-distribution features for the effective detection of non-authentic images.

Keywords: Benford's law · Digital image analysis · Image manipulation detection · Image analysis

1 Introduction

Image manipulation and falsification are significant concerns in this digital age. Advances in technology have enabled the creation of realistic yet falsified content, posing the risk of disinformation [1]. Studies have shown that people struggle to recognize manipulated images, and techniques such as deepfakes have become highly sophisticated [2, 3]. Modern tools and deep learning algorithms facilitate the creation of ultra-realistic yet fictional faces and scenes [4]. Manipulated visual content can severely impact public opinion and democratic processes [5]. Hence, the development of effective methods for detecting inauthentic images is crucial.

2 Overview of Digital Image Authenticity Problems

Image forgers use various manipulation techniques, ranging from simple cropping and retouching to advanced deep learning methods [6]. Modifications can affect both semantic content (e.g., adding or removing objects) and signal-level information (e.g., retouching color or brightness) [7]. No single feature can definitively indicate manipulation because changes can be subtle and challenging to detect. Algorithms must analyze pixel changes, colors, and textures. Images vary owing to lighting, angle, and compression, complicating the distinction between natural and manipulated changes [8]. Developing a universal method for verifying the authenticity of images remains a challenge.

3 Introduction to Benford's Law

Benford's law is based on the observation that in many natural datasets, the first digits are not evenly distributed; instead, some appear first more often than others. For example, digit 1 appears first approximately 30 per cent of the time, which is much more frequent than the other digits. This law has applications in fields ranging from geology to economics and is used to detect anomalies in data that may suggest manipulation or fraud, such as in financial data or election results. The main premise of Benford's law can be mathematically expressed as:

$$P(d)=\log\_10\ [(d+1)-\log\_10(d)]\qquad(1)$$

where P(d) is the probability that the given datasets start with digit (d) [9, 10].

In the context of digital image analysis, Benford's law can be used to detect manipulations in JPEG images stored in compressed format. However, analysis based on Benford's law requires consideration of the effect of JPEG compression on the distribution of the pixel values. To effectively apply this law, it is necessary to convert images into a format that allows direct analysis of pixel values, one possibility being conversion to grayscale or RGB values [11, 12]. This opens the way to using Benford's law to identify inauthenticity or image modification.

4 Literature Review

In the literature review section, we discuss various applications of Benford's law and its generalizations in the contexts of digital image analysis, forgery identification, and digital forensics. The first article introduced a novel algorithm that uses the traditional and generalized Benford's law to construct a feature vector for detecting forgeries in digital images. This method, based on Mean Absolute Deviation (MAD) analysis and the distribution of pixel values, shows higher accuracy than existing solutions, as confirmed by tests on CASIA V1.0 and V2.0 datasets - a significant advance in the field [13].

Another article focuses on the application of Benford's Law in No-Reference Image Quality Assessment (NR-IQA), analysing features based on the distribution of first digits in different domains, such as wavelet coefficients and Discrete Cosine Transform (DCT). Experimental results on seven large benchmark databases show that these features can reach or even surpass the state-of-the-art, highlighting their value in the context of image quality assessment [14].

A study on the identification of adversarial images shows that they have a distribution of first-digit pixels that deviate from those predicted by Benford's Law, which offers a new method for detecting these images without having to modify convolutional neural network (CNN) classifiers. This method can be applied to increase the robustness of image classifier systems against various types of adversarial attacks [15].

The analysis of the detection capabilities of Generative Adversarial Network (GAN)-generated images using Benford's Law opens new perspectives in the field of forgery analysis and detection. This study proves that statistical traces that differentiate GAN images from natural photographs can be effectively detected, which is an important step towards understanding and countering the use of GAN technology for fraudulent purposes [16].

The article 'Double-Crossing Benford's Law' and 'Generalized Benford's Law for Fake Fingerprint Detection' extends the discussion of the capabilities and limitations of Benford's Law in the context of forgery detection, including the manipulation of data for legitimacy and detection of false fingerprints. These studies emphasize the need for careful application of Benford's law and suggest its potential applications in biometric systems [17, 18].

Further work, such as 'A generalized Benford's law for JPEG coefficients and its applications in image forensics' and 'Benford's law in image processing, demonstrate the application of Benford's law in forensic analysis of digital images, JPEG compression detection, double compression, and steganalysis. These studies demonstrate the effectiveness of a statistical model based on Benford's law in various aspects of image analysis, from manipulation identification to hidden message detection [19, 20].

The article 'Detecting Double Compression and Splicing using Benford's First Digit Law' presents methods using Benford's First Digit Law to detect image manipulation, including double compression and image splicing, in the JPEG format. The proposed techniques offer both supervised and unsupervised detection methods, achieving high Area Under the Curve (AUC) values, indicating their superiority over other digital forensic methods [21].

Next, an Analysis of Benford's law for image processing explores the generalization of Benford's law in the context of digital modification detection and counterfeit banknote authentication. The results show that deviation from the Benford curve can serve as an effective indicator of counterfeiting, confirming the effectiveness of Benford's law in digital image forensics [22].

Recent studies have focused on the use of Benford's law and machine learning techniques, including convolutional neural networks and Bayes classifiers, to classify and identify the sources of biometric images and fingerprints. These studies show high classification accuracy and potential for application in biometric security systems, highlighting the importance of Benford's Law in combination with modern technologies for detecting forgery and ensuring data authenticity [23, 24].

In the context of financial fraud detection, Goh's article explores the application of Benford's Law and visual analytics in an accounting context, demonstrating a practical approach to identifying potential fraud using tools such as tableau. This study demonstrates the wide range of applications of Benford's law, from image analysis to financial forensics [25].

5 Aims of the Study

This study aimed to investigate the usefulness of Benford's law for identifying manipulations in digital photographic images. This study focuses on analyzing the distribution of the first digits of pixel values after applying the discrete cosine transform (DCT) and comparing it with the distribution predicted by Benford's law. The main research question is whether possible differences in these distributions can be used as markers to identify manipulated images. To this end, several statistical methods and machine learning techniques were tested on 137 pairs of authentic and modified JPEG images, including Receiver Operating Characteristic (ROC), k-means clustering, chi-square test, and Principal Component Analysis (PCA). However, the results obtained indicate that Benford's law alone proved insufficient to effectively detect image manipulation in the studied dataset.

6 Methodology

6.1 Application of Benford's Law and DCT in Image Analysis

Benford's law was applied to digital JPEG images by converting them using Python libraries to perform a Discrete Cosine Transform (DCT) and extract the first digits of the resulting values. OpenCV, NumPy, SciPy, Matplotlib, and Sklearn were used for the experiments. Grayscale conversion reduces image complexity by focusing on luminance analysis and simplifying the data for further processing.

The difference between the distribution of the first digits in the image data and the expected distribution according to Benford's law was a key element of this study. However, despite the relevance of analyzing the differences in distributions, attention must be paid to potential errors, such as false positives and false negatives, which can affect the reliability of the results. False positives are situations in which the model incorrectly identifies the original images as manipulated (i.e., the original images are above the designated threshold). False negatives are situations in which the model incorrectly identifies manipulated images as original (i.e., manipulated images below the threshold).

Figure 1 shows the data-preparation algorithm. The DCT is used to extract key features from images by transforming the pixel space into a frequency space. This allows for the identification of patterns that may not be apparent in direct pixel analysis. Processing the image to grayscale and then applying DCT can reveal hidden regularities or anomalies in the data that can be analyzed using Benford's law.

Fig. 1. Algorithm for data preparation

In the article 'Fighting Deepfakes by Detecting GAN DCT Anomalies, the authors describe how the application of the DCT can improve the detection of anomalies in GAN-generated image data. Analyzing GAN Specific frequencies (GSFs) using DCT allows the detection of anomalies, which is a key element in verifying the authenticity and integrity of image data [26].

6.2 Data Preparation

As part of the Benford's law compliance study, digital images were selected from a single source to ensure data consistency. The 16 megapixel images were taken with a Canon 700D camera, which stored the images directly in JPEG format with a size of 5184 × 3456 pixels. Each image was characterized by a 24-bit color depth and sRGB color reproduction standard. From the entire dataset, 137 images were selected for further analysis.

Subsequently, these images were loaded in grayscale using the OpenCV library, and the pixel luminance values from the grayscale channel were transformed into numerical form. Then, using Discrete Cosine Transform (DCT), the images were transformed from pixel space to frequency space, which facilitated the extraction of key features related to the intensity of light in the images.

The first digit for each non-zero pixel was extracted from the transformed DCT values. The resulting series of first digits were analyzed by calculating their actual incidence ratios. These were then compared with the theoretical proportions predicted using Benford's law. This analysis made it possible to investigate whether or how much the distribution of the first digits differed from the theoretical proportions for the original and manipulated images.

Two datasets were used in this study (Fig. 2). The first was the original images, which were ripped directly from the camera memory. The second set consisted of the same images.

Fig. 2. Original photo (left) and retouched photo (right)

7 Presentation of Results

7.1 ROC Curve

ROC curves are graphical representations of the performance of binary classifiers, showing the tradeoff between true positives and false positives at different decision thresholds. The area under the curve (AUC) value is a measure of a classifier's ability to discriminate between classes, with a value of 1.0 indicating excellent classification ability and a value of 0.5 indicating no ability [27–29]. In the context of image retouching analysis, where the aim is to distinguish between the original and modified images, ROC curves were used to assess the effectiveness of Benford's law for this type of task.

The discriminative classifier between the original and manipulated images did not achieve a high performance. The AUC values for all four graphs were very close to 0.5, indicating a lack of clear classification ability, a level comparable to that of random guessing. The optimal thresholds selected based on the best trade-off between sensitivity and specificity remained close to 0.5, further emphasizing the lack of discrimination between classes. In addition, the lack of a significant change in AUC as the dataset size increased (Fig. 3) indicates that the method used may not be suitable for detecting manipulation in images based on Benford's law in the context of the dataset used.

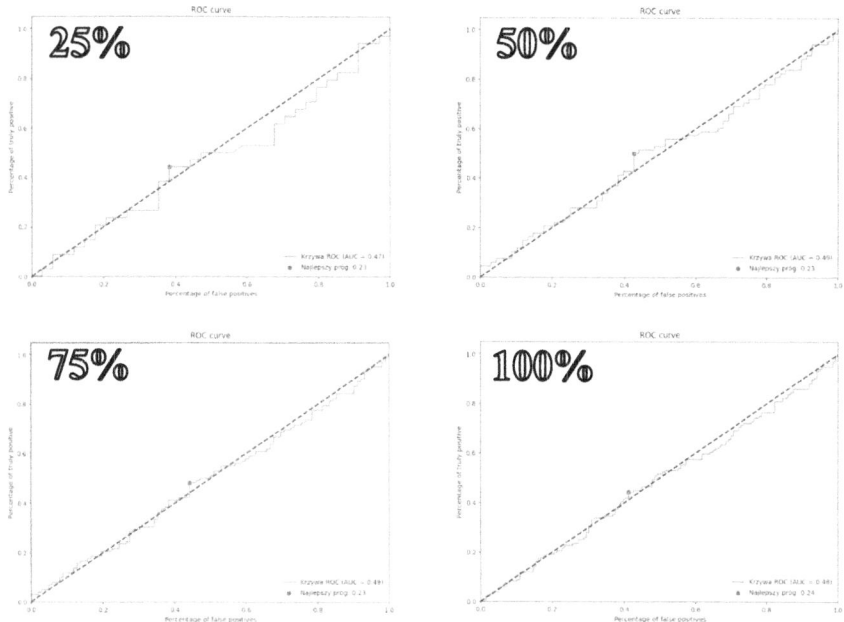

Fig. 3. ROC curves for different collection sizes.

The numerical results are summarized in Table 1, which shows the key performance metrics of the classifier in the context of increasing the data size.

Table 1. Analysis of classifier performance at different data sampling points

Threshold value	25%	50%	75%	100%
maximum difference	0.3836	0.3836	0.3836	0.4098
mean + standard deviation	0.2794	0.2851	0.2828	0.2903
median	0.2181	0.2211	0.2222	0.2261
percentile 95	0.3112	0.3354	0.3365	0.3382
ROC curve	0.2260	0.2263	0.2263	0.2350
AUC value	0.4702	0.4948	0.4916	0.4848

Theoretically, an AUC value of 0.5 indicates that the classifier lacks discriminative ability, equivalent to random guessing. In the presented data, the AUC values ranged from 0.4701 to 0.4948, suggesting that the classifier effectively discriminated between the original and the manipulated images.

The maximum difference indicates the greatest difference in classification ability between the samples. These values remained relatively constant as the percentage of data increased, suggesting that the performance of the classifier did not increase significantly with additional data.

The mean plus standard deviation provides information regarding the dispersion of the results around the mean. Small changes in these values may indicate the stability of the classifier across different dataset sizes.

The median, which is the middle value of the data, also shows little change, supporting the conclusion that the classifier results are stable.

The 95th percentile shows a value below which 95% of the results were obtained. A slight increase in this value may indicate that more extreme results occur with larger datasets; however, they are not sufficiently significant to improve the overall performance of the classifier.

From this table, it can be concluded that the classification method used did not significantly improve its performance as the data sample size increased. The results are consistent but do not exceed the random level of accuracy, suggesting the need for further research or a change of approach.

7.2 Cluster Analysis

K-means algorithms are commonly used to group data based on similarity. Their popularity is owing to their simplicity, efficiency, and proven effectiveness in practice [30]. The k-means algorithm is a popular tool used for image segmentation that groups pixels based on their similarity, allowing areas with similar visual characteristics to be extracted [31].

By extracting areas with similar pixel brightness, the actual distribution of the first digits was compared with the expected distribution according to Benford's law.

The graphs in (Fig. 4) illustrate the clustering results for percentage divisions of the dataset. These graphs visualize the distinction between the original (red) and manipulated (purple) images based on an analysis of the differences in the distributions of the first digits of the pixel values.

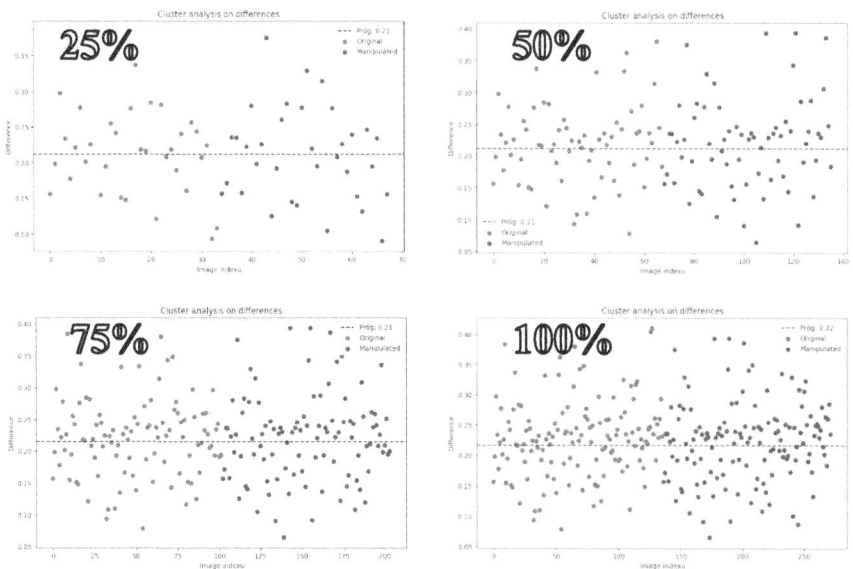

Fig. 4. Cluster analysis of the differences in the distribution of the first digit of pixel values for the original and manipulated images. (Color figure online)

The data below present the key metrics for evaluating classifier performance: precision, completeness, F1 measure, and accuracy, which characterize the quality of the distinction between the original and manipulated images.

Precision:	0.4875
Recall:	0.5735
F1 Score:	0.5270
Accuracy:	0.4853

Based on these results, the k-means model shows limited effectiveness. The low recall indicates a problem with false negatives, that is, the model often fails to recognize manipulated images as such. The precision of 49% is also unsatisfactory, which means that almost half of the images recognized by the model as manipulated are in fact original (false positives or false positives). The accuracy (precision) is only slightly better than that of random guessing, which is far from the level required in practical applications where much higher performance is expected.

The low F1 value indicates that the model has not found a good compromise between precision and completeness; therefore, it is not a well-balanced model in terms of these two criteria.

7.3 Chi-Square Test

The chi-squared test is often used to assess whether the observed frequency distribution differs from the expected distribution. It is used to compare the observed frequencies with expected frequencies to determine whether there is a statistically significant difference between the two [32]. In the context of Benford's law, which predicts a specific logarithmic distribution of the first digits in natural datasets, the chi-square test was used to assess whether the distribution of the first digits of image pixels differs from the distribution predicted by this law. The threshold is calculated as the mean plus one standard deviation of the value of the chi-square statistic for the original images, which provides a criterion to distinguish between the original and potentially manipulated images.

Table 2 presents the results of the chi-squared test for the selected images. These values and the corresponding p-values for the original and manipulated images provided the data necessary to assess whether the distribution of the first pixel digits of these images was significantly different from the theoretical distribution predicted by Benford's law.

Table 2. Example chi-square and p-value statistics for original and manipulated images

No.	Filename	Original_Chi2	Original_p_val	Manipulated_Chi2	Manipulated_p_val
1	IMG_7973.JPG	0.442989	0.999916	0.560935	0.999794
2	IMG_3586.JPG	0.462213	0.999901	0.177992	0.999998
3	IMG_0554.JPG	0.467146	0.999897	0.378875	0.999954
...	...	...	...	...	...
134	IMG_3626.JPG	0.338112	0.999970	0.338112	0.999970
135	IMG_3364.JPG	0.390958	0.999948	0.466048	0.999898
136	IMG_7098.JPG	0.450583	0.999910	0.752545	0.999381

The above statistical values of the chi-square test are also visualized in a bar chart (Fig. 5), which illustrates the distribution of the chi-square values for each image, with the statistical threshold marked to distinguish between the original (blue) and manipulated (red) images.

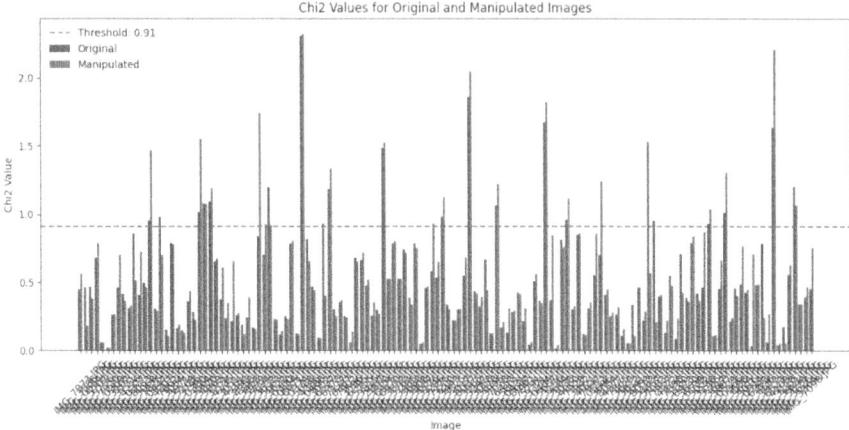

Fig. 5. Chi2 Values for Original and Manipulated images (Color figure online)

The dashed line indicates the set threshold above which the images can be considered manipulated. The threshold was determined from the mean value of the chi-square statistic for the original images, to which one standard deviation was added. A threshold value of 0.912215653330346 serves as a decision criterion for identifying potential manipulations. It was observed that some manipulated images had higher chi-square values than the original images, which may indicate non-compliance with Benford's law and potential manipulation. However, there are also original images with values above the threshold, suggesting that the chi-square statistic alone may not be sufficiently discriminative to reliably distinguish authentic from manipulated images without additional analysis or other supporting data.

7.4 Principal Component Analysis

According to the theory presented by Kurita, PCA is a data analysis tool that identifies meaningful bases to represent a set of data, uncovering hidden structures in the data, and reducing noise. PCA effectively reduces the dimensionality of the data while retaining the most relevant statistical information [33].

Using Benford's law as a tool to analyze the first digits of the pixel values in the images, we obtained a dataset that is difficult to interpret directly, particularly because we deal with a large number of pixels and images. PCA reduces this complexity by focusing on the most important features of the distributions, which facilitates visualization and further analysis of the data. In the context of determining the authenticity of images, PCA aims to capture key features that can differentiate authentic from manipulated images.

Each image was transformed into a feature vector containing calculated differences. Dimensionality reduction was performed on these vectors by using PCA, which allowed the main patterns of variation in the dataset to be extracted and highlighted. With PCA, it was possible to visualize and evaluate the scatter of the images in the principal component space, making it possible to see that the distribution of points did not clearly separate the original from the modified images. These findings highlight the need to look for more advanced analysis methods or to combine PCA with other techniques to improve the discriminative ability of the model.

Figure 6 shows the transformed feature vectors of the images in the principal component space, revealing the key patterns of differences between the original and potentially modified images.

The division of the dataset into successive fractions (25%, 50%, 75%, and 100%) provides detailed insight into the stability and scalability of the principal component analysis (PCA) methods used. Overlapping scores are observed at all fractional levels, suggesting that analysis of the first digits of pixel values in the context of Benford's law alone is not sufficient for identifying image authenticity, regardless of sample size.

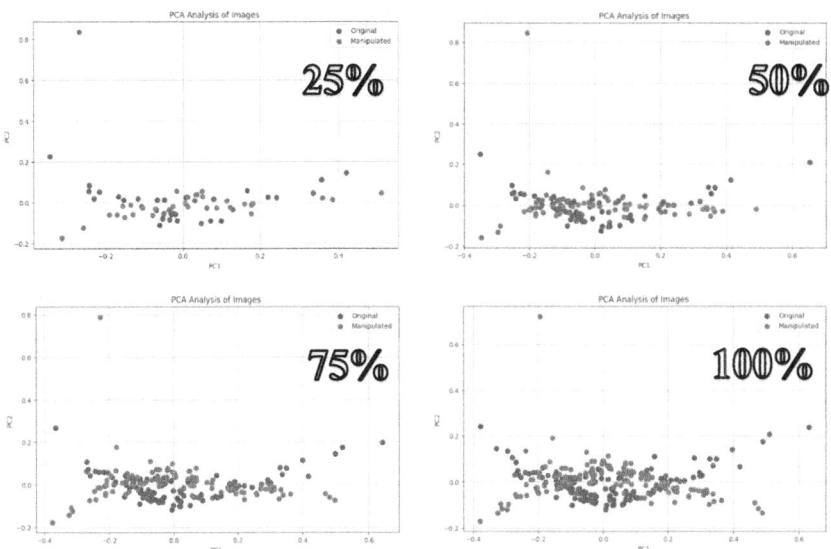

Fig. 6. PCA Analyys of images

As part of the analysis, the disparities between the empirical distributions of the first digits of the pixel values and the distributions predicted by Benford's law were used as descriptors to characterize the digital images. Visualizing these disparities using principal component analysis (PCA) provides important information regarding the structure of the data. The observations for authentic and digitally processed images show a spatial distribution of the two dominant components (PC1 and PC2). However, it is noticeable that the point visualizations for the two categories of images partially overlap, implying potential challenges in distinguishing images based solely on the analysis of the first digits of the pixel values. The point distribution in the PCA graphics did not show a clear separation between sets of genuine and manipulated images, suggesting that PCA analysis, although a guide, may not be sufficiently diagnostic to reliably differentiate between genuine and manipulated images. The overlap of points on the PCA plane indicates significant similarities in the characteristics of the images from both categories, highlighting the need for more sophisticated analytical methods to improve the identification of image manipulation.

8 Results

8.1 Presentation of Results

The ROC curve and AUC analysis showed low classifier performance, with AUC values near 0.5, indicating poor classification ability, comparable to random guessing. The k-means algorithm also failed with 49% precision and low recall, indicating issues with false positives and negatives. Further research is required to improve the accuracy of this model.

The chi-square test, used to assess the differences between the observed and expected distributions of the first digits of pixel values, also failed to sufficiently discriminate between genuine and manipulated images. The values of the chi-square statistic for some of the manipulated images were higher than those of the original images, which may indicate manipulation. However, observations of the original images exceeding a set threshold suggest that the chi-square statistic itself may not be sufficiently discriminative.

Principal component analysis (PCA) allowed us to reduce the dimensionality of the data and visualize the main patterns of variation in the dataset. However, the overlap of scores for authentic and manipulated images on the PCA plane indicated significant similarities in the characteristics of images from both categories, highlighting the need for more sophisticated analytical methods to improve the performance of image manipulation identification.

8.2 Effectiveness of Benford's Law

The analysis conducted as part of the study showed that the application of Benford's law to identify inauthentic digital images can be helpful but is not sufficiently effective in every case. The results obtained using various statistical methods, such as ROC curves, k-means clustering, chi-square test, and principal component analysis (PCA), did not show high effectiveness in distinguishing the original from manipulated images.

Despite these limitations, Benford's law may be valuable in combination with other image-analysis techniques. Further research could focus on integrating Benford's law with advanced image-processing methods, such as machine learning or texture analysis, which could increase the effectiveness of manipulation detection.

Benford's law has the potential to identify inauthentic digital images, but its effectiveness in the studied dataset is limited. Further work is required to develop and refine this method to increase its effectiveness for practical applications. The exploration of additional image features and their relationship to Benford's law may contribute to a better understanding of the mechanisms behind the distribution of the first digits of pixel values in the context of digital image authenticity.

9 Limitations and Application of Benford's Law

The study of the application of Benford's law to the identification of inauthentic digital images, although promising, faces several limitations that need to be considered when interpreting the results and planning further research. One of the main limitations is the specificity of the image data, which may be susceptible to a variety of manipulations that do not directly affect the distribution of the first digits of the pixel values, thereby limiting the effectiveness of the method. In addition, image compression, especially in the JPEG format, introduces additional distortions that may affect the distribution of pixel values and thus comply with Benford's law.

Another limitation is the complexity of digital images, which can contain a wide range of visual and semantic information that is difficult to capture by statistical analysis based solely on the first digits of the pixel values. This highlights the need to combine Benford's law with other image analysis methods such as texture analysis, pattern recognition, and machine learning techniques to increase the effectiveness of manipulation identification.

Additionally, this study is based on the assumption that authentic digital images follow the distribution predicted by Benford's law, which may not always be true in practice. A variety of image sources, recording conditions, and processing processes may lead to deviations from this distribution, even for images that have not been manipulated.

In terms of practical application, the method requires further adaptation and calibration to be effective in different scenarios and for a variety of datasets. This requires extensive research and testing on larger and more diverse datasets, which is another limitation of this study.

The application of Benford's law in the identification of inauthentic digital images opens new perspectives in digital forensics, and it is important to consider the aforementioned limitations and to continue research to develop and optimize this method.

10 Conclusion

The analysis showed that although the application of Benford's law alone to the identification of non-authentic digital images faces some limitations, it opens up new research perspectives. In particular, this study provides valuable insights into the opportunities and challenges of using first-digit distributions of pixel values to verify image integrity.

The results obtained indicate that analysis based on Benford's law should be considered as part of a broader image manipulation detection system rather than as a stand-alone technique. Nevertheless, this study represents an important step towards understanding the statistical properties of authentic and falsified digital images. It points to directions for further work on the development of methods that combine the assumptions of Benford's law with image processing and analysis techniques, such as texture analysis or machine learning. Thus, this article contributes to the knowledge in the area of combating the ever-improving techniques of digital image forgery.

References

1. Guera, D., Delp, E.J.: Deepfake video detection using recurrent neural networks. In: 2018 15th IEEE International Conference on Advanced Video and Signal Based Surveillance (AVSS), Auckland, New Zealand, pp. 1–6. IEEE (2018). https://doi.org/10.1109/AVSS.2018.8639163
2. Nightingale, S.J., Wade, K.A., Watson, D.G.: Can people identify original and manipulated photos of real-world scenes? Cogn. Res. **2**(1), 30 (2017). https://doi.org/10.1186/s41235-017-0067-2
3. Tolosana, R., Vera-Rodriguez, R., Fierrez, J., Morales, A., Ortega-Garcia, J.: Deepfakes and beyond: a survey of face manipulation and fake detection. Inf. Fusion **64**, 131–148 (2020). https://doi.org/10.1016/j.inffus.2020.06.014
4. Karras, T., Aila, T., Laine, S., Lehtinen, J.: Progressive growing of GANs for improved quality, stability, and variation. arXiv http://arxiv.org/abs/1710.10196 (2018). Accessed 09 Feb 2024
5. Vaccari, C., Chadwick, A.: Deepfakes and disinformation: exploring the impact of synthetic political video on deception, uncertainty, and trust in news. Soc. Media + Soc. **6**(1), 205630512090340 (2020). https://doi.org/10.1177/2056305120903408
6. Verdoliva, L.: Media forensics and DeepFakes: an overview. IEEE J. Sel. Top. Signal Process. **14**(5), 910–932 (2020). https://doi.org/10.1109/JSTSP.2020.3002101
7. Farid, H.: Image forgery detection. IEEE Signal Process. Mag. **26**(2), 16–25 (2009). https://doi.org/10.1109/MSP.2008.931079
8. Abbott, J.: The Digital Darkroom: The Definitive Guide to Photo Editing. Ilex Press, Lewes (2021)
9. De Kok, R., Rotundo, G.: Benford networks. Stats **5**(4), 934–947 (2022). https://doi.org/10.3390/stats5040054
10. Anderson, K.M., Dayaratna, K., Gonshorowski, D., Miller, S.J.: A new benford test for clustered data with applications to American elections. Stats **5**(3), 841–855 (2022). https://doi.org/10.3390/stats5030049
11. Singh, N., Bansal, R.: Analysis of Benford's law in digital image forensics. In: 2015 International Conference on Signal Processing and Communication, ICSC 2015, pp. 413–418 (2015). https://doi.org/10.1109/ICSPCom.2015.7150688
12. Póth, M., Trpovski, Ž.: Analysis of JPEG digital image compression process. J. Appl. Tech. Educ. Sci. **9**(4) (2019). ISSN: 2560-5429. https://doi.org/10.24368/JATES.V9I4.119
13. Parnak, A., Baleghi Damavandi, Y., Kazemitabar, S.J.: A novel image splicing detection algorithm based on generalized and traditional Benford's law. IJE **35**(04), 626–634 (2022). https://doi.org/10.5829/IJE.2022.35.04A.02
14. Varga, D.: Analysis of Benford's law for no-reference quality assessment of natural, screen-content, and synthetic images. Electronics **10**(19), 2378 (2021). https://doi.org/10.3390/electronics10192378
15. Zago, J.G., Antonelo, E.A., Baldissera, F.L., Saad, R.T.: Benford's law: what does it say on adversarial images? J. Vis. Commun. Image Represent. **93**, 103818 (2022)
16. Bonettini, N., Bestagini, P., Milani, S., Tubaro, S.: On the use of Benford's law to detect GAN-generated images. In: 2020 25th International Conference on Pattern Recognition (ICPR), Milan, Italy, pp. 5495–5502. IEEE (2021). https://doi.org/10.1109/ICPR48806.2021.9412944
17. Kazemitabar, J.: Double-crossing Benford's law. arXiv http://arxiv.org/abs/2105.09812 (2021). Accessed 06 Feb 2024
18. Satapathy, G., Bhattacharya, G., Puhan, N.B., Ho, A.T.S.: Generalized Benford's law for fake fingerprint detection. In: 2020 IEEE Applied Signal Processing Conference (ASPCON), Kolkata, India, pp. 242–246. IEEE (2020). https://doi.org/10.1109/ASPCON49795.2020.9276660

19. Fu, D., Shi, Y.Q., Su, W.: A generalized Benford's law for JPEG coefficients and its applications in image forensics. Presented at the Electronic Imaging 2007, San Jose, CA, United States, p. 65051L (2007). https://doi.org/10.1117/12.704723
20. Perez-Gonzalez, F., Heileman, G.L., Abdallah, C.T.: Benford's law in image processing. In: 2007 IEEE International Conference on Image Processing, San Antonio, TX, USA, pp. I-405–I-408. IEEE (2007). https://doi.org/10.1109/ICIP.2007.4378977
21. Frick, R.A., Liu, H., Steinebach, M.: Detecting double compression and splicing using Benfords first digit law. In: Proceedings of the 15th International Conference on Availability, Reliability and Security, Virtual Event Ireland, pp. 1–9. ACM (2020). https://doi.org/10.1145/3407023.3409200
22. Bodke, M., Mishra, D., Vasani, K., Janjua, J.: Analysis of Benford's law for image processing, vol. 9, no. 6, p. 7 (2021)
23. Iorliam, A., Orgem, E., Shehu, Y.I.: An investigation of Benford's law divergence and machine learning techniques for intra-class separability of fingerprint images. Gazi Univ. J. Sci. Part A: Eng. Innov. **9**(3), 211–224 (2022). https://doi.org/10.54287/gujsa.1077430
24. Iorliam, A., Ho, A.T.S., Waller, A., Zhao, X.: Using Benford's law divergence and neural networks for classification and source identification of biometric images. In: Shi, Y.Q., Kim, H.J., Perez-Gonzalez, F., Liu, F. (eds.) IWDW 2016. LNCS, vol. 10082, pp. 88–105. Springer, Cham (2017). https://doi.org/10.1007/978-3-319-53465-7_7
25. Goh, C.: Applying visual analytics to fraud detection using Benford's law. J. Corp. Account. Finance **31**(4), 202–208 (2020). https://doi.org/10.1002/jcaf.22440
26. Giudice, O., Guarnera, L., Battiato, S.: Fighting deepfakes by detecting GAN DCT anomalies. J. Imaging **7**(8), 128 (2021). https://doi.org/10.3390/jimaging7080128
27. Werner, P., Lopez-Martinez, D., Walter, S., Al-Hamadi, A., Gruss, S., Picard, R.W.: Automatic recognition methods supporting pain assessment: a survey. IEEE Trans. Affect. Comput. **13**(1), 530–552 (2022). https://doi.org/10.1109/TAFFC.2019.2946774
28. Von Borries, G.F., Quadros, A.V.C.: ROC app: an application to understand ROC curves. Braz. J. Biom. **40**(2) (2022). https://doi.org/10.28951/bjb.v40i2.566
29. Parodi, S., Verda, D., Bagnasco, F., Muselli, M.: The clinical meaning of the area under a receiver operating characteristic curve for the evaluation of the performance of disease markers. Epidemiol. Health **44**, e2022088 (2022). https://doi.org/10.4178/epih.e2022088
30. Jain, A.K.: Data clustering: 50 years beyond K-means. Pattern Recogn. Lett. **31**(8), 651–666 (2010). https://doi.org/10.1016/j.patrec.2009.09.011
31. Celebi, M.E., Kingravi, H.A., Vela, P.A.: A comparative study of efficient initialization methods for the k-means clustering algorithm. Expert Syst. Appl. **40**(1), 200–210 (2013). https://doi.org/10.1016/j.eswa.2012.07.021
32. Sharpe, D.: Your chi-square test is statistically significant: now what? **20**(8) (2015)
33. Kurita, T.: Principal Component Analysis (PCA). In: Kurita, T. (ed.) Computer Vision, pp. 1–4. Springer, Cham (2020). https://doi.org/10.1007/978-3-030-03243-2_649-1

Efficient Moving Object Detection from Ultra-High Resolution Omnidirectional Video

Takuro Ohashi and Shohei Yokoyama(✉)

Graduate School of Systems Design, Tokyo Metropolitan University, Tokyo, Japan
ohashi-takurou@ed.tmu.ac.jp, shohei@tmu.ac.jp

Abstract. With advancements in panoramic camera technology, resolutions have significantly improved [1], capturing distant objects more clearly. The Insta360 Titan, for instance, supports up to 11k resolution (10560×5280), offering unprecedented detail. However, current object recognition methods struggle with such ultra-high-resolution footage. This paper presents a novel approach for detecting moving objects in 11k panoramic videos from the Insta360 Titan. Our method involves downsampling and background subtraction to detect moving objects quickly and accurately. These regions are then cropped into smaller images for high-precision detection, reducing computational load. This technique, inspired by proxy methods in video editing, maintains result quality while easing processing burdens. Experiments demonstrate our method's ability to accurately detect humans at distances up to 60 m, achieving 15 fps, thus proving its effectiveness for ultra-high-resolution panoramic footage.

Keywords: Ultra-High Resolution Video · Computer Vision · Moving Object Detection · Background Subtraction

1 Introduction

The possibility of high-definition video, made possible by the dramatic increase in resolution of digital cameras, is an advantage for photographers and a source of inspiration for the future of object recognition technologies based on machine learning techniques. With the ability to capture distant objects in high resolution, these images have significantly enhanced digital imaging and opened up new possibilities in the field.

A significant technical hurdle in leveraging the advantage of high-resolution videos is the disparity in image resolution. Image recognition technology is typically designed for images of lower resolution than those captured by digital cameras. For instance, while image sizes used in image machine learning are less than Full HD (2.1 megapixels), the iPhone has a 48-megapixel camera, highlighting the substantial difference and the complexity of the problem.

However, current systems have yet to fully capitalize on these high-resolution sensors' capabilities. Object recognition, a typical task in computer vision, often utilizes deep convolutional neural network models trained on datasets such as

ImageNet [2]. These models tend to focus on low-resolution images for several reasons:

1. Certain scenarios can be adequately addressed with low-resolution images.
2. Processing low-resolution images is faster.
3. Publicly available training datasets consist of low-resolution images (e.g., ImageNet, CIFAR100 [3], Caltech 256 [4]).

On the other hand, the broadcasting industry has been pushing the envelope with ultra-high-definition video standards. For instance, NHK's 8K broadcasting technology research demonstrates the industry's commitment to leveraging high-resolution capabilities for superior video quality and immersive experiences [5]. These advancements highlight the growing importance and potential of high-resolution video technology.

The omnidirectional camera is the technology that has benefited most from the increasing resolution of cameras. It is a device that uses multiple sensors to capture images of all 360° around it. The direct correlation between higher resolution and video quality is a testament to the impressive technological strides, fostering a sense of appreciation for the advancements in the field.

Figures 1 and 2 show 2K (3.7 megapixels) and 11K (60 megapixels) omnidirectional images taken with the Insta 360 Titan [6], a high-resolution omnidirectional camera known for its exceptional image quality. At a 10 m distance, there is little difference between the two images, but at a 30 m distance, it is not easy to distinguish the person in the 2K image because of the blurriness.

This is also true for machines; identifying distant subjects in low-resolution video is a complex problem. On the other hand, using high-resolution images with state-of-the-art machine learning techniques without down-sampling requires a tremendous amount of computing resources. The challenge lies in the fact that processing high-resolution images in real-time, especially in the context of video, is computationally intensive. Video cameras have to process about 10 to 30 frames per second, which further exacerbates this issue.

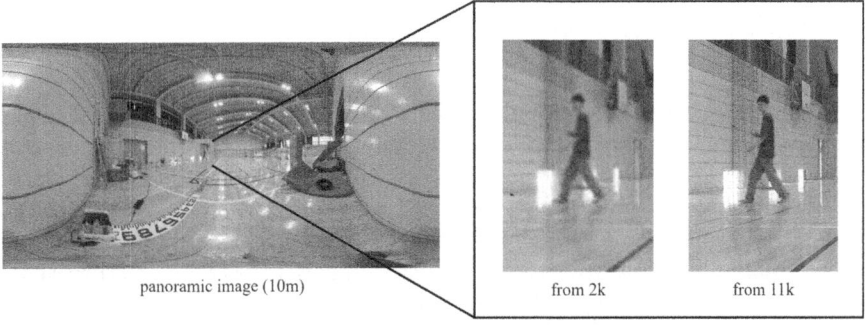

Fig. 1. Comparison of images cropped from 2k and 11k resolution videos taken at 10 m from the person. The image on the left is the original panoramic view. The cropped images on the right show details from the 2k video (left) and the 11k video (right)

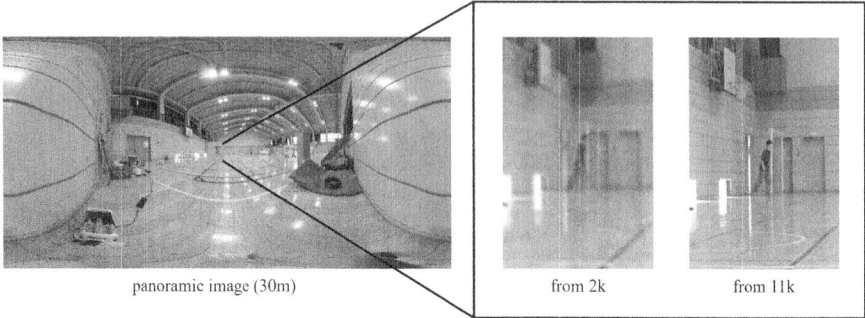

Fig. 2. Comparison of images cropped from 2k and 11k resolution videos taken at 30 m from the person. The image on the left is the original panoramic view. The cropped images on the right show details from the 2k video (left) and the 11k video (right)

This study addresses these challenges by proposing a method for detecting moving objects in ultra-high-resolution panoramic videos. Our method involves several steps. First, we use background subtraction to accurately detect moving objects. We then crop these regions into smaller images to reduce the computational load. Finally, we perform low-latency, high-accuracy object detection on these smaller images. Our proposed method reduces computational load while maintaining detection accuracy, achieving an average processing speed of 15 fps for 11k resolution video. Most impressively, it successfully detects humans at a distance of 30 m, a feat challenging for conventional methods, leaving the audience impressed by the method's capabilities.

The structure of this paper is as follows. Section 2 discusses related work. Section 3 details the proposed method. Section 4 presents experimental results and validates the effectiveness of the proposed method. Finally, Sect. 5 concludes the paper, emphasizing the need for continuous research and discussing future research directions.

2 Related Work

2.1 History of Moving Object Detection

Moving object detection has been a significant research topic in computer vision. Initial research focused on detecting objects in still images, but as video sequences became prevalent, the demand for detecting objects in dynamic scenes increased. This led to the evolution of various methods for moving object detection, with numerous approaches proposed over the years. Classical methods such as frame differencing and background subtraction have been extensively used. A seminal work in background subtraction is the Gaussian Mixture Model (GMM) based BackgroundSubtractorMOG. Stauffer and Grimson [7] first proposed using GMM for real-time object tracking, modeling each pixel's background with multiple Gaussian distributions, which proved effective in handling illumination changes and moving backgrounds. Zivkovic [8] later improved this model's adaptability, making it widely used in practice.

Frame Differencing Method. The frame differencing method is a classical technique that detects motion by calculating the pixel-wise difference between consecutive frames. This method is computationally simple and suitable for real-time processing, making it popular in surveillance and tracking systems [7]. However, it is sensitive to illumination changes and background movements, which can lead to frequent false detections.

Background Subtraction Method. Background subtraction involves modeling the static background of a scene and detecting moving objects by subtracting this model from each frame. This method is particularly effective for fixed-camera systems like surveillance cameras, providing relatively high accuracy in detecting moving objects [8]. Nonetheless, it faces challenges in adapting to background changes such as weather variations or day-night transitions, complicating long-term surveillance.

2.2 Object Detection in High-Resolution Video

With the proliferation of high-resolution video, there is a growing need for object detection in 4K and 8K resolution videos. Notable research in this area includes work by Růžička and Franchetti, who proposed a fast and accurate object detection method using YOLOv2 for 4K and 8K videos [9]. Their approach involves dividing 4K images into multiple square segments and performing object detection in two stages: first, identifying regions of interest through coarse segmentation, and second, performing detailed detection in these regions at high resolution. This method achieves processing speeds of 3–6 fps for 4K resolution and 2 fps for 8K resolution, demonstrating higher efficiency compared to processing the entire image at once.

Other approaches have also tackled high-resolution video processing. For example, Tran et al. introduced a method for fast object detection in high-resolution videos using modern hardware and detection techniques, which significantly enhances processing efficiency [10]. Mattela et al. proposed a pipeline for distant person detection and identification specifically targeting 4K videos, demonstrating effective usage of GPU acceleration for high-speed processing [11]. These works, while focused on different resolutions, contribute important insights into efficient object detection in large-scale video data.

Our research advances this field in several critical ways. First, in alignment with advancements in camera technology, we have adopted the latest version of YOLO (YOLOv8 [12]) rather than the older YOLOv2. This upgrade is essential to match the capabilities of modern, high-resolution cameras, ensuring that our detection methods are both accurate and efficient. Second, our study targets 11K resolution, enabling more extensive and detailed object detection. Third, while prior work focused on general high-resolution videos, we concentrate on omnidirectional panoramic videos captured with an omnidirectional camera, allowing comprehensive monitoring of wide areas. Lastly, instead of coarse segmentation for initial object detection, we use a background subtraction algorithm to identify moving regions and crop these areas, effectively extracting regions of interest and enabling detailed object detection at high resolution.

Additionally, Haidi Zhu et al. proposed a moving object detection method for 4K resolution real-time processing, leveraging specialized hardware for high-speed processing and effective object detection [13]. However, the limitation of 4K resolution constrains the detection of small or distant objects and fine details. In contrast, our study employs 11K resolution for non-real-time processing, aiming for higher detail and broader field coverage. This allows improved detection accuracy for distant objects and subtle movements. Similarly, Nakaizumi et al. proposed a method to divide high-resolution video based on regions of interest, demonstrating an efficient technique to handle high-resolution video regardless of object positioning [14], while Li et al. introduced lightweight object detection using Tiny-DSOD for resource-constrained environments, an approach aligned with efficient detection under limited computational resources [15].

Our research uniquely employs an omnidirectional camera as the input device, capturing omnidirectional video simultaneously in all directions, making it suitable for wide-area monitoring. By adopting non-real-time processing, we distribute the computational load while analyzing ultra-high-resolution data in detail. This approach is valuable for long-term monitoring and detailed analysis scenarios. By incorporating the strengths of previous research while overcoming the limitations of 4K resolution, our approach offers significant improvements in resolution, detection accuracy, and application scope.

In summary, our study significantly advances object detection in ultra-high-resolution videos by targeting 11K resolution panoramic videos, achieving higher accuracy and efficiency, and providing comprehensive monitoring capabilities.

3 Proposed Method

In this section, we detail our proposed method for moving object detection. This method consists of three main steps: creation of background subtraction video, tracking and cropping from the difference video, and object detection in the cropped video. Each step is described in detail using images and diagrams.

3.1 Creation of Background Subtraction Video

The first step is to downsample the 11K resolution panoramic video to 2K resolution. This is inspired by the technology called "proxy" used in video editing software such as Adobe Premiere Pro, which is used to edit high-resolution video [16]. This is done to reduce computational load while maintaining high resolution. The downsampled 2K video is then processed using the background subtraction algorithm (cv2.cuda.BackgroundSubtractorMOG()) to convert it into a binary video where moving objects are highlighted in white. Please refer to the schematic diagram in Fig. 3 for a visual representation of whole process.

In this study, we adopt BackgroundSubtractorMOG for moving object detection in ultra-high-resolution videos. This method is a type of background subtraction method that models each pixel with a mixture of multiple Gaussian distributions, allowing it to handle dynamic backgrounds and changes in illumination. The BackgroundSubtractorMOG algorithm is detailed as follows:

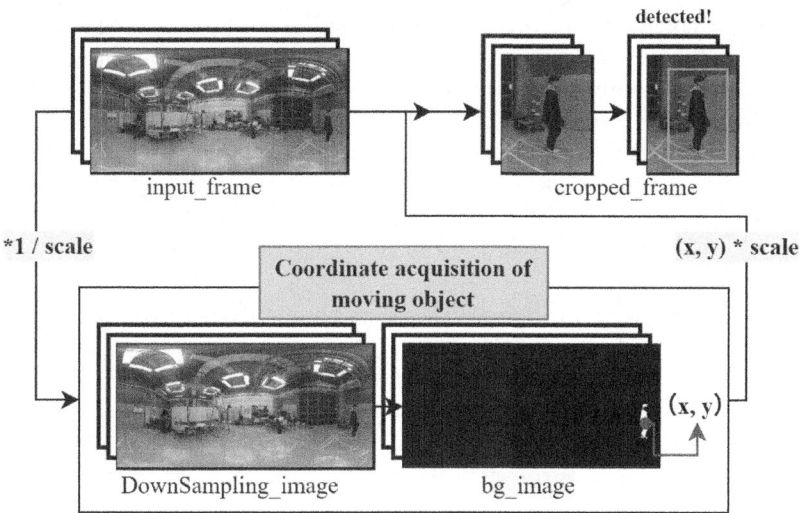

Fig. 3. Detection results at various distances using the 11k resolution central portion of the video (Frame 120 of a 300-frame video). The left side shows the input videos captured at 40 m, 50 m, and 60 m distances. The right side shows the corresponding detected objects with confidence scores

1. **Initialization**: The Gaussian mixture model is initialized using the initial frame. Each pixel is assigned multiple Gaussian distributions, each initialized with mean, variance, and weight.
2. **Frame Input**: As new frames are input, the Gaussian mixture model for each pixel is updated.
3. **Foreground Detection**: Each pixel in the current frame is checked against the background model's Gaussian distributions. If the pixel does not belong to any of the distributions, it is marked as foreground (moving object).
4. **Background Update**: After foreground detection, the parameters of the Gaussian distributions (mean, variance, weight) are updated. When new data points are added, the oldest Gaussian distribution is replaced by a new one.

Using this method, robust moving object detection is possible even in the presence of wide-ranging motion and changes in illumination. A specific application example is the detection of moving objects in 11K resolution omnidirectional panoramic videos.

This process generates a binary video where moving objects are highlighted, forming the basis for the next step of tracking and cropping.

3.2 Tracking and Cropping from the Difference Video

Next, using the binary difference video, we perform tracking and cropping of moving objects. This step proceeds as follows:

1. **Noise Removal**: Morphological transformations are used to remove noise from the binary video, enhancing detection accuracy.

2. **Contour Extraction and Ranking**: Contours of objects in the difference video are extracted and ranked based on their size. Since we are targeting ground objects, only objects above a certain size are considered.
3. **Tracking**: The coordinates of objects in the previous frame are saved, and objects within a threshold distance in the current frame are tracked as the same object. If there is only one moving object, the largest object is tracked. If there are multiple objects, the number of objects detected in the initial frame is registered, and each object is assigned an ID (e.g., object_1, object_2) for tracking

Parameter Setting. To improve the accuracy of tracking, the following two parameters need to be appropriately set. These parameters are adjusted based on the video resolution.

- Distance threshold for recognizing the same object between the previous and current frames: `distance_threshold`
- Minimum contour area threshold for moving objects: `min_contour_area`.

3.3 Object Detection in Cropped Video

In the final step, the tracked moving objects are centered and cropped into 400×400 pixel images, and object detection is performed using YOLO v8. This method enables high-accuracy and high-speed object detection.

By applying the YOLO v8 model to the cropped images, moving objects are accurately detected and their positions are identified. This step leverages the excellent performance of YOLO v8, allowing for near-real-time object detection.

3.4 Post-processing

The YOLO v8 model internally uses a non-maximum suppression (NMS) algorithm during object detection to automatically integrate overlapping bounding boxes. This post-processing step ensures optimal detection results.

The proposed method aims to improve the efficiency and accuracy of moving object detection in ultra-high-resolution omnidirectional panoramic videos. Starting with initial detection using background subtraction, followed by tracking and cropping, and culminating in final object detection, this sequence of processes yields high-precision detection results. This approach enables the coverage of wide areas and near-real-time detection of moving objects.

4 Experiments

This section details the system specifications and measurement criteria used in our experiments, followed by the results in terms of accuracy and performance. We utilized a high-performance PC for these experiments, which was equipped with Ubuntu 22.04.3 LTS (64-bit) as the operating system. The hardware configuration included a 13th generation Intel Core i9-13900k-32 CPU, an NVIDIA A6000 Ada Generation GPU, and 128 GB of RAM. These specifications ensured efficient handling of high-resolution video processing and accurate object detection.

4.1 Distance and Accuracy

For the experiments, we used omnidirectional panoramic videos captured with the Insta360 Titan. The videos were recorded at five different resolutions: 2k, 4k, 6k, 8k, and 11k. Given the nature of panoramic videos and the fact that the moving objects were ground-based, we divided the entire image into upper, middle, and lower thirds and used only the central portion. This preprocessing step allowed us to investigate the relationship between distance and accuracy effectively.

The recordings took place at the gymnasium of Tokyo Metropolitan University Hino Campus, where the distances between the camera and the subjects were set to 5 m, 10 m, 15 m, 20 m, 25 m, and 30 m. Due to indoor distance limitations, additional recordings were performed outdoors at the same campus with the same distance settings. This dual setting enabled us to evaluate accuracy at various distances comprehensively.

Accuracy was measured using two key metrics. The first metric was the average confidence score, calculated by averaging the confidence scores of detection results across all frames of the cropped videos. The YOLO confidence threshold was set to 0.01. This metric provided an overall assessment of the system's reliability. The second metric was the proportion of high-confidence detections, defined as those with a confidence score of 0.8 or higher. Both the average confidence score and the proportion of high-confidence detections were tracked by following the IDs of the detected persons, excluding other objects. A higher proportion indicated better system accuracy.

4.2 Evaluation of Resolution, Processing Speed, and FPS

We assessed the impact of video resolution on processing speed and frames per second (FPS). The panoramic videos used for this evaluation were captured with the Insta360 Titan at 2k, 4k, 6k, 8k, and 11k resolutions. The recordings took place at Tokyo Metropolitan University Hino Campus, with moving objects being humans recorded from a fixed distance of 30 m.

For performance measurement, we used the unedited videos described previously as input. We evaluated the execution time (in seconds) and processing speed (FPS) of the program, which involved several steps: downsampling the input video, creating background differences, generating cropped videos focused on moving objects, and performing object detection on these cropped videos.

By measuring these processing times and FPS, we could clearly demonstrate the system's performance across different resolutions. For Sect. 4.2, the performance measurement was conducted by limiting the moving object to one per frame, ensuring precise evaluation of processing speed and FPS (Table 1).

Table 1. Bitrate settings for the videos used in Experiments 1 and 2

Resolution in 1	Bitrate in 1	Resolution in 2	Bitrate in 2
11k (10560,1760)	150 Mbps	11k (10560,5860)	455 Mbps
8k (7680, 1280)	80 Mbps	8k (7680, 3340)	240 Mbps
6k (6400, 1068)	55 Mbps	6k (6400, 3200)	165 Mbps
4k (3840, 640)	40 Mbps	4k (3840, 1980)	60 Mbps
2k (1980, 330)	20 Mbps	2k (1980, 990)	25 Mbps

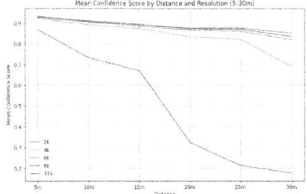
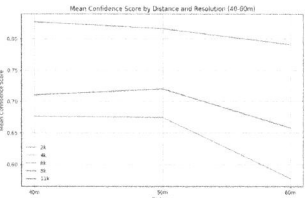

Fig. 4. Mean Confidence Score by Distance and Resolution (5–30 m)

Fig. 5. Mean Confidence Score by Distance and Resolution (40–60 m)

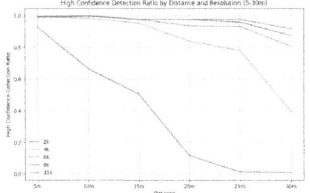
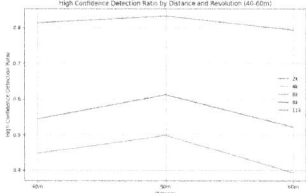

Fig. 6. High Confidence Detection Ratio by Distance and Resolution (5–30 m)

Fig. 7. High Confidence Detection Ratio by Distance and Resolution (40–60 m)

5 Results and Discussion

5.1 Results and Discussion for Experiment 4.1

Results. In Experiment 4.1, we evaluated the accuracy of moving object detection at different distances and resolutions. The evaluation criteria used were the mean confidence score and the ratio of high-confidence detections. The graphs below show the results for each distance and resolution.

Figure 8 shows the detection results at various distances using the 11k resolution central portion of the video (Frame 120 of a 300-frame video). The left side of the figure displays the input videos captured at 40 m, 50 m, and 60 m distances, while the right side shows the corresponding detected objects with confidence scores. These results highlight the effectiveness of our method in accurately detecting moving objects at different distances in high-resolution video.

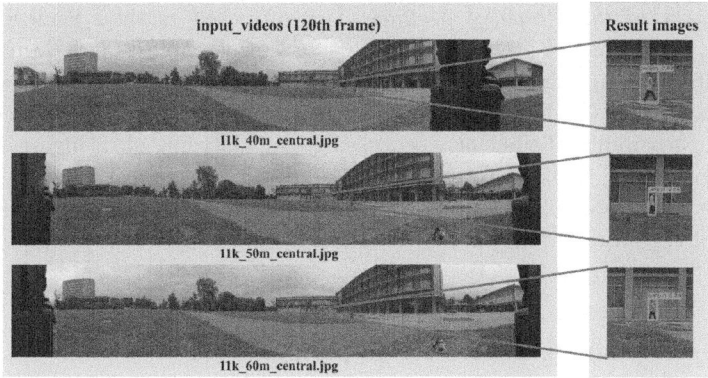

Fig. 8. Detection results at various distances using the 11k resolution central portion of the video (Frame 120 of a 300-frame video). The left side shows the input videos captured at 40 m, 50 m, and 60 m distances. The right side shows the corresponding detected objects with confidence scores

Discussion. Based on these results, we can draw several key observations:

High Confidence Detection Ratio. The high-confidence detection ratio tends to decrease as the distance increases (Fig. 6). This trend is particularly pronounced for 2k and 4k resolutions, where the ratio approaches zero at 30 m. In contrast, the 11k resolution maintains a relatively consistent high-confidence detection ratio, close to 0.8, regardless of the distance (Fig. 7). This indicates that high resolution helps to maintain detection accuracy even at longer distances.

Mean Confidence Score. The mean confidence score also shows a declining trend with increasing distance (Figs. 4 and 5). For 2k resolution, the score drops sharply, reaching about 0.2 at 30 m. On the other hand, the decline is more gradual for 8k and 11k resolutions, which maintain relatively high confidence scores. This suggests that higher resolutions are more effective for detecting objects at greater distances.

Relationship Between Resolution and Distance. Higher resolutions are less affected by distance. Specifically, 8k and 11k resolutions maintain high detection accuracy even as the distance increases (Figs. 7 and 5). Conversely, 2k and 4k resolutions show a steep decline in detection accuracy with increasing distance, indicating that these resolutions are better suited for close-range detection.

Practical Implications. The superior performance of high-resolution videos in detecting moving objects at long distances has significant practical implications for fields such as surveillance and sports analysis, where detailed information from a distance is crucial. Combining mean confidence scores and high-confidence detection ratios allows for a comprehensive evaluation of the system's reliability and accuracy. This provides valuable insights for future research and practical applications.

Effectiveness of the Proposed Method. The proposed method achieves high-precision, low-latency object detection using downsampling and frame differencing. It maintains an average processing speed of 15 fps for 11k resolution videos and sustains high detection accuracy at distances up to 30 m. This demonstrates the feasibility of efficiently processing and analyzing ultra-high-resolution panoramic videos, marking a significant step towards practical implementation.

These results and discussions underscore the effectiveness and potential applicability of the proposed method, leveraging the advantages of high resolution to achieve efficient object detection.

5.2 Results and Discussion for Experiment 4.2

Results. In Experiment 4.2, we measured the processing time required to handle 8 s of video under different resolutions and input frame rates (FPS) and calculated the corresponding processing speed (FPS). The table below presents the processing time and processing speed for each resolution and input FPS combination (Table 2).

Table 2. Processing speed (FPS) for each resolution and input video FPS

Resolution\fps	5	10	15	20	25	30
11k	8.587111	13.017160	14.013631	14.532249	15.591522	15.534487
8k	13.862548	18.790959	20.887579	22.399784	23.239280	24.073252
6k	16.512666	21.839234	25.504624	26.909611	28.700124	29.675951
4k	21.857072	33.038024	38.707572	44.167106	46.355777	49.190616
2k	24.291875	36.330278	41.910038	47.947087	51.082116	53.514783

The following 3D surface plots visually depict the processing time and processing speed for various resolutions and input FPS.

Discussion. Based on these results, we can draw several key observations:

Relationship Between Resolution and Processing Speed. As the resolution increases, the processing speed significantly decreases. For 11k resolution, the processing speed at the highest input FPS (30 FPS) is limited to 15.53 FPS, the lowest among all tested resolutions. In contrast, at 2k resolution, the processing speed is much higher, reaching 53.51 FPS at 30 FPS input. This trend is due to the increased computational demand for processing higher resolution images, which requires more resources and time. This relationship is clearly illustrated in Figs. 9 and 10. Figures 9 and 10 only have data points obtained from the experiment at the intersection of the three axes, and the rest of the mesh graph is linearly interpolated. All the videos used have a total length of 8 s, differing only in resolution and FPS.

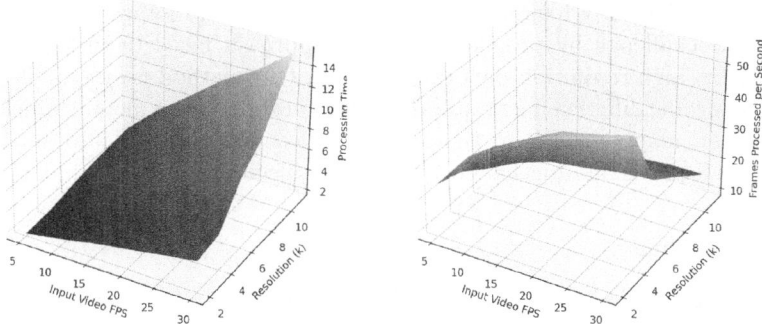

Fig. 9. Processing Time vs Resolution and Input FPS

Fig. 10. Processing Speed vs Resolution and Input FPS

Impact of Input FPS on Processing Speed. Across all resolutions, an increase in input FPS generally leads to an increase in processing speed. This trend is particularly noticeable at 4k and 2k resolutions, where the processing speed at 30 FPS input reaches 49.19 FPS and 53.51 FPS, respectively. This demonstrates the system's capability to efficiently handle higher input rates, up to a certain threshold determined by the resolution. This relationship is visually depicted in Fig. 10.

Processing Capacity Limits. At 11k resolution, the increase in processing speed with higher input FPS becomes less pronounced, especially between 20 FPS and 30 FPS input, where the processing speed shows minimal change. This suggests that the system is reaching its processing capacity limits at high resolutions, likely due to hardware constraints or the need for further algorithmic optimization to manage the high computational load. This trend is confirmed in Figs. 9 and 10.

Effectiveness of the Proposed Method. The proposed method achieves high-precision, low-latency object detection using downsampling and frame differencing. It maintains an average processing speed of 15 fps for 11k resolution videos and sustains high detection accuracy at distances up to 30 m. This demonstrates the feasibility of efficiently processing and analyzing ultra-high-resolution panoramic videos, marking a significant step towards practical implementation.

These results and discussions underscore the effectiveness and potential applicability of the proposed method, leveraging the advantages of high resolution to achieve efficient object detection.

6 Summary and Implications

The evolution of camera devices has significantly increased their resolution, particularly with devices like the Insta360 Titan that supports up to 11k (10560×5280) resolution. However, conventional object recognition methods are not designed to efficiently handle such ultra-high-resolution footage. This study addresses this challenge by proposing a novel approach for detecting moving objects in ultra-high-resolution panoramic videos. Our method leverages downsampling and frame differencing to quickly and accurately detect moving objects, which are then mapped back to the original video and cropped into smaller images for high-precision object detection with reduced computational load.

6.1 Key Findings

Our findings highlight the significance of ultra-high-resolution videos in various applications. The 11k resolution video provides the capability to capture fine movements and small objects at long distances, offering significant advantages in fields such as surveillance, sports analysis, and event recording. High-resolution footage is particularly valuable for detecting objects at greater distances, providing details that are not discernible at lower resolutions like 2k or 4k.

The experiments demonstrated that higher resolutions maintain high detection accuracy even at greater distances. For instance, the 11k resolution maintained a high-confidence detection ratio close to 0.8 at distances up to 60 m, whereas 2k and 4k resolutions showed a steep decline in accuracy with increasing distance. This finding is crucial for applications requiring detailed information over long distances. Additionally, the mean confidence scores indicated that higher resolutions exhibit a more gradual decline in accuracy with increasing distance, with 8k and 11k resolutions consistently maintaining higher scores compared to lower resolutions.

In terms of processing speed and efficiency, our analysis revealed that higher resolution images demand more computational resources. Despite this, our method achieved an average processing speed of 15 fps for 11k resolution videos, demonstrating the feasibility of near-real-time processing for ultra-high-resolution footage. The relationship between input FPS and processing speed indicated that our system efficiently handles higher input rates, particularly at resolutions of 4k and below. However, at 11k resolution, the improvements in processing speed plateau, suggesting a need for further optimization and potential hardware limitations.

6.2 Practical Implications

The superior performance of high-resolution videos in detecting moving objects at long distances has significant practical implications across various fields. In surveillance systems, the monitoring efficiency of public spaces and critical infrastructure is greatly enhanced. High-resolution cameras cover broader areas and detect subtle movements and small objects, improving the ability to quickly identify and respond to security threats. For instance, in high-traffic areas such as airports, train stations, and shopping malls, high-resolution surveillance systems enable detailed identification and behavioral analysis, enhancing overall security.

In sports analysis, capturing detailed movements of athletes in large stadiums allows for precise performance analysis and tactical evaluation. High-resolution footage can detect subtle differences in athletes' form and movements, providing valuable feedback for improvement. Coaches and analysts can use high-resolution videos to evaluate overall game strategies and player positioning, contributing to the enhancement of team tactics.

Event recording also benefits from high-resolution videos, as they can capture the entire scope of large events while recording detailed activities. This is particularly useful for concerts and sports events, where the high-resolution footage can preserve detailed audience reactions and intricate performance details. Post-event analysis benefits from the ability to focus on specific moments or perspectives in detail, aiding in the improvement of future event management and performance planning.

7 Conclusion

The proposed method effectively utilizes ultra-high-resolution panoramic videos to achieve high-precision and efficient moving object detection. This study demonstrates the practical viability of processing 11k resolution footage and provides a solid foundation for further advancements in the field of computer vision.

Future research should focus on several key areas. First, there is a need to develop more efficient algorithms to improve processing speeds and accommodate higher resolutions. This includes enhancing existing frame differencing and background subtraction algorithms to reduce computational costs while maintaining accuracy. Integrating advanced machine learning and deep learning models could also enhance detection capabilities and processing efficiency. Second, implementing dedicated hardware and parallel processing techniques is crucial for achieving real-time detection. While it is currently possible to detect multiple objects simultaneously, the processing speed decreases proportionally with the number of detections. Therefore, parallelization is essential. Utilizing GPUs and FPGAs for parallel processing can significantly expedite the handling of large-scale data. Distributed computing in cloud environments can further enhance real-time capabilities by leveraging multiple nodes for parallel processing, making large-scale surveillance and live event analysis more feasible.

Finally, adapting the proposed method for other high-resolution sensors and different application domains, such as autonomous vehicles and robotics, is a promising direction. In autonomous vehicles, ultra-high-resolution cameras can detect distant objects and fine obstacles early, improving safety. In robotics, high-resolution imaging enables precise operations and remote control, benefiting sectors like manufacturing and healthcare. Additionally, drones equipped with high-resolution cameras can enhance wide-area surveillance and inspection tasks.

References

1. Blahnik, V., Schindelbeck, O.: Smartphone imaging technology and its applications. Adv. Opt. Technol. **10**(3), 145–232 (2021)
2. Deng, J., Dong, W., Socher, R., Li, L.-J., Li, K., Fei-Fei, L.: ImageNet: a large-scale hierarchical image database. In: 2009 IEEE Conference on Computer Vision and Pattern Recognition, pp. 248–255. IEEE (2009)
3. Krizhevsky, A., Nair, V., Hinton, G.: CIFAR-100 (Canadian Institute for Advanced Research). http://www.cs.toronto.edu/~kriz/cifar.html. Accessed 21 June 2024
4. Griffin, G., Holub, A., Perona, P.: Caltech-256 object category dataset. California Institute of Technology (2007)
5. Aihara, S.: Overview of 8K satellite broadcasting experiment. https://www.nhk.or.jp/strl/english/publica/bt/63/4.html. Accessed 21 June 2024
6. Insta360: Product Comparison - Insta360. https://www.insta360.com/jp/product/compare. Accessed 21 June 2024
7. Stauffer, C., Grimson, W.E.L.: Adaptive background mixture models for real-time tracking. In: Proceedings of the IEEE Computer Society Conference on Computer Vision and Pattern Recognition (CVPR 1999), vol. 2, pp. 246–252. IEEE (1999)
8. Zivkovic, Z.: Improved adaptive gaussian mixture model for background subtraction. In: Proceedings of the 17th International Conference on Pattern Recognition (ICPR 2004), vol. 2, pp. 28–31. IEEE (2004)
9. Růžička, V., Franchetti, F.: Fast and accurate object detection in high resolution 4K and 8K video using GPUs. In: 2018 IEEE High Performance Extreme Computing Conference (HPEC), pp. 1–7. IEEE (2018)
10. Tran, R., Kanaujia, A., Parameswaran, V.: Fast object detection in high-resolution videos. In: Proceedings of the IEEE/CVF International Conference on Computer Vision Workshops (ICCVW), pp. 1461–1470. IEEE (2023)
11. Mattela, G., Tripathi, M., Pal, C., Dhiraj, R.S., Acharyya, A.: An efficient pipeline for distant person detection and identification in 4K video using GPUs. In: Proceedings of the International Conference on Communication Systems & Networks (COMSNETS), pp. 744–749. IEEE (2020)
12. Jocher, G., Chaurasia, A., Qiu, J.: Ultralytics YOLOv8. https://github.com/ultralytics/ultralytics. Accessed 21 June 2024
13. Zhu, H., Wei, H., Li, B., Yuan, X., Kehtarnavaz, N.: Real-time moving object detection in high-resolution video sensing. Sensors **20**(12), 3591 (2020)
14. Nakaizumi, Y., Shishido, H., Kameda, Y.: Video dividing method for high-resolution video regardless of people position. In: Proceedings of Other Conferences (2021)
15. Li, Y., Li, J., Lin, W., Li, J.: Tiny-DSOD: lightweight object detection for resource-restricted usages. In: Proceedings of the British Machine Vision Conference (BMVC). BMVA (2018)
16. Adobe: Proxy workflow in Premiere Pro. https://helpx.adobe.com/premiere-pro/using/proxy-workflow.html. Accessed 21 June 2024

Evaluation of the Clustering Method Used to Analyze the Proximity of Mobile Devices Using Indirect Geolocation Indicators

Jaroslaw Kobiela(✉) and Piotr Urbaniec

Institute of Computer Science, University of Opole, Opole, Poland
{jaroslaw.kobiela,urbanip}@uni.opole.pl

Abstract. This study introduces a new methodology for clustering mobile devices to determine their geographical proximity without using direct geolocation data. Using the DBSCAN algorithm, we aim to identify significant spatial patterns while preserving user privacy. The dataset used includes information on device manufacturers and network interactions. Clustering was performed after data preprocessing, with DBSCAN effectively grouping devices in proximity. Our results show that this method successfully identifies clusters that reflect meaningful geographical relationships among the devices. The evaluation included calculating the average and maximum distances within the clusters, demonstrating the robustness of the method. Despite its effectiveness, the success of the method depends on the quality and completeness of the input data. Future research should explore additional data sources and refine used algorithms to enhance accuracy and efficiency.

Keywords: Clustering Algorithms · Geographical Proximity · Mobile Devices

1 Introduction

1.1 Background

The extensive use of mobile devices in contemporary society has generated vast amounts of data, offering unique insights into various social phenomena, particularly in public health and safety sectors. This study addresses a significant gap in current research by evaluating the efficacy of device-clustering methods for establishing geographic proximity without relying on geolocalization data.

The primary objective of this study was to assess the effectiveness of various clustering methodologies in pinpointing the geographical proximity of devices, specifically in scenarios in which direct geolocation data might not be available. This study aimed to provide empirical evidence of the applicability and limitations of these methods.

It is hypothesized that diverse clustering techniques can successfully determine the geographical proximity among devices. However, the precision of these methods is expected to diminish when direct access to geolocalization data is unavailable.

This study employed a mixed-methods approach that combines quantitative data analysis with algorithmic testing to assess the accuracy of device clustering. The data utilized in this research comprised anonymized and aggregated mobile device data collected from various sources, to ensure compliance with data protection laws. Several clustering algorithms, including k-means, hierarchical clustering, and Density-Based Spatial Clustering of Applications with Noise (DBSCAN), have been evaluated for their ability to group devices based on synthetic proximity indicators derived from the data. In this article, we describe the use of only the DBSCAN algorithm, due to the more unambiguous results we obtained.

This study has the potential to support the creation of innovative applications and systems that aim to improve public health monitoring and community safety, while ensuring the protection of individual privacy.

1.2 Motivation

One of the key challenges in analyzing data from mobile devices is determining the geographical proximity of devices without using direct geolocation data.

The aim of this study is to develop and evaluate the effectiveness of methods for clustering mobile devices in the context of determining their geographical proximity without using direct geolocation data.

Our motivation stems from the need for more efficient and secure data-analysis methods that can be used in publicly available applications. We aim to fill a gap in existing research by providing empirical evidence of the effectiveness of clustering techniques in scenarios where direct geolocalization data are unavailable or incomplete. Additionally, our research aims to understand the limitations of these methods and provide guidance for further development of privacy-preserving technologies in mobile data analytics.

2 Literature Review

Boutet and Cunche (2021) proposed a privacy-preserving method for Wi-Fi location systems that reduces the amount of data exposed to untrusted systems through caching and random sampling [1]. Jhon Jairo Castro Afanador and colleagues (2020) aimed to enhance GPS geolocalization accuracy by integrating supporting signals and cooperative networks. Their study highlighted the significance of geopositioning methods in improving location accuracy in applications such as engineering and urban planning [2]. Yuichi Sei and Akihiko Ohsugi addressed the issue of location anonymity by proposing privacy metrics that account for location errors and the concept of (k,w)-anonymisation to enhance user privacy. Lorenzo Schwittmann, Matthäus Wander, and Torben Weis (2019) introduced a method for determining user locations through embedded sensors in smartphones, allowing for geographical area identification without user knowledge or consent [3]. Shun Zhang and colleagues (2022) introduced DPIVE, a location obfuscation scheme that allows users to set individual privacy levels after 2D space discretisation and the QK-means algorithm [4]. S. Zhang and colleagues (2022) suggested the Geo-MOEA system, which utilises a multi-objective evolutionary algorithm to optimise service availability and privacy in the context of Spatial Crowdsourcing [5]. Bashar

M. Nemy and Ali Nafaa Jaafar developed a mobile device location system using GSM and UMTS networks to track devices without additional hardware [6]. A. Al-Hamad and N. El-Sheimy recommended using smartphones as an affordable mobile mapping system (MMS) to revolutionize future GIS applications and mapping [7]. Yali Ji and colleagues investigated the application of k-anonymity algorithm and grid method for safeguarding the location privacy of mobile users during crowdsensing tasks. On the other hand, Hongtao Li and co-workers proposed a two-stage approach for securing location queries in mobile social networks by involving privacy processors and service providers [8]. Vidyasagara Sadhu et al. developed an integrated mobile location platform called CollabLoc, which incorporates sensor-critical data for enhancing location privacy [9]. Feilong Tang and colleagues proposed the use of soft computing techniques for generating false paths in cloud-based mobile services to ensure long-term location privacy [10]. Anon Sukstrienwong from Bangkok University presented an algorithm for forming geolocalisation groups to optimise travel for mobile co-working activities [11]. Finally, Yang et al. introduced an advanced method for location privacy known as semantic k-anonymity that protects sparse location data from semantic attacks [12].

The value of these studies lies in their ability to advance the field of location privacy technology by showcasing diverse methodologies and techniques that are effective for practical applications.

3 Data Collection and Clustering Methodology

This study relies on information gathered from mobile devices during the pre-production phase of the CyberEva project, financed by The Polish National Center for Research and Development, and utilizes data from a test database that includes 904 541 scans conducted using mobile devices in a designated region of Poland. This information was de-identified and screened to guarantee compliance with existing data protection regulations.

3.1 Data Collection Process

A team of testers and volunteers operating within a specific voivodeship (and partly for reference purposes during subsequent testing and research, outside it) in Poland collected the data used in this study. Data collection was facilitated by 2023 using the CyberEva mobile application, which was developed as part of the project. This application was designed to perform comprehensive scans of the mobile device and its connected networks, including Wi-Fi, GSM, and Bluetooth networks.

During each scan, the application collected a wide range of available information, including:

- **IP Addresses**: The application captured the IP addresses associated with the device and the network to which it was connected.
- **Device Names**: Names of devices detected within the network, providing an additional context for identifying and categorizing devices.
- **DNS Addresses**: Information about DNS servers used by the devices, which can offer insights into network configurations and usage patterns.

- **Device Manufacturer IDs**: Unique identifiers for device manufacturers that help categorize and differentiate between different types of devices.
- **Scan Time**: Timestamp for each scan, allowing for temporal analysis of device proximity and movement.
- **Network Types**: Details concerning the types of networks (Wi-Fi, GSM, Bluetooth) to which the device was connected during the scan.

The data collection process was carefully designed to ensure that all the collected information was anonymized and aggregated to protect user privacy.

3.2 Database Structure

The information for this study was carefully stored in a comprehensive database designed to manage the various details collected from the mobile devices. The database is divided into several sections, each with a specific function, to ensure that the data are immutable and managed effectively. For example, one section stores network-related information, including GSM, Bluetooth, and Wi-Fi details, and captures elements such as network standards, operators, IP addresses, and device statuses. The database also stores separate records for manufacturer-specific details, allowing the categorization and differentiation of devices. In addition, several sections contain information on various network services, including HTTP, FTP, and SMTP services, which store details such as port numbers, service names, versions, and security attributes. This well-organized design facilitated robust data collection and processing, enabling accurate and efficient grouping and proximity analysis.

4 Geospatial Data Analysis and Clustering Techniques

4.1 Proximity Analysis Without Direct Geolocation

One of the more intriguing issues addressed in this study is the ability to determine the geographical proximity of devices (and indirectly their users) based on selected data collected and shared by these devices in everyday life, often without user awareness. Our approach evaluates the possibility of grouping users (their devices) such that the group members are in the same location within a specified time window. In the most general case, the exact locations of such places need not be known; however, our method can still provide socially valuable information, for example, in modeling the spread of infectious diseases or public safety.

The authors did not focus on known methods of geolocation and identification, such as the analysis of BTS points, IP addresses, access points, SSID names, or the analysis of metadata hidden in packets. Instead, interest lies in seemingly insensitive and ostensibly meaningless data that can be collected by a mobile application (even an amateur one) installed on mobile devices. After transferring this information to a server and processing it appropriately, it is used for the grouping described later.

4.2 Formal Description of the Problem

The issue presented can be described as the problem of identifying devices in close proximity based on certain subsets of data collected and shared by them. The identification procedure, from data acquisition to verdicting on proximity, proceeds as follows:

1. Scans are conducted using a collection of mobile devices, obtaining a collection C of scans numbered s belonging to the set S.
2. After processing scan number s, the data can be described using an ordered set of keys [keys] $K = (k_1, k_2, \ldots, k_n)$ and a set of corresponding values [values] $V(s) = (v[k_1](s), v[k_2](s), \ldots, v[k_n](s))$; it is assumed that K is constant for all scans in a specified time period T.
3. From the set K, an ordered $I = (i_1, i_2, \ldots, i_m)$ is chosen, where $m < n_m < n$, called the proximity indicator. The value of indicator I for scan s, denoted $V(s)$, is the set of values corresponding to the indicator keys for the scan s.
4. For the given indicator, a *prediction algorithm* A_I is developed which may, for example, decide whether two devices performing scans were geographically close to each other (according to a given criterion) within a time interval ΔT (where ΔT is a subset of T) or divide the set of indicator values into clusters grouping those indicator values that correspond to scans performed by devices close to each other in the interval ΔT.

In particular, the authors noted promising results from the analysis of a very simple and natural situation where the proximity indicator I is a one-element set having a manufacturers key, whose value for the scan $s \in S$ is the sequence (of variable length) $V_I(s) = (i_1(s), i_2(s), \ldots, i_{n(s)}(s))$, composed of the manufacturer names of the devices detected in the wireless network environment during the s-scan. The remainder of this article is devoted to an analysis of this particular situation. Note that in the indicated situation specifying the time interval ΔT in which we want to detect the proximity of scanning devices only results in narrowing the initial data set, without affecting the ideas of the methods used. For this reason, and to increase the size and diversity of the analyzed data, in what follows we assume that $\Delta T = T$.

4.3 Selection of Data for Problem Analysis

From the database, it was necessary to select scans that contained the correct and complete information: 1. manufacturer names for all devices detected in the environment, and 2. geolocation of the device performing the scan (let us emphasize that geolocations are not used at the clustering stage, but only during the final verification of the effectiveness of the proposed method). After selection, a set of 6 926 scans were obtained, covering a total of 41 956 devices from 152 manufacturers (excluding the devices carrying out the scan). The names of the manufacturers have been replaced with natural numbers. Selected characteristics of the data are shown in the following three charts (Fig. 1 and 2):

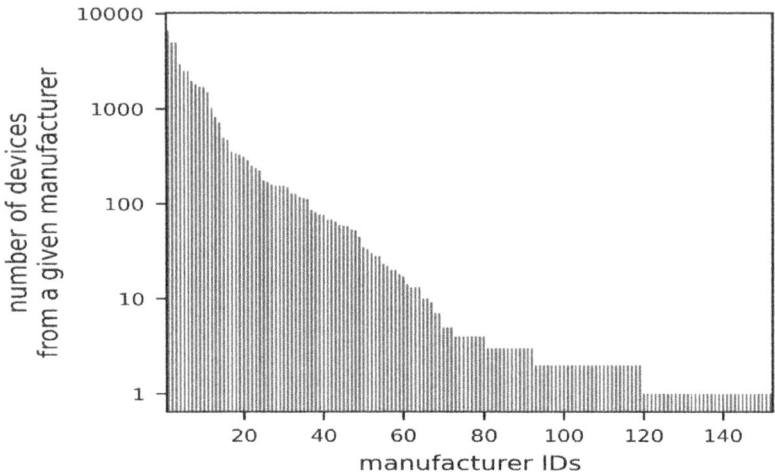

Fig. 1. Distribution of the number of devices by manufacturer

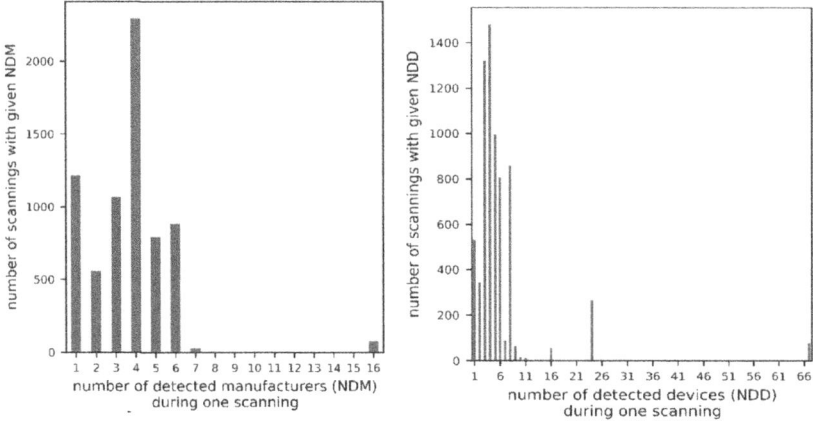

Fig. 2. Distribution of the number of manufacturers detected during the scans (left) and a distribution of the number of devices detected during the scans (right).

Remark 1. The average number of devices observed in the device environment per scan is $M_{dev} = 6.06$. The 95% confidence interval for the M_{dev} obtained by the percentile bootstrap method is [5.86, 6.26]. Therefore, we can say that there were an average of 7 "active" devices in the place where the scan was performed (6 observed + the one that performed the scan). This is an interesting result in its own way because, as noted in [13], the average number of IoT devices connected to the local network for a local resident in Poland was seven in 2023.

4.4 Enhanced GPS Data Analysis

Given the geographic coordinates obtained from mobile devices, a critical decision involves determining when two positions are sufficiently proximate. The Global Positioning System (GPS), which is part of the broader suite of global navigation satellite systems (GNSS), plays a pivotal role in providing the necessary data for mobile phones to ascertain their geolocation. The World Geodetic System 1984 (WGS 84) is the standard employed, which defines an Earth-centered, Earth-fixed coordinate system using a reference ellipsoid that approximates Earth's geoid [14, 15].

However, the conversion between WGS 84 and other coordinate systems requires careful attention, particularly when using programming libraries designed for geospatial calculations. This is crucial for accurately computing the distances between two GPS-determined geolocations [16]. It is essential to consider that GNSS-determined locations by nature are approximations and subject to potential errors, notably when device scanning occurs indoors, such as in homes, offices, and shopping malls [17].

The reduced signal-to-noise ratio caused by signal attenuation and the multipath phenomenon, where signals reflect and refract, causing multiple echoes, are significant technical challenges in indoor environments [18]. These factors can drastically affect the accuracy of geolocation measurements, despite advances in mobile GNSS receiver technology that attempt to compensate for these detrimental effects.

As a result of analyzing extensive data sets, the "Law of Urban Multipath" was proposed in [19], which allows predicting GNSS outdoor position accuracy based on the heights of nearby buildings:

$$\text{Mean Accuracy}(m) = \text{Building height(floors)} + 5\,m \tag{1}$$

This equation highlights the correlation between building height and the accuracy of position measurements, emphasizing the challenges and necessary consideration of location-based services in urban areas. Figure 3 illustrates the RMS 2D positioning error and the corresponding horizontal DOP.

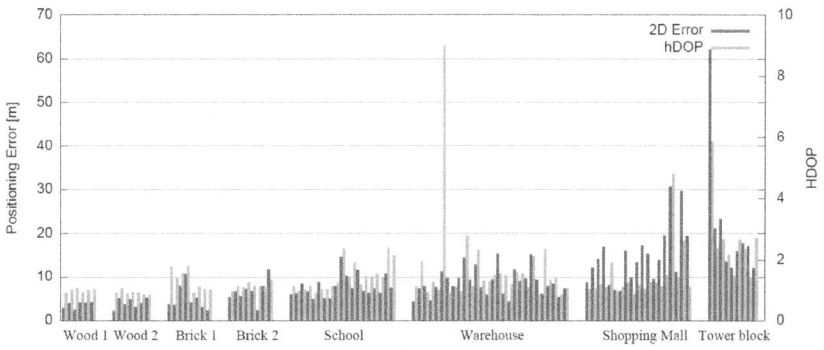

Fig. 3. RMS 2D positioning error and respective horizontal DOP [18]

With this rationale in mind, this study assumes that the positions of the two devices are considered close if the horizontal distance (determined using the Karney method) of their GPS-derived geolocalizations does not exceed $\Delta d = 25$ m.

4.5 Application of Clustering Techniques

Our methodology utilizes the DBSCAN clustering algorithm to analyze a dataset of selected mobile device scans, as described in Sect. 4.3. This algorithm clusters sequences representing the scan results in the form $(m_1, m_2, ..., m_N)$, where m_k denotes the number of devices (detected during scanning) from a given manufacturer and N denotes the total number of manufacturers. For each manufacturer, the position of the number of products in the sequence is fixed. Clustering is based on the Manhattan ($=$ Minkowski with $p = 1$ power) metric d_M, which is a natural choice for measuring similarity in this context [19].

It is well known that the choice of the control parameters (*eps* and *min_samples*) of the chosen scanning algorithm is crucial for obtaining the results. In our case, the number of clusters obtained and their sizes are of secondary importance. However, similarity in the structures of the elements classified into one cluster is important.

The greatest chance for the actual proximity of scanning devices included in one cluster is when their corresponding sequences $(m_1, m_2,..., m_N)$ are equal or slightly different. From this point of view, for d_M metric, *eps* < 2 are worth considering; observe, that for any point $v \in V$ its eps-neighborhoods $N_{eps}(v) = \{w \in V: d_M(v,w) \leq eps\}$ (these objects are crucial to the DBSCAN algorithm, see [20]) are identical for *eps* $\in (0,1)$ and, similarly, $N_{eps}(v)$ are identical for *eps* $\in [1, 2)$. Therefore, we limited our consideration to the representative values of *eps* $= 0.5$ and *eps* $= 1.0$. Furthermore, the data we analyzed are formally multidimensional (dimension is $N = 152$); however, the homogeneity and discreteness of the coordinates of the data points must be considered. It is clear that a cluster size of just a few does not necessarily disqualify it compared to clusters with several dozens or hundreds of elements, which may simply indicate that several scans were performed in a unique network environment. Therefore, we considered *min_samples* $\in [2, 4]$ to be the appropriate initial values for DBSCAN (this is one of the cases in which we should not follow the standard recommended setting of the *min_samples* parameter, such as 2 * dimension; see comments in [20]).

5 Results

Following the clustering process, we determined (using known geolocations now) the actual intra-cluster distances as well as the empirical probability that two points within a cluster were closer than the predefined distance $\Delta d = 25$ m. To quantify this empirical probability, we use the following formula to calculate the *overall index of inner proximity* (*C*) for each cluster C, where:

$$P(C) = \#\{(s, t): s, t \in C, s \neq t, d_M(s, t) < \Delta d\} / \#\{(s, t): s, t \in C, s \neq t\} \quad (2)$$

The formula above measures the proportion of all possible pairs of points within a cluster that are closer than the threshold distance Δd, providing a robust statistical measure of cluster density and separation.

This analysis is supported by Table 1.

Table 1. Characteristics of Clusters Detected by the DBSCAN Algorithm (*eps* = 1, *min_samples* = 4)

Cluster index	Cluster size	P(C)	Actual maximum distance in cluster [km]	Actual average distance in cluster [km]
−1	192	0,08	540,56	47,32
0	3 469	0,40	548,62	67,01
1	807	0,98	0,45	<*Δd*
2	77	1,00	<*Δd*	<*Δd*
3	139	0,65	62,84	10,02
4	5	1,00	<*Δd*	<*Δd*
5	6	1,00	<*Δd*	<*Δd*
6	10	0,49	0,79	0,35
7	4	0,00	0,22	0,13
8	1 807	1,00	<*Δd*	<*Δd*
9	25	0,92	0,04	<*Δd*
10	7	1,00	<*Δd*	<*Δd*
11	35	1,00	<*Δd*	<*Δd*
12	7	1,00	<*Δd*	<*Δd*
13	6	1,00	<*Δd*	<*Δd*
14	8	1,00	<*Δd*	<*Δd*
15	57	1,00	<*Δd*	<*Δd*
16	265	1,00	<*Δd*	<*Δd*

This granular analysis underscores the practical applications of our clustering approach, particularly when considering the indoor GPS positioning challenges. By effectively categorizing the device proximity without relying on precise geolocation data, our methodology extends the utility of mobile device data to urban planning and public health monitoring.

It is worth focusing on Cluster 8 (Table 1). Many users of the scanning application tested it in the project building, which was equipped with a specific set of wireless devices; this is where the above-mentioned cluster corresponds.

Figures 4 and 5 show the results of the clustering analysis performed using the DBSCAN algorithm on network device data. The graph contains the proximity rates for different types of clusters.

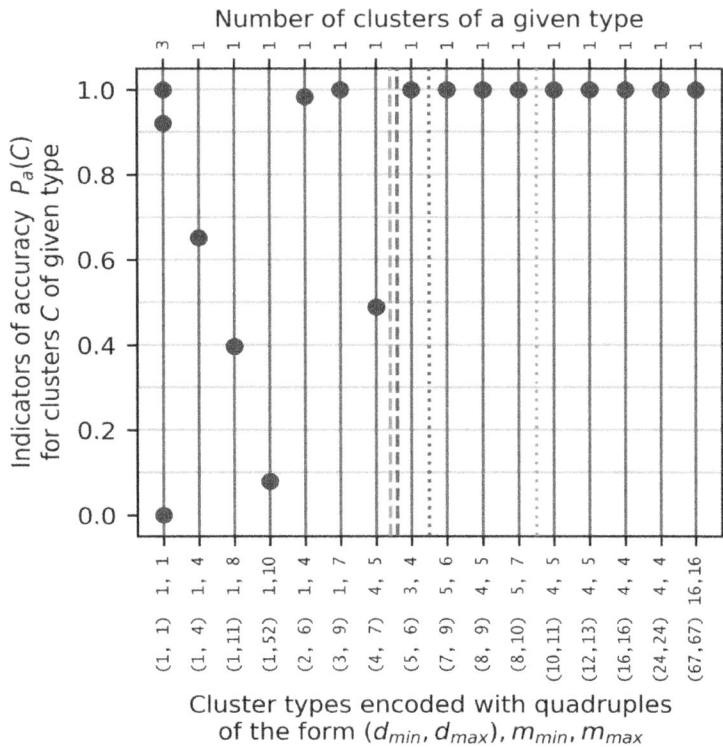

Fig. 4. Clustering results using the DBSCAN algorithm for the parameters $eps = 1$ and $min\_sample = 4$.

The horizontal axis shows the different cluster types coded as fours (d_{min}, d_{max}), m_{min}, m_{max}, where d_{min} and d_{max} are the minimum and maximum number of devices detected (NDD) in the scans belonging to the cluster, respectively, and m_{min} and m_{max} are the minimum and maximum number of device manufacturers detected (NDMD) in the scans belonging to the cluster, respectively. The vertical axis shows the overall inner proximity indices, $P(C)$, for cluster C of a given type. These values range from 0 to 1, where 1 represents the highest accuracy for identifying clusters containing close scans. The blue points in the graph represent the proximity rates for all detected clusters. The distribution of points illustrates the accuracy of the DBSCAN algorithm in identifying clusters of different types. The numbers above each vertical group of points represent the number of clusters for a given type. A description of the dashed and dotted lines is provided in the next section.

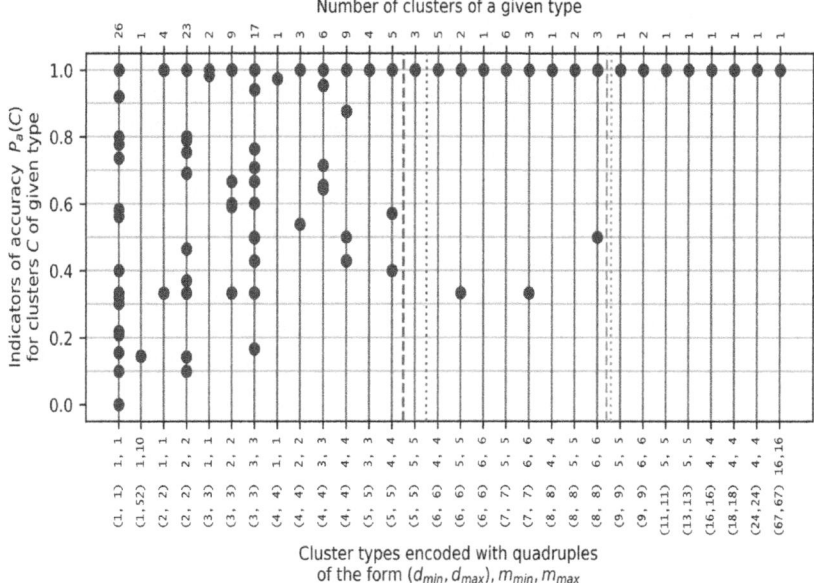

Fig. 5. Clustering results using the DBSCAN algorithm for parameters *eps* = 0.5 and *min_samples* = 4.

5.1 Analysis of Results and Cluster Category Prediction Algorithm

From Figs. 4 and 5, we can distinguish three categories of clusters, represented by points located in three areas separated by dashed red and green lines. Clusters of *the low category*, represented by points lying to the left of the dashed red line, generally have low overall index of inner proximity, and the vast majority of them contain distant scans. Clusters of *the medium category* (sometimes not present), represented by points between dashed lines, generally have various overall indices of inner proximity and may contain both close and distant scans. Clusters of *high category*, represented by points lying to the right of the dashed green line, generally have the maximum overall index of inner proximity and therefore contain close scans. The challenge is to predict the location of the mentioned red and green dashed guide lines, or more precisely, to find the conditions that the quadruple $(d_{min}, d_{max}, m_{min}, m_{max})$ of a given type should meet in order to classify the clusters of this type into the appropriate category.

Here, we propose what seems to be a natural and straightforward approach. Because the distributions of sequences s_M and s_D of NDMD-s and NDD-s, respectively, are far from normal (see Fig. 2), we used Yoe-Johnson transformations T_M and T_D to obtain a normal distribution in both cases. We then calculated the mean values μ_M and μ_D and the standard deviations δ_M and δ_D for the transformed sequences $T_M(s_M)$ and $T_D(s_D)$, respectively. Let us put:

$$M_{med} = T_M^{-1}(\mu_M), \quad M_{high} = T_M^{-1}(\mu_M + \delta_M) \qquad (3)$$

$$D_{med} = T_D^{-1}(\mu_D), \quad D_{high} = T_D^{-1}(\mu_D + \delta_D). \qquad (4)$$

For the data analyzed in this study, the values were $M_{med} = 3.37$, $M_{high} = 5.56$, $D_{med} = 4.28$, and $D_{high} = 8.59$. We now present the following prediction algorithm (scheme).

1. clusters with $d_{min} \leq D_{med}$ or $m_{min} \leq M_{med}$ are predicted to be in the low category;
2. clusters with $d_{min} \geq D_{high}$, $m_{min} > M_{med}$, $d_{max} - d_{min} \leq 2*eps$ and $m_{max} - m_{min} \leq 2*eps$ are predicted to be in the high category;
3. In other cases, we predicted that the clusters were in the medium category.

The areas to the left of the red dotted lines in Fig. 3 and 4 contain clusters predicted by the algorithm to be in the low category, the areas between the dotted lines contain clusters predicted to be in the medium category, and the areas to the right of the red dotted line contain clusters predicted to be in the high category.

The clusters predicted to belong to the high category were highly likely to contain close scans.

6 Discussion

The developed methodology for detecting groups of close mobile devices using clustering without direct geolocation data has proven to be effective. This finding is significant because it suggests that an accurate proximity analysis can be performed without compromising user privacy. As described, the authors did not have access to information regarding the specific device models detected during the scan. Simulations performed by the authors showed that access to such data significantly increased the accuracy of the device grouping. The authors were surprised by the effectiveness of the method described herein. Of course, tests of the method were carried out on random subsets of various sizes of the existing scan database; equally good results were obtained, but that was to be expected considering the specificity of the clustering algorithms. Truly reliable verification of the method will be possible after collecting the next batch of scans.

Evidently, the effectiveness of the described method depends significantly on the quality and completeness of the input data. Missing or inaccurate data can noticeably affect the clustering accuracy. In addition, as data volumes increase, performance optimization may be necessary to maintain the processing efficiency. The current implementation may require improvements to handle larger datasets without compromising the speed and accuracy.

7 Conclusions and Future Work

Future research could focus on improving the clustering algorithm, predicting algorithms, and exploring alternative approaches to further improve the accuracy and efficiency. Incorporating additional data sources, such as temporal traffic patterns and network interactions, can provide deeper insights (that are partially confirmed by ongoing research). Additionally, real-world applications of this methodology should be tested to verify its practicality and scalability in different scenarios.

Further refinement and optimization have significant potential for practical applications in various domains. The ability of this method to effectively group devices without direct geolocation data addresses critical privacy concerns and opens up new possibilities for proximity analysis.

Acknowledgements. This work was supported by the Polish National Centre of Research and Development under the CyberSecIdent Programme within CYBERSECIDENT/489912/IV/NCBR/2021 project.

References

1. Boutet, A., Cunche, M.: Privacy protection for Wi-Fi location positioning systems. J. Inf. Secur. Appl. **58**, 102635 (2021). https://doi.org/10.1016/j.jisa.2020.102635
2. Castro Afanador, J.J., Lopez Rivero, A.J., Roman Gallego, J.A.: Analysis of geolocation accuracy by GPS: dedicated support signal integration and collaborative network in location-based services. In: 2020 15th Iberian Conference on Information Systems and Technologies (CISTI), Seville, Spain, pp. 1–8. IEEE (2020). https://doi.org/10.23919/CISTI49556.2020.9140929
3. Schwittmann, L., Wander, M., Weis, T.: Mobile devices as digital sextants for zero-permission geolocation. In: Proceedings of the 5th International Conference on Information Systems Security and Privacy, Prague, Czech Republic: SCITEPRESS - Science and Technology Publications, pp. 55–66 (2019). https://doi.org/10.5220/0007254000550066
4. Zhang, S., Lan, P., Duan, B., Chen, Z., Zhong, H., Xiong, N.N.: DPIVE: a regionalized location obfuscation scheme with personalized privacy levels. ACM Trans. Sen. Netw. **20**(2), 1–26 (2024). https://doi.org/10.1145/3572029
5. Zhang, S., Zhang, T., Chen, Z., Xiong, N.: Geo-MOEA: a multi-objective evolutionary algorithm with geo-obfuscation for mobile crowdsourcing workers. (2022). arXiv http://arxiv.org/abs/2201.11300. Accessed 06 May 2024
6. Nema, B.M., Nafaa Jaafar, A.: Geo location of mobile device. In: Mitra, P. (ed.) Recent Trends in Communication Networks. IntechOpen (2020). https://doi.org/10.5772/intechopen.92154
7. Al-Hamad, A., El-Sheimy, N.: Smartphones based mobile mapping systems. Int. Arch. Photogramm. Remote Sens. Spatial Inf. Sci. **XL-5**, 29–34 (2014). https://doi.org/10.5194/isprsarchives-XL-5-29-2014
8. Li, H., Gong, L., Wang, B., Guo, F., Wang, J., Zhang, T.: k-anonymity based location data query privacy protection method in mobile social networks. In: 2020 International Conference on Networking and Network Applications (NaNA), Haikou City, China, pp. 326–334. IEEE (2020). https://doi.org/10.1109/NaNA51271.2020.00063
9. Sadhu, V., Zonouz, S., Sritapan, V., Pompili, D.: CollabLoc: privacy-preserving multi-modal collaborative mobile phone localization. IEEE Trans. Mob. Comput. **20**(1), 104–116 (2021). https://doi.org/10.1109/TMC.2019.2937775
10. Tang, F., Li, J., You, I., Guo, M.: Long-term location privacy protection for location-based services in mobile cloud computing. Soft. Comput. **20**(5), 1735–1747 (2016). https://doi.org/10.1007/s00500-015-1703-8
11. Sukstrienwong, A.: Geolocation-based group formation and its mobile application prototype. TEM J. 1154–1164 (2022). https://doi.org/10.18421/TEM113-21
12. Yang, X., Gao, L., Wang, H., Zheng, J., Guo, H.: A semantic k-anonymity privacy protection method for publishing sparse location data. In: 2019 Seventh International Conference on Advanced Cloud and Big Data (CBD), Suzhou, China, pp. 216–222. IEEE (2019). https://doi.org/10.1109/CBD.2019.00047
13. Internet of things market in Poland. Market analysis and development forecasts for 2024–2029. PMR Market Experts. https://mypmr.pro/products/internet-of-things-market-in-poland. Accessed 28 May 2024
14. Eldredge, L.: WAAS Performance Standard (2008)

15. Global Positioning System Standard Positioning Service Performance Standard. Department of Defense USA, GP Navstar (2008). https://www.gps.gov/technical/ps/2008-SPS-performance-standard.pdf
16. DMA Technical Report, Second Edition. DMA TR 8350.2, no. 94-17382 (1991). https://apps.dtic.mil/sti/tr/pdf/ADA280358.pdf
17. Januszewski, J.: Sources of error in satellite navigation positioning. TransNav **11**(3), 419–423 (2017). https://doi.org/10.12716/1001.11.03.04
18. Kjærgaard, M.B., Blunck, H., Godsk, T., Toftkjær, T., Christensen, D.L., Grønbæk, K.: Indoor positioning using GPS revisited. In: Floréen, P., Krüger, A., Spasojevic, M. (eds.) Pervasive Computing. LNCS, vol. 6030, pp. 38–56. Springer, Heidelberg (2010). https://doi.org/10.1007/978-3-642-12654-3_3
19. van Diggelen, F., Enge, P.: The World's First GPS MOOC and Worldwide Laboratory Using Smartphones, pp. 361–369 (2015)
20. Schubert, E., Sander, J., Ester, M., Kriegel, H.P., Xu, X.: DBSCAN revisited, revisited: why and how you should (still) use DBSCAN. ACM Trans. Database Syst. **42**(3), 1–21 (2017). https://doi.org/10.1145/3068335

Software and System Intelligence

Cross-Project Software Defect Prediction Using Ensemble Model with Individual Data Balancing and Feature Selection

Vitaliy Yakovyna[1,2](✉) and Oleh Nesterchuk[2]

[1] University of Warmia and Mazury in Olsztyn, Oczapowskiego Str. 2, 10-719 Olsztyn, Poland
yakovyna@matman.uwm.edu.pl
[2] Lviv Polytechnic National University, Bandery Str. 12, Lviv 79013, Ukraine

Abstract. The quality of software significantly influences its safety and security. With the rapid expansion of software development, the issue of coding quality has become increasingly critical. The manual and resource-intensive nature of error detection in software and its inherent unreliability underscores the necessity for automation. Consequently, a burgeoning interest is employing machine learning methods for software defect prediction. This study introduces a novel stacking software cross-project defect prediction model. Each weak classifier undergoes a learning process incorporating individual data balancing and feature selection techniques. The efficacy of the model was evaluated using accuracy and F1 score metrics on multiple project datasets sourced from the PROMISE repository. The application of the proposed model yielded a classification accuracy of 0.839 and an F1 score of 0.909, surpassing the average performance of single classifiers.

Keywords: Cross-project Defect Prediction · Code Metric · Machine Learning · Ensembling · Feature Selection · Data Balancing

1 Introduction

The growth of empirical software engineering techniques has led to increased interest in software defect prediction approaches. These approaches predict areas of software projects likely to be defect-prone: areas with a high incidence of defects. Software defect prediction models (SDP) are widely used to identify defect-prone modules in software systems. SDP can be divided into three main classes: within-project, cross-project and heterogeneous [1]. The SDP model can help reduce testing costs and resource allocation and improve software quality.

The main contributions of this paper can be summarized as follows:

- We develop a new ensemble software defect prediction model using a random forest as a metamodel, where each weak classifier – viz., logistic regression, decision tree, support vector machines, Naïve Bayes classifier, k-nearest neighbors, and random forest – undergoes a learning process using individual data balancing and feature selection methods.

- We demonstrate the efficiency of individual data balancing and feature selection application in stacking ensemble, both with the predictions of the weak classifiers and with a sum of the predictions of weak classifiers and the initial dataset features as input to a metamodel.
- We experimentally establish an increase in the classification accuracy based on the developed ensemble software defect prediction model compared with other existing models.

The remainder of the paper is structured as follows. Section 2 presents the results of a review and critical analysis of existing work on software defect prediction models, data balancing, and feature selection. Section 3 introduces the research methods along with the dataset description. Section 4 presents the numerical results of software defect prediction using consequently (i) different single classifiers, (ii) a random forest with feature selection methods, (iii) a random forest with data balancing, (iv) voting and stacking ensembles, finishing with the developed stacking ensemble with individual feature selection and data balancing. Our conclusions are presented in Sect. 5.

2 Related Works

The main problems that prevent effective prediction of software defects include [1]:

- Data imbalance.
- Redundancy of features of datasets.
- The impossibility of predicting defects at the early stages of software development.

In solving classification problems, data imbalance is a widespread problem that directly affects the decrease in the effectiveness of learning the algorithm. The solution to this problem may be redundant class sample elimination, duplicating samples of a few classes, or generating samples of a few data. Each option has drawbacks, as it can significantly distort the original dataset.

Several works are devoted to solving the data imbalance problem and predicting software defects. In [2], a detailed empirical comparative analysis of the impact of data balancing methods on software defect prediction was carried out. Gao et al. [3] overview the problem of interpretability in software defect prediction since interpretation from rule-based interpretable models can provide high-quality insights about past defects. In [4], Balogun et al. studied the deployment of data sampling and ensemble techniques in alleviating the class imbalance problem in software defect prediction, particularly the influence of data balancing methods on the effectiveness of software defect prediction ensemble methods. Zhang et al. [5] introduced a new value, the relative density, which indicates the importance of each dataset sample (whether it is an outlier, is on the border of the class, or is a noise). Based on this value, fuzzy membership functions were introduced to replace the weights in the Weighted Extreme Learning Machine algorithm used to solve the imbalanced data problem. Several well-known data balancing methods, viz., undersampling, oversampling, and SMOTE, as well as their shortcomings, are overviewed in [6]. The authors of [7] developed a semi-automatic learning algorithm for data generation. With this approach, it is possible to predict software defects at the early stages of system development when the dataset contains several samples of different classes. Zhang et al. [8] proposed a new model for solving the problem of data imbalance for classification – an anomaly detection model for predicting software defects based on a bidirectional generative adversarial network. Izonin et al. [9] improved the implementation of the Probabilistic Neural Network based on a new method of forming the outputs of the Probabilistic Neural Network's summation layer. The authors [9] show the advantages of the practical use of such an approach in the case of processing a short set of unbalanced data.

In turn, the dataset features describing the software modules are essential. Many available ready-made datasets are "noisy"; they contain too many features, some of which are irrelevant for finding modules with defects. Different feature selection methods are used to overcome this problem, some based on mathematical and statistical principles and some based on implementing a specific classification algorithm.

Several works have been devoted to solving the feature selection problem to increase the effectiveness of software defect prediction. Catal and Diri [10] investigated feature selection for shallow ML models using public NASA datasets from the PROMISE repository [11]. They concluded that Random Forests provides the best prediction performance for large datasets and Naive Bayes is the best algorithm for small datasets in terms of the AUC. Bala et al. [12] propose a transformation and feature selection approach to reduce the distribution difference and high-dimensional features in cross-project defect prediction. The article [13] used the F1 score as a metric in combination with such classifiers as the NN filter, ANN filter, random forest ensemble model, and genetic algorithm. Li et al. [14] investigate the problem of Effort-Aware Defect Prediction and the influence of feature selection methods on the quality of software defect prediction. In the paper [15], research was carried out on filter-based feature selection, where the authors mention the shortcomings of the main existing algorithms. Balogun et al. [16] focus on wrapper-based feature selection, where a family of algorithms is used to select a combination of features on which the classifier is trained. Ali et al. [17] attempted to solve the problem of predicting software defects by using several known feature selection methods, forming three datasets containing different subsets of features from one initial dataset. A study of the effectiveness of tree-based algorithms for solving the problem of software defect prediction was conducted in [18]. Zhao et al. [19] aim to research cross-project prediction of software defects using the manifold feature transformation method. Paper [20] raises the issue of using deep learning methods. Kumar and Chaturvedi [21] propose a specific optimized deep neural network framework to develop an SDP system.

Only a few works study the combination of feature selection and data balancing, particularly for ensemble prediction methods. Therefore, this paper aims to increase the accuracy of software defect prediction by creating a new ensemble classifier that considers individual feature selection and data balancing approaches.

3 Materials and Methods

3.1 Research Methods

As already described in the previous section, existing research on software defect prediction using machine learning methods is based on the following approaches:

- Reducing the size of the dataset by removing redundant features that do not have beneficial information.
- Balancing samples of both classes in a dataset.
- Developing own algorithm of a prediction model.

Most studies have focused on one of the approaches, but none have attempted to combine all the ways to improve prediction results. In addition, one should not focus on one specific machine learning method since conclusions about the effectiveness of the methods in most cases can be made based on empirical studies. In this case, work must be done to determine such combinations of data dimensionality reduction and data balancing algorithms that give the best results for specific machine learning methods.

Ensemble machine learning methods, mainly stacking, should be used to improve the results further, allowing generalizing predictions from previously trained models. The systematic review of SDP by ensemble learning is presented by Matloob et al. in [22]. It is also rational to study two options for training classifiers included in stacking:

- Training on the same sets of training data that underwent dimensionality reduction and balancing on the same combination of algorithms.
- Training on a dataset that undergoes different pre-processing for different classifiers.

For this research, we utilized the most widely used classification methods: logistic regression (LR), decision tree (DT), support vector machines (SVM), Naïve Bayes classifier (NB), k-nearest neighbors (KNN), and random forest (RF). The most used within- and cross-project software defect prediction classifiers were used in this study. E.g., LR was used in [12], DT in [4, 16, 17], SVM in [12, 17], NB in [4, 17], KNN in [12, 17], and RF in [12, 17, 18].

The data balancing methods can be conditionally divided into three groups: oversampling, undersampling, and combination.

In this study, we used the following oversampling algorithms: Random Oversampling, Synthetic Minority Oversampling Technique (SMOTE), KMeansSMOTE (the SMOTE modification, where instances of the minority class are grouped using the k-means clustering algorithm), and SMVSMOTE (the SMOTE method that uses the SVM algorithm to detect instances of a class that generally fail to be correctly classified).

The undersampling algorithms tested in this paper are Random Undersampling, Near Miss, Tomek Links, and Edited Nearest Neighbors.

Two combined algorithms were utilized: SMOTEENN (a combination of SMOTE and Edited Nearest Neighbours) and SMOTETomek (a combination of SMOTE and Tomek Links).

The software features reflect the characteristics of software modules [12]. However, some software contains many features, some of which are irrelevant and contribute to decreasing the prediction performance of software defect prediction models. Therefore, introducing a feature selection technique to select more relevant features can improve the predictive performance of the software defect prediction model (see, e.g., [12] and references therein). The Analysis of Variance F-value (ANOVA F-value), Recursive Feature Elimination (RFE), and Principal Component Analysis (PCA) feature selection methods were applied.

To evaluate the effectiveness of machine learning models, traditional metrics for the binary classification problem will be used: Accuracy and F1 score. This research only discusses the performance measures for the defective class as we predict the defective modules, not the non-defective ones [17].

The F1 score does consider how many negative examples were classified or how many negative examples are in the dataset at all; instead, e.g., the balanced accuracy metric gives half its weight to how many positives were labeled correctly and how many negatives were labeled correctly. However, the problem is not only in the imbalanced data but in detecting the minority class as precisely as possible. Hence, we used an F1 score instead of balanced metrics, e.g., balanced accuracy. Further, all the models were tuned and trained to obtain the maximum value of the F1 score.

The Python programming language and the Google Colab cloud code execution environment were used for software defect prediction. The sklearn library was used to work with the classification algorithms given in the previous section. Features were scaled using StandardScaler, which brings the variance of all features to the value of 1. Cross-validation was performed using the 5-fold method. Each algorithm was run three times to compute each result reported below.

3.2 The Dataset

Five datasets from the PROMISE repository were selected for experiments: CM, JM1, KC1, KC2, and PC1 [11]. All datasets represent different NASA software products written in C and C++ programming languages. In working with these datasets, modules are units of programming language, such as functions. Table 1 summarizes the details of the used datasets.

Table 1. Datasets description.

Dataset	Description	Number of instances	Class distribution
CM1	A NASA spacecraft instrument written in C	498	true: 49 false: 449
JM1	A real-time predictive ground system written in C	10,885	true: 2,106 false: 8,779
KC1	A C++ system implementing storage management for receiving and processing ground data	2,109	true: 326 false: 1,783
KC2	Data from C++ functions. Science data processing, another part of the same project as KC1, has different personnel than KC1. Shared some third-party software libraries with KC1, but no other software overlap	522	true: 105 false: 415
PC1	Data from C functions. Flight software for earth orbiting satellite	1,109	true: 77 false: 1,032

Each dataset consists of 21 features (code metrics) and one Boolean target field indicating whether the software module contains a defect [11]. The dataset includes the following features: McCabe's line count of code; McCabe's cyclomatic complexity; McCabe's essential complexity; McCabe's design complexity; Halstead's total operators + operands; Halstead's volume; Halstead's program length; Halstead's difficulty; Halstead's intelligence; Halstead's effort; Halstead's delivered bugs; Halstead's time estimator; Halstead's line count; Halstead's count of lines of comments; Halstead's count of blank lines; Halstead's Count of lines of code that also contain a comment; Halstead's Unique operators; Halstead's Unique operands; Halstead's Total operators; Halstead's Total operands; Number of branches in the flow graph.

In contrast to other research, in this paper, we combine all used PROMISE datasets into a single dataset, which will be used further for training the models and testing. This approach simulates a real-world ML pipeline, where a predictive model is continuously trained using available and newly appeared data sources and then is used to make predictions. Thus, this is a cross-project defect prediction approach using a combined dataset instead of training one dataset and predicting another, as it is utilized in most papers.

4 Results and Discussion

4.1 The Efficiency of Single Classifiers

Here and in the future, single classification methods will be considered methods without using a feature selection mechanism, data balancing, or hyperparameter optimization. First, the effectiveness of such classification algorithms as logistic regression, decision trees, support vector machines, Naïve Bayes classifier, k-nearest neighbors, and the random forest was tested. These methods used the hyperparameter values that *sklearn* defines as default. The obtained results from the test sample of data are shown in Table 2.

Table 2. Single classification methods evaluation.

Classifier	Accuracy	F1 score
Logistic Regression	0.806	0.890
Decision Tree	0.721	0.827
SVM	**0.825**	**0.904**
Naïve Bayes Classifier	0.817	0.897
k-nn	0.778	0.871
Random Forest	0.810	0.892

From the above results, it can be concluded that single classification methods cope with their task quite well. The best values of the F1 score and accuracy metrics were achieved using the SVM and the Naïve Bayes classifier.

4.2 The Efficiency of Feature Selection Methods

The following sequence of steps was carried out to reduce the number of features without significantly decreasing the prediction efficiency:

- The selection of K features described in the previous section using the Fisher criterion (*SelectKBest* class), recursive feature extraction (*RFE* class), and the method of principal components (*PCA* class) were used as feature selection methods. All classes are taken from the *sklearn* library.
- 5–16 features were selected.
- A random forest is chosen as the classification algorithm that will perform prediction.

The obtained results are shown in Table 3.

Table 3. The efficiency of feature selection methods based on F1 score.

Number of features	SelectKBest	RFE	PCA
5	0.898	0.895	0.898
6	0.899	0.896	0.900
7	0.900	0.897	0.900
8	0.902	0.900	0.901
9	0.902	0.899	0.901
10	0.903	0.901	0.902
11	0.902	0.900	0.902
12	0.901	0.899	0.903
13	0.902	0.900	0.904
14	0.903	0.900	0.905
15	0.904	0.901	0.905
16	0.905	0.902	0.905

Data from Table 3 indicate that feature selection methods slightly improved the results of the F1 score when solving a given predicting problem. For further experiments, it was decided to use all three feature selection methods with a given value of features 7, 8, and 9. The explained variance level of above 95% can be achieved with eight components using PCA. In our previous paper [23], the most significant features were obtained as follows:

1. McCabe's cyclomatic complexity.
2. McCabe's design complexity.
3. Halstead's total operators & operands.
4. Halstead's volume.
5. Halstead's line count.
6. Halstead's count of lines of comments.
7. Halstead's Total operators.
8. Number of branches in the flow graph.

4.3 The Efficiency of Data Balancing

The average ratio of the number of modules without and with defects in the datasets is 5:1. Hence, we used data balancing algorithms to improve the classifier's results in this case. For this, the data balancing algorithms described in the previous section were selected from the *imblearn* library, represented by the following classes: NearMiss, TomekLinks, EditedNearestNeighbors, RandomUnderSampler, RandomOverSampler, SMOTE, SMOTEENN, KMeansSMOTE, SVMSMOTE, and SMOTETomek. The efficiency of the classification algorithm on the dataset using these data balancing methods is shown in Table 4.

Table 4. Data balancing methods evaluation.

Data balancing method	F1 score
KMeansSMOTE	0.904
TomekLinks	0.902
RandomOverSampler	0.889
SVMSMOTE	0.889
SMOTE	0.887
SMOTETomek	0.885
EditedNearestNeighbors	0.851
SMOTEENN	0.804
RandomUnderSampler	0.766
NearMiss	0.422

The analysis of Table 4 shows that for predicting software defects, using such methods as EditedNearestNeighbors, SMOTEENN, RandomUnderSampler, and NearMiss is inappropriate. Instead, the selected effectiveness indicators were increased using the following two methods: KMeansSmote and TomekLinks. To further improve the classification results, the following actions were taken:

- Various combinations of data balancing algorithms and feature selection methods defined in the previous subsection are created.
- A random forest is chosen as the classification algorithm that will perform prediction.

The *Pipeline* class of the *imblearn* library was used to create combinations of different algorithms, constructing a new machine learning model by combining the steps of various algorithms. The efficiency of data balancing methods was evaluated based on the F1 score value. The top ten out of thirty combinations are listed in Table 5.

The results of Table 5 show that using data balancing algorithms in combination with feature selection algorithms almost did not increase prediction effectiveness. Further research is needed to explain this behavior.

Table 5. The efficiency of data balancing methods in combination with feature selection.

Data balancing method	Feature selection method	Number of features	F1 score
KMeansSMOTE	SelectKBest	8	0.902
KMeansSMOTE	SelectKBest	7	0.901
KMeansSMOTE	PCA	9	0.900
KMeansSMOTE	SelectKBest	9	0.900
KMeansSMOTE	PCA	7	0.900
KMeansSMOTE	PCA	8	0.900
KMeansSMOTE	RFE	9	0.900
KMeansSMOTE	RFE	8	0.898
TomekLinks	PCA	9	0.898
TomekLinks	SelectKBest	8	0.897

4.4 The Efficiency of Ensemble Methods

Experiments using ensemble machine learning methods were carried out to improve the prediction effectiveness further. It was decided to test and compare such ensemble methods as voting-based ensemble and stacking. For each of these methods, different pre-processing of the training data was applied:

- Data balancing and feature selection are the same for all weak classifiers.
- Data balancing is the same for all weak classifiers, but feature selection differs.
- Data balancing and feature selection are individual for all weak classifiers.

Classical classification problems usually involve a random set of instances. On the other hand, from the software engineering point of view, there is no proof that software defect-prone modules are indeed random. Moreover, there needs to be proof (despite the increasing number of publications) that the defect-proneness depends on code metrics. The datasets for each project differ significantly in their class ratio, e.g., for PROMISE repository datasets used in this study, the part of defect modules varies from 6.94% for the PC1 dataset to 20.5% in the case of the KC2 dataset. Besides, there is no specific proof that the proposed cross-project defect prediction can be efficient because, in this case, the learning and test sets are mixed with data from different projects, where other code metrics may play an important role. That's why we apply different feature selection and data balancing techniques in our ensemble method.

Testing of the above options started with voting. Six previously defined machine learning algorithms became the weak classifiers: logistic regression, decision tree, support vector machines, Naïve Bayes classifier, k-nearest neighbors, and random forest. Table 6 shows the experimental results for the voting model. The average values of the evaluation metrics are listed in the Table, while the variation of the corresponding values was less than 0.48%.

Next, various stacking options were tested. As known, stacking differs from voting ensemble in that a different classification method (metaclassifier) is responsible for

Table 6. Voting ensemble results.

Data balancing method	Feature selection method	Number of features	Accuracy	F1 score
KMeansSMOTE	SelectKBest	8	0.830	0.905
TomekLinks	SelectKBest	8	0.833	0.905
KMeansSMOTE	Individual	–	0.829	0.905
TomekLinks	Individual	–	0.832	0.905
Individual	Individual	–	**0.833**	**0.906**

decision-making. A classic stacking version involves making this decision based only on the predictions of the weak classifiers. Another version adds the results of weak classifiers to the features of the input dataset.

The *StackingClassifier* class from the *sklearn* library was used to test stacking. Using the *passthrough* parameter allows for determining whether features from the input dataset should be added to the prediction results of the weak classifiers (*passthrough* = True) or not (*passthrough* = False). Table 7 shows the results of using stacking, where the metaclassifier is logistic regression. The number of features was set to 8 in the case of the SelectKBest feature selection method. When the feature selection method was applied individually for each primary classifier, the number of features varied. The average values of the Accuracy and F1 score evaluation metrics are listed in Table 7, while the variation of the corresponding values was less than 0.36%.

Table 7. Results of stacking with logistic regression as a metaclassifier.

Data balancing method	Feature selection method	Passthrough	Accuracy	F1 score
KMeansSMOTE	SelectKBest	False	0.830	0.905
KMeansSMOTE	SelectKBest	True	0.827	0.905
TomekLinks	SelectKBest	False	0.834	0.905
TomekLinks	SelectKBest	True	0.835	0.906
KMeansSMOTE	Individual	False	0.829	0.906
KMeansSMOTE	Individual	True	0.828	0.905
TomekLinks	Individual	False	0.837	0.907
TomekLinks	Individual	True	0.838	0.908
Individual	Individual	False	0.835	0.907
Individual	Individual	True	**0.837**	**0.908**

Recent studies show that ML classifiers underperform when default settings are used. Tantithamthavorn et al. [24] studied the impact of parameter optimization on defect prediction models. They showed that ML techniques like C5.0 and neural networks can outperform widely used ones after applying optimization. In this study, we applied the grid search method to hyperparameter tuning. Besides, different variants of data balancing methods (KMeansSMOTE and TomekLinks) and feature selection (7–9 features) were used for a grid search. The best hyperparameter combinations were chosen and used for the developed stacking model.

As shown in Table 7, stacking, for which weak classifiers use different data balancing and feature selection algorithms, shows the most significant effect on F1 score and Accuracy. However, it is worth noting that the increase in results is still relatively small. However, considering stacking to be a relatively weak ensemble, these results are within the expected range. Future research will focus on other ensembling techniques to obtain further improvement in software module classification. We can also note the impact of using the Passthrough option on all staking options.

Next, experiments were conducted using an ensemble of similar compositions, but the random forest was used as a metaclassifier instead of logistic regression. The number of features was set to 8 in the case of the SelectKBest feature selection method. The number of features varied when the feature selection method was applied individually for each weak classifier. The results of the experiment are given in Table 8.

Table 8. Results of stacking with a random forest as a metaclassifier.

Data balancing method	Feature selection method	Passthrough	Accuracy	F1 score
KMeansSMOTE	SelectKBest	False	0.830	0.906
KMeansSMOTE	SelectKBest	True	0.828	0.906
TomekLinks	SelectKBest	False	0.829	0.901
TomekLinks	SelectKBest	True	0.834	0.905
KMeansSMOTE	Individual	False	0.827	0.905
KMeansSMOTE	Individual	True	0.829	0.906
TomekLinks	Individual	False	0.834	0.905
TomekLinks	Individual	True	0.838	0.907
Individual	Individual	False	**0.839**	**0.909**
Individual	Individual	True	0.838	0.909

From Table 8, we can conclude that using the TomekLinks balancing method allows us to achieve almost the same F1 score value but with slightly higher Accuracy than when using KMeansSMOTE.

In addition, it can be concluded that the best metrics were obtained when using stacking, the metaclassifier of which is a Random Forest. The weak classifiers use individual methods of data balancing and feature selection, and the metaclassifier additionally uses the features from the initial dataset. The highest accuracy value obtained is 0.839, and the F1 score is 0.909.

The comparison of the obtained classification metrics with those published in the literature is summarized in Table 9. Table 9 contains both within-project and cross-project results obtained using different datasets. The closest to our research results were reported in [7, 15, 17], where the same datasets and similar approaches were used. In contrast to those papers, we studied a combined dataset instead of the separate datasets and introduced the described ensembling method with individual feature selection and data balancing. Results show that the proposed ensemble outperformed all classifiers and ensembles from published papers in F1 score and is close in terms of the Accuracy metric to papers [7, 15]. Article [17] reported the highest Accuracy value for the PC4 dataset; however, the F1 score value was low, which is more important in the case of very imbalanced data, as we mentioned above. It is worth noting that the accuracy values for other datasets in [17] were comparable to those of our study.

Hence, the proposed ensembling model solved the main classification issues and can be applied to both within- and cross-project software defect prediction on imbalanced datasets. Thus, we demonstrated that in contrast to the commonly used approach, individual data balancing and feature selection can improve the classification metrics for ensemble models.

Table 9. Summary of the software defect prediction results.

Paper	Dataset	Model	Accuracy	F1 score
[12]	AEEEM	KNN	–	0.69
		SVM	–	0.78
		RF	–	0.79
		LR	–	0.66
[16]	25 datasets from PROMISE, NASA, AEEEM, and ReLink repositories	NB	0.826	0.821
		DT	0.831	0.826
[6]	40 datasets from tera-PROMISE repository	AdaBoost	0.85	0.85
		DT	0.83	0.83
		Extra Tree	0.83	0.83
		Gradient Boost	0.85	0.85
		KNN	0.83	0.82
		LR	0.85	0.84
		NB	0.82	0.78
		RF	0.88	0.88
[3]	47 datasets from different sources	3 rule-based interpretable models	–	0.523
[20]	Columba, Bugzilla, JDT, Mozilla, Platform and PostgreSQL	Denoising autoencoder CNN JIT defect prediction (DAECNN-JDP)	0.763	0.802
[17]	NASA JM1	Voting: SVM+RF+KNN	0.849	0.507
	NASA KC1	Voting: SVM+RF+KNN	0.839	0.548

(*continued*)

Table 9. (*continued*)

Paper	Dataset	Model	Accuracy	F1 score
	NASA PC4	Voting: SVM+RF+KNN	**0.919**	0.68
	NASA PC5	Voting: SVM+RF+KNN	0.878	0.75
[15]	NASA CM1, KC1, KC2, KC3, MW1, PC1, PC3, PC4, PC5	NB	0.824	0.815
		DT	0.853	0.830
[7]	NASA CM1, KC1, KC2, PC1	Tri_SSDPM	0.874	0.855
		DT	0.832	0.320
		NB	0.748	0.379
		AdaBoost	0.855	0.304
		S4VM+	0.866	0.314
This paper	NASA CM1, JM1, KC1, KC2, PC1	Proposed ensemble: LR+DT+SVM+NB+KNN+RF	0.839	**0.909**

5 Conclusion

A novel cross-project software defect prediction method is introduced in this article based on stacking, the weak classifiers of which use individual methods of data balancing and feature selection. The method was examined with CM, JM1, KC1, KC2, and PC1 datasets from the PROMISE repository. Accuracy values of up to 0.839 and F1 score values of up to 0.909 were achieved using individual data balancing and feature selection methods for the underlying stacking classifiers rather than one-size-fits-all. Results show that the proposed ensemble outperformed all classifiers and ensembles from published papers in the F1 score. The proposed ensembling model solved the main classification issues and can be applied to both within- and cross-project software defect prediction on imbalanced datasets. The paper demonstrates that in contrast to the commonly used approach, individual data balancing and feature selection can improve the classification metrics for ensemble models.

The generalizability of the model across different software projects is demonstrated by combining all used PROMISE datasets into a single dataset to simulate a real-world ML pipeline for cross-project software defect prediction.

Further studies using different data sets, analyzing metrics in detail, and comparing more algorithms will serve to prove the results obtained in this paper. Future research will also focus on other ensembling techniques to improve software module classification. Besides, some activities will be performed to explain the results of single classifiers in combination with data balancing and feature selection.

Acknowledgments. Vitaliy Yakovyna thanks the U4U Non-Residential Fellowship Program for the financial support of this study.

Disclosure of Interests. The authors have no competing interests to declare that are relevant to the content of this article.

References

1. Jing, X.-Y., Chen, H., Xu, B.: Intelligent Software Defect Prediction. Springer, Singapore (2024). https://doi.org/10.1007/978-981-99-2842-2
2. Odejide, B.J., et al.: An empirical study on data sampling methods in addressing class imbalance problem in software defect prediction. In: Silhavy, R. (ed.) CSOC 2022. LNNS, vol. 501, pp. 594–610. Springer, Cham (2022). https://doi.org/10.1007/978-3-031-09070-7_49
3. Gao, Y., Zhu, Y., Zhao, Y.: Dealing with imbalanced data for interpretable defect prediction. Inf. Softw. Technol. **151**, 107016 (2022). https://doi.org/10.1016/j.infsof.2022.107016
4. Balogun, A.O., et al.: Empirical analysis of data sampling-based ensemble methods in software defect prediction. In: Gervasi, O., Murgante, B., Misra, S., Ana, M.A., Rocha, C., Garau, C. (eds.) ICCSA 2022, pp. 363–379. Springer, Cham (2022). https://doi.org/10.1007/978-3-031-10548-7_27
5. Zheng, S., Gai, J., Yu, H., Zou, H., Gao, S.: Software defect prediction based on fuzzy weighted extreme learning machine with relative density information. Sci. Program. **2020**, 1–18 (2020). https://doi.org/10.1155/2020/8852705
6. Bejjanki, K.K., Gyani, J., Gugulothu, N.: Class imbalance reduction (CIR): a novel approach to software defect prediction in the presence of class imbalance. Symmetry **12**(3), 407 (2020). https://doi.org/10.3390/sym12030407
7. Meng, F., Cheng, W., Wang, J.: Semi-supervised software defect prediction model based on tri-training. KSII Trans. Internet Inf. Syst. **15**(11) (2021). https://doi.org/10.3837/tiis.2021.11.009
8. Zhang, S., Jiang, S., Yan, Y.: A software defect prediction approach based on BiGAN anomaly detection. Sci. Program. **2022** (2022). https://doi.org/10.1155/2022/5024399
9. Izonin, I., Tkachenko, R., Greguš, M.: I-PNN: an improved probabilistic neural network for binary classification of imbalanced medical data. In: Strauss, C., Cuzzocrea, A., Gabriele Kotsis, A., Tjoa, M., Khalil, I. (eds.) DEXA 2022. LNCS, pp. 147–157. Springer, Cham (2022). https://doi.org/10.1007/978-3-031-12426-6_12
10. Catal, C., Diri, B.: Investigating the effect of dataset size, metrics sets, and feature selection techniques on software fault prediction problem. Inf. Sci. **179**(8), 1040–1058 (2009). https://doi.org/10.1016/j.ins.2008.12.001
11. The PROMISE repository of software engineering databases. http://promise.site.uottawa.ca/SERepository. Accessed 29 Dec 2023
12. Bala, Y.Z., Samat, P.A., Sharif, K.Y., Manshor, N.: Improving cross-project software defect prediction method through transformation and feature selection approach. IEEE Access **11**, 2318–2326 (2022). https://doi.org/10.1109/ACCESS.2022.3231456
13. bin Faiz, R., Shaheen, S., Sharaf, M., Rauf, H.T.: Optimal feature selection through search-based optimizer in cross project. Electronics **12**(3), 514 (2023). https://doi.org/10.3390/electronics12030514
14. Li, F., Lu, W., Keung, J.W., Yu, X., Gong, L., Li, J.: The impact of feature selection techniques on effort-aware defect prediction: an empirical study. IET Softw. **17**(2), 168–193 (2023). https://doi.org/10.1049/sfw2.12099
15. Balogun, A.O., et al.: Empirical analysis of rank aggregation-based multi-filter feature selection methods in software defect prediction. Electronics **10**(2), 179 (2021). https://doi.org/10.3390/electronics10020179
16. Balogun, A.O., et al.: Software defect prediction using wrapper feature selection based on dynamic re-ranking strategy. Symmetry **13**(11), 2166 (2021). https://doi.org/10.3390/sym13112166
17. Ali, U., Aftab, S., Iqbal, A., Nawaz, Z., Bashir, M.S., Saeed, M.A.: Software defect prediction using variant based ensemble learning and feature selection techniques. Int. J. Mod. Educ. Comput. Sci. **12**(5) (2020). https://doi.org/10.5815/ijmecs.2020.05.03

18. Naseem, R., et al.: Investigating tree family machine learning techniques for a predictive system to unveil software defects. Complexity **2020**, 1–21 (2020). https://doi.org/10.1155/2020/6688075
19. Zhao, Y., Zhu, Y., Yu, Q., Chen, X.: Cross-project defect prediction method based on manifold feature transformation. Future Internet **13**(8), 216 (2021). https://doi.org/10.3390/fi13080216
20. Zhu, K., Zhang, N., Ying, S., Zhu, D.: Within-project and cross-project just-in-time defect prediction based on denoising autoencoder and convolutional neural network. IET Softw. **14**(3), 185–195 (2020). https://doi.org/10.1049/iet-sen.2019.0278
21. Kumar, R., Chaturvedi, A.: A framework for software defect prediction using optimal hyperparameters of deep neural network. In: Tanveer, M., Agarwal, S., Ozawa, S., Ekbal, A., Jatowt, A. (eds.) ICONIP 2022. CCIS, pp. 163–174. Springer, Singapore (2023). https://doi.org/10.1007/978-981-99-1648-1_14
22. Matloob, F., et al.: Software defect prediction using ensemble learning: a systematic literature review. IEEE Access **9**, 98754–98771 (2021). https://doi.org/10.1109/ACCESS.2021.3095559
23. Shakhovska, N., Yakovyna, V.: Feature selection and software defect prediction by different ensemble classifiers. In: Strauss, C., Gabriele Kotsis, A., Tjoa, M., Khalil, I. (eds.) DEXA 2021. LNCS, pp. 307–313. Springer, Cham (2021). https://doi.org/10.1007/978-3-030-86472-9_28
24. Tantithamthavorn, C., McIntosh, S., Hassan, A.E., Matsumoto, K.: The impact of automated parameter optimization on defect prediction models. IEEE Trans. Softw. Eng. **45**(7), 683–711 (2019). https://doi.org/10.1109/TSE.2018.2794977

AUTO-DataGenCARS+: An Advanced User-Oriented Tool to Generate Data for the Evaluation of Recommender Systems

María del Carmen Rodríguez-Hernández[1(✉)], Sergio Ilarri[2(✉)], Marcos Caballero[1], Raquel Trillo-Lado[2], Ramón Hermoso[2], and Rafael del-Hoyo-Alonso[1]

[1] Technological Institute of Aragón (ITA), María de Luna 7, Zaragoza, Spain
{mcrodriguez,mcaballero,rdelhoyo}@ita.es
[2] I3A, Universidad de Zaragoza, María de Luna 1, Zaragoza, Spain
{silarri,raqueltl,rhermoso}@unizar.es

Abstract. Context-Aware Recommender Systems (CARS) offer context-based suggestions that are particularly crucial in the tourism domain, where personalized experiences significantly enhance user satisfaction. However, the evaluation of CARS is a challenge, partly due to the scarce availability of appropriate datasets that fulfill a variety of evaluation purposes. For example, to evaluate CARS, we need datasets that incorporate context data, but in practice existing datasets provide very little contextual information.

This paper presents AUTO-DataGenCARS+, a graphical user-oriented tool designed to generate synthetic data for evaluating both Recommender Systems and CARS. Some of the relevant features of the tool include: a flexible definition of user profiles, user, item and context schemas; a realistic generation of ratings and item attributes; the possibility to mix real and synthetic datasets; functionalities for analyzing and evaluating existing datasets; and an extendable architecture for advanced users. We illustrate the benefits of AUTO-DataGenCARS+ through several examples and experimental evaluations.

Keywords: Recommender systems · Context-aware recommender systems · Mobile users · Synthetic dataset generation · Evaluation

1 Introduction

Due to the high amount of information available, which can easily overwhelm users when they need to take a decision that involves choosing among a variety of options, there is a high interest in developing solutions that can filter the data and offer personalized suggestions to users (adapted to their preferences and current circumstances). In particular, *Recommender Systems* (*RS*) [20], that suggest relevant items to the users (e.g., books, music, movies, news, touristic destinations, points of interest in a city, friends in social networks), are a consolidated and hot research area within the information management field [6] and the mobile computing field [19]. From an abstract perspective, a recommender system estimates if a given item is relevant for a specific user (e.g., by predicting the rating that the user would provide for that item). Whereas traditional recommender systems tackle the problem from a two-dimensional perspective, based on users and items ($User \times Item$), the so-called *Context-Aware Recommender Systems* (*CARS*) [1] add the context as a third dimension ($User \times Item \times Context$), based on the idea that by exploiting information about the context of the user it is possible to provide recommendations that are better adapted to that context. An example of a context variable with a clear impact is the location of the user, which is exploited by *Location-Aware Recommender Systems* (*LARS*) [5] (a popular type of mobile CARS). As another example, the weather conditions can be an important context variable to consider when providing recommendations for outdoor activities.

An intensive research effort has been performed in the area of RS. However, there are still research issues to solve. One of the key challenges is the difficulty to evaluate a proposed recommender system [25]. For example, how can we estimate whether the proposed system will provide suitable recommendations to a mobile user in an unobtrusive way? Evaluating this in a real scenario is usually not possible, as recommender systems frequently depend on the availability of a significant user base, but users will not want to use a recommender system that is not effective enough. Besides, emulating in a real scenario a variety of situations that may be relevant from the evaluation perspective is not easy. So, alternatives different from field tests are needed for large-scale evaluations.

Most researchers assess their proposed recommendation algorithms through experiments by using popular datasets (e.g., MovieLens [7]). Whereas the availability of those datasets is very relevant for the research community, they can limit the types of experiments that can be performed and lead to the implementation of specific dataset-driven improvements over the proposed algorithms, which could bring good results with those datasets but not with others. Instead, it could be more appropriate if we could evaluate the performance of the RS approaches under different conditions by considering datasets that exhibit any behavior that may be required for our evaluation purposes, including behaviors that can be observed in real situations, inspired by real data, or simply envisioned in hypothetical scenarios that could arise in the future.

As if this were not enough, if what we want to evaluate is a CARS approach then we need datasets with context data, which are really scarce in the community. For example, according to the study presented in [10], only a few datasets include context attributes (e.g., *DePaulMovie, LDOS-CoMoDa, InCarMusic, Frappé, STS*). Moreover, the context data available in those datasets are in general very sparse. As an example, the dataset with a higher number of context attributes is STS [3], with 14 context attributes, but most of them are actually empty: 89.37% of the context values are unknown and the attribute with the highest number of known values (the distance between the user and the item) is available only in 17.96% of the ratings. This is probably because most users prefer not to disclose their context when they rate items (e.g., due to privacy concerns); besides, in cases where the context values are not obtained automatically from sensors and have to be entered manually in an app form by the user (when rating an item), users may be lazy to do all this effort using their mobile devices.

Therefore, we argue that the availability of a tool that can generate suitable synthetic datasets for the evaluation of CARS would be relevant and useful for research. With such a tool we could generate as much contextual data as needed and also cover all the possible potential scenarios that researchers may need to consider to prove the validity and generality of their recommendation approaches. Motivated by this, we have developed the tool *AUTO-DataGenCARS+ (Advanced User-orienTed tOol DataGenCARS)*, whose goal is to help the designer of recommender systems to generate data that can be used to evaluate his/her proposed recommender systems under any desired condition. It offers functionalities relevant to researchers in the field of RS, such as the ability to define, generate, import and export relevant files for evaluation (synthetic datasets, schemas, and configuration files), preprocess existing datasets (whether original or synthetic), and integrate data analysis and evaluation of RS and CARS approaches in the tool itself. The development of this tool has been motivated by the interest of researchers in the previous DataGenCARS library [4], which unfortunately was not easy to use due to the lack of a graphical user interface (GUI) as well as the need to manually edit all the (quite complex) configuration files and to define all the required data generation process by coding (using the DataGenCARS API). The AUTO-DataGenCARS+ tool provides step-by-step help information for each of its available functionalities, includes many improvements, and represents a significant step forward for the research community.

The structure of the rest of this paper is as follows. First, in Sect. 2, we present some related work. Afterwards, in Sect. 3, we summarize the main capabilities of AUTO-DataGenCARS+. Then, in Sect. 4, we present some example evaluation scenarios using the tool. Finally, in Sect. 5 we summarize our conclusions and outline some plans for future work.

2 Related Work

The most related work is the DataGenCARS library [4], which allows the generation of datasets for the evaluation of CARS. It has attracted the interest of researchers, but it has some weaknesses. The most relevant weak point of DataGenCARS is that its use requires significant knowledge about its API (in order to program the required data generation strategy) and defining all the configuration and schema files, which are quite complex to be edited manually. Thus, DataGenCARS is just a Java library rather than a tool developed for end users. It lacks a user-friendly graphical interface, which makes it unsuitable for non-developer researchers. Additionally, it does not integrate data analysis and RS evaluation functionalities. These shortcomings limit the tool's usability and flexibility, prompting the need for a more advanced and user-centric solution. This motivated us to develop a completely-new modern tool, that we call AUTO-DataGenCARS+.

There are also other data generation approaches focused on recommender systems (see Table 1), like SynRec [21], which uses data generation techniques with the final goal of allowing companies to release recommender system data to the research community without revealing sensitive information (e.g., by replacing original values in the user-item matrix with synthetic values or by artificially generating new users). SynRec is actually a data protection framework and it does not consider context data, so it is not suitable to evaluate solutions for pervasive and mobile computing environments (it could be used in the context of classical RS rather than CARS). Another example is GANRS [2], where the authors propose the use of a Generative Adversarial Network (GAN) to generate collaborative filtering datasets (without considering context data). The approach presented in [24] is also worth mentioning, as it proposes a method to generate synthetic ratings in the context of group recommender systems in order to protect information about the individual preferences of the members of each group. Also with a focus on privacy, a method to generate synthetic interaction data for users based on their privacy preferences is presented in [14]. The purpose of these approaches, as well as other proposals [13,15,16], is different from ours, and they focus solely on traditional RS and not on CARS.

Concerning the synthetic generation of context data in the field of recommender systems, we can mention works such as [12,17]. In [17], an abstract methodology to build context-aware collections of data (in terms of item ratings and context attributes) is presented; however, that work mainly focuses only on the application of different Probability Distribution Functions (PDFs), it does not offer a tool to researchers, and advanced functionalities and an empirical evaluation seem to be missing. In [12], random contexts are generated for the evaluation of a recommender system that suggests appropriate TV content; in that paper, an ad hoc synthetic data generation for a specific use case is presented. Up to the author's knowledge, besides AUTO-DataGenCARS+, there is no other graphical full-fledged tool for flexible and easy generation of synthetic data suitable to evaluate the performance of CARS.

3 Main Functionalities

AUTO-DataGenCARS+ offers a comprehensive tool designed to enhance the development and evaluation of traditional RS and CARS. It is a powerful GUI implemented in Python and accessible through any web browser. Previously, we developed a version of the graphical tool in Java, but while performing a major software overhaul we eventually re-designed it and implemented it in Python. The current tool features three main modules: generating a completely synthetic dataset, preprocessing an existing dataset, and visualizing and evaluating RS.

Table 1. Overview of synthetic data generation frameworks with a focus on RS.

Framework	Goal	Language	License	Field	Type	Input	Output	User-Friendly	Latest Update
SynRec [21]	Protection of sensitive information in the user-item matrix by replacing the original values with synthetic values or, alternatively, completely synthesizing new users	R	N/A	RS (protection data)	Framework	Original user-item data (ratings), CART parameters	Synthetic dataset		2020 (GitHub)
GANRS [2]	A Generative Adversarial Network (GAN)-based method to generate synthetic collaborative filtering RS (CFRS) datasets	N/A	N/A	CFRS	Approach	User and item count, sample size, stochastic variability	Synthetic dataset		2023 (paper)
CART and PrivBayes [24]	Systematic analysis of synthetic data influence on recommendations to protect user privacy in Group RS (GRS)	N/A	CC BY 4.0	GRS	Approach	User-item interaction data, group preferences, privacy requirements	Synthetic dataset (preserving original data's statistical ensuring user privacy)		2022 (paper)
UPC-SDG (User Privacy Controllable Synthetic Data Generation) [14]	Generation of synthetic user-item interaction data from a real dataset, considering user privacy preferences	Python, C++	N/A	RS (privacy-preserving)	Approach	User-item interaction data, privacy preferences, model hyperparameters	Privacy-aware synthetic dataset		2022 (GitHub)
Clustering-based approach [15]	Generation of synthetic datasets for offline evaluation of recommender systems, mimicking the characteristics of existing datasets	N/A	N/A	RS	Approach	User preferences, number of clusters, distribution	Synthetic dataset		2019 (paper)
DaGzang [16]	Synthetic data generator for Cross-domain Recommendation Services	Java	GPLv3	RS (cross-domain)	Web application (not available)	User and item count, sparsity, rating scale, distribution, real dataset, common user count	Synthetic dataset	✓	2021 (GitHub)
TalkThe Walk [13]	Generation of synthetic conversational data	N/A	N/A	RS (music)	Approach	Corpus of items	Simulated conversational RS responses		2023 (paper)
SDG (Synthetic Data Generator) by Pasinato et al. [17]	Generation of synthetic datasets in order to evaluate CARS	Plan to release SDG as a Matlab Toolbox	N/A	CARS	Methodology	User count, destinations, evaluations	Synthetic dataset		2013 (paper)
Context-aware TV content data generator [12]	Generation of synthetic data to simulate user-TV content interactions for system testing and evaluation	C#, HTML, JavaScript, CSS, ASP	N/A	CARS (TV content)	Approach	User profiles, context labels, TV content	Synthetic dataset		2014 (paper)
DataGen CARS [4]	Generation of data for the evaluation of RS	Java	GPL	RS and CARS	Library	Schema, config and user profile files	CSV		2018 (source code)
AUTO-DataGen CARS+	Generation of data for the evaluation of RS	Python	GPL	RS and CARS	Web application	Web forms	CSV	✓	2024 (source code)

The first module provides robust functionalities for generating completely synthetic datasets, such as the definition and creation of users, items and contexts through schema and configuration files. Through its GUI, this user-oriented tool supports an easy creation of attributes for user, item and context schemas. The generation of user, item and context files can be configured to include a certain percentage of null values in the overall dataset, or to introduce specific percentages of null values for each attribute.

The second module of AUTO-DataGenCARS+ is designed to support a comprehensive range of workflows for preprocessing datasets, whether they are original or synthetic. These workflows offer different functionalities, such as generating or removing unknown contextual information (replacing it by values), increasing the number of ratings or recalculating rating values in an existing dataset, generating a synthetic dataset similar to an existing one, creating user profiles (both manually and automatically from the GUI), and transforming attributes (e.g., converting categorical attributes to numerical ones or changing preferential ratings to binary ratings, and vice versa). Additionally, the tool facilitates the visualization of these workflows, making it easy to understand the sequence of actions required to achieve the desired final dataset. For instance, the workflow for generating user profiles (see Fig. 1) is composed by three actions: replacing unknown item attribute values in an item file by actual values and/or replacing unknown context attribute values in a context file, and generating a user profile (automatically or manually) considering both item and context files. The workflow highlights (in red-colored rectangles) actions that could be optional for the user. For example, the user could need to perform both actions ("Replace NULL Values <item>" and "Replace NULL Values <context>"), or choose to execute one or none of them from the options available within the "Replace NULL values" workflow. Afterwards, the user could decide between automatically generating the user profile ("Generate User Profiles <Automatic>") or creating it manually ("Generate User Profiles <Manual>"). This approach not only enhances the tool's usability but also provides a clear visual representation of how different workflows, like the "Replace NULL values" workflow, is integrated into the "Generate user profile" workflow.

The tool includes a third module dedicated to analysis, which provides functionalities for visualizing datasets, whether pre-existing or synthetically generated by the tool. These functionalities enable the display of general statistics for user, item, context, and rating files, as well as the identification of missing values per attribute to highlight data quality issues. It also facilitates obtaining a detailed overview of the dataset by displaying attribute names, data types, and value ranges. Advanced features, such as the analysis of the information of users, items and contexts per attribute, the number of ratings by user, the histogram of ratings or the evolution of user preferences through graphs, allow users to explore data distribution and variability. Similarly, analyzing the correlation among attributes helps to uncover interrelationships between variables, by using correlation coefficients such as the Pearson, Kendall, and Spearman coefficients. These analytical features enable users to conduct a comprehensive exploratory study of the data, revealing interesting patterns and anomalies.

Additionally, it integrates evaluation functionalities, which allows configuring the required experimental settings and evaluating recommendation algorithms on synthetic or real datasets. For evaluating traditional RS, the tool includes a variety of Collaborative Filtering algorithms (e.g., KNN, SVD, SVD++, Non-negative Matrix Factorization, Slope One, Co-clustering, etc.), all available in the Surprise library [8]. In the case of evaluating CARS, different paradigms such as Contextual Modeling, Pre-filtering, and Post-filtering can be configured.

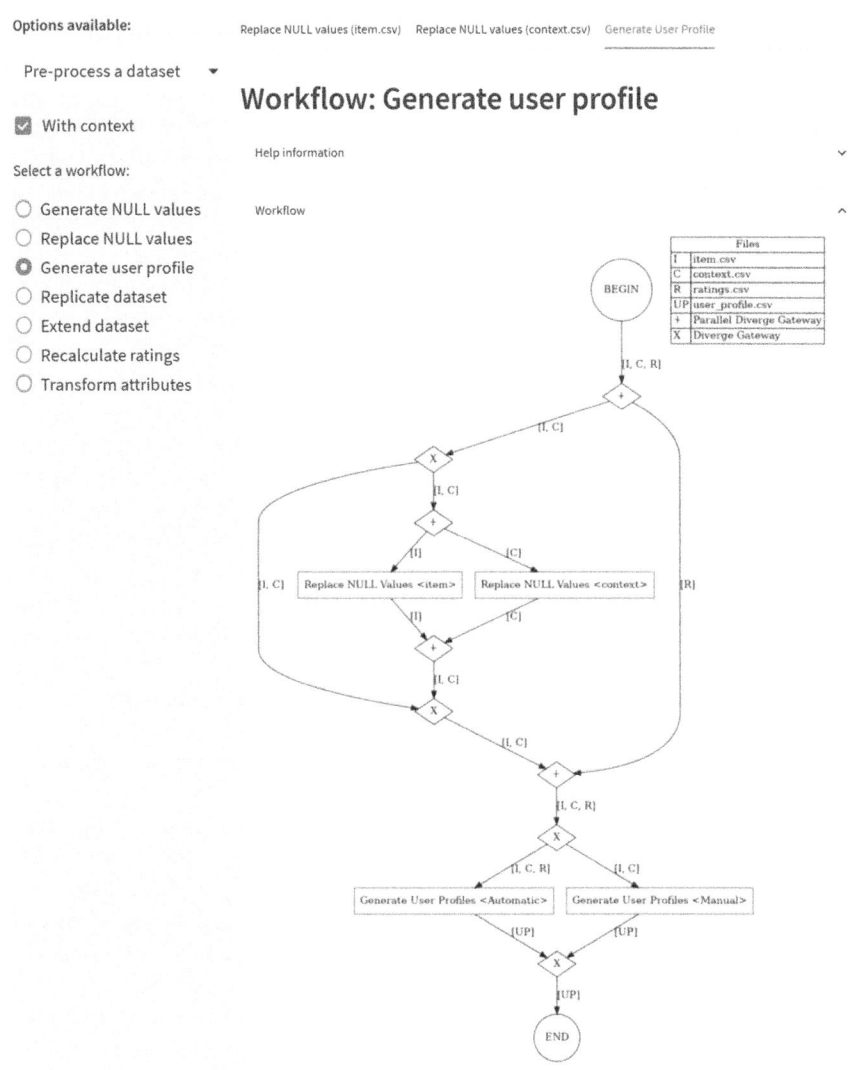

Fig. 1. Workflow example defined using AUTO-DataGenCARS+.

Specifically, Contextual Modeling relies on classification algorithms (e.g., SVM, Gaussian Naïve Bayes, Random Forest, K-Means, Hist Gradient Boosting, and KNN), accessible in the Scikit-learn library [18]. In this paradigm, the context variables and the attributes of items are considered as features, and ratings are the target classes, which can be binary or multi-class. Additionally, this module allows users to set evaluation metrics (e.g., MAE, Precision, Recall, F1-Measure, RMSE, MAP, NDCG, etc.), and choose a split strategy, such as K-fold, Repeated K-Fold, Shuffle Split, and Leave One Out, specifying the required number of folds.

4 Experimental Evaluation

In this section, we describe some example use case scenarios that we have defined to illustrate the use of AUTO-DataGenCARS+ and evaluate its benefits.

4.1 Enlarge an Existing Dataset

In this scenario, we will show how the tool can be used to increase the number of ratings in an existing dataset. For clarity, we will use the popular MovieLens dataset [7], and more specifically the MovieLens 100k (ml-100k) distribution, which was reduced to 20k ratings for this experiment. First, we will load the dataset in AUTO-DataGenCARS+ and visualize the histogram of ratings (see the left of Fig. 2). Then, using a 10-fold cross-validation, we will compute the performance metrics precision, recall, and F-measure, using AUTO-DataGenCARS+ and considering the following classical recommender approaches: user-based collaborative filtering (UBCF), item-based collaborative filtering (IBCF), and SVD (Singular Value Decomposition). The tool uses by default the implementation of those approaches provided by the library Surprise [8]. On the right of Fig. 2, we present the evaluation results.

Fig. 2. Visualization (left) and evaluation (right) of a MovieLens 20k dataset.

Then, we will use AUTO-DataGenCARS+ to extend the number of ratings from 20k to 30k, using the "Extend dataset" workflow of the "Pre-process a dataset" module. To achieve this, a user profile file that includes features from this dataset is required. Therefore, through this workflow, we automatically generate user profiles by integrating the "Generate User Profile" workflow and loading the user, item, and rating files from the MovieLens 20k dataset. Once the new dataset has been generated, we can visualize the histogram of ratings (this histogram, and several other graphs, are created automatically after the dataset generation ends and shown in the "Analyze a dataset / Visualization" option), which should be similar to the one of the original dataset (as we have not defined variations, like additional noise or uncertainty, in the process). In addition, we evaluate the performance of the original dataset and the newly enlarged dataset (see Fig. 3).

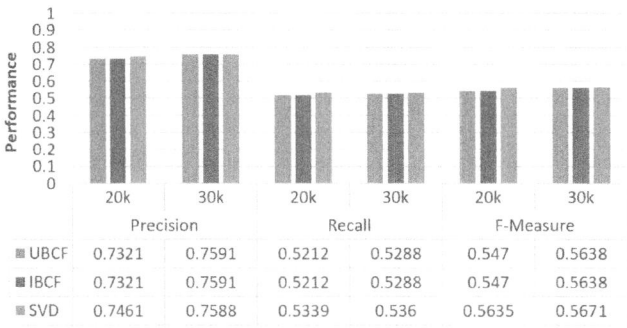

Fig. 3. Metrics obtained with the original dataset (20k) and the enlarged dataset (30k).

As can be seen in Fig. 3, the performance metrics in the new enlarged dataset are comparable to those obtained using the original dataset, for all the algorithms, which shows that enlarging the dataset did not affect the conclusions that can we obtained from the performance results. The improved performance observed in the larger dataset (ml-30k) compared to the original (ml-20k) could be due to the increased number of ratings, which enriches the recommender system's knowledge base. This experiment highlights the importance of the dataset size, confirming that a larger volume of data can lead to more precise recommendations.

4.2 Incorporate Context Data Into an Existing Dataset

In this scenario, we will show how the tool can be used to add context into a dataset where no context data is available. For this purpose, we will use again the MovieLens 100k dataset, which contains no context. The following context attributes will be added: *room_comfort* of the room where the movie was watched (with possible values *very good*, *good*, *adequate*, *bad*, and *very bad*), *room_occupancy* (with possible values *high*, *medium*, and *low*), *room_cleanliness* (with possible values *high*, *medium*, and *low*), *eating_allowed* (with possible values *only drinks*, *only food*, *food and drinks*, and *none*), *place_in_room* where the spectator was located (with possible values *far from the screen*, *close to the screen*, *center*, and *corner of the room*), and the existing *weather_conditions* (with possible values *sunny*, *windy*, *rainy*, and *cloudy*).

The intuition behind this is that some of these context variables may have an impact on how a person perceives a movie; for example, watching a movie in a dirty cinema room may lead to a lower rating than if the room was clean, and some types of movies (e.g., kid movies) may be better rated especially when popcorn is allowed in the room. The choice of these specific attributes is just an example, as the important point here is to illustrate how we can do this kind of context extensions by using AUTO-DataGenCARS+.

To define the aforementioned attributes, the context schema will first be created using the AUTO-DataGenCARS+ tool, and then this file will be used to create the context data file. The schema can be filled with the necessary context attributes (defined above) in the "Generate a synthetic dataset / Context" tab, and in the "Generation settings" option the different percentages of null context values and the number of contexts to be generated can also be chosen; in this case, we will generate 2000 context instances without null values. This newly created file will be used to perform a synthetic generation of a dataset from the original MovieLens dataset. To generate the ratings, a user profile will be generated focusing exclusively on context attributes as important features.

Now, we will generate four additional datasets based on the one we have generated, but emulating that contextual information is not available for all the ratings; specifically, each dataset will have a different number of context configurations (20%, 40%, 60% and 80%). To achieve this, we use the "Generate NULL values" workflow within the "Pre-process a dataset" module. Then, we will evaluate all resulting datasets using the "Analyze a dataset / Evaluation" option (Fig. 4). Specifically, we will apply a CM (Contextual Modelling) recommendation approach (based on the Naïve Bayes classifier from Scikit-learn [18]), considering context attributes as features, 5 possible target classes (an integer rating from 1 to 5), and choosing the use of a 10-fold cross-validation.

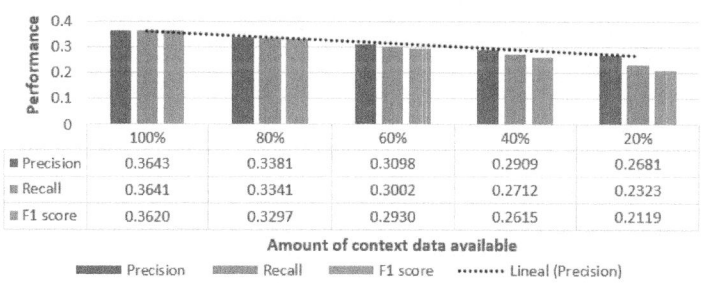

Fig. 4. Performance evaluation depending on the amount of context data available.

As can be seen in Fig. 4, when there are more context data available the performance improves, as in this scenario some context variables have an impact on the ratings provided by the users. Therefore, in this hypothetical scenario the availability of context data could be exploited by CARS to provide more suitable recommendations, adapted to the existing circumstances.

4.3 Reduce Bias in an Existing Dataset

For this example, the COMPAS (Correctional Offender Management Profiling for Alternative Sanctions) dataset [11] will be used. Even though this is not a dataset used to evaluate recommender systems, we use it because of its popularity and due to the fact that it has been proved to be biased in favor of white defendants and against black inmates, when calculating the risks of recidivism. Even though there are no user preferences involved, an application using COMPAS could be seen as a recommender that, based on the probability of repeating a crime, suggests a specific action (e.g., release the person or keep him/her in prison). To carry out this experiment, low recidivism risk values have been substituted for the value of 1, medium for 2, and high for 3; in this way, we transformed risk values into ratings.

To generate a dataset that behaves as the original one but removing some bias, items (which in this case are criminals) will be generated synthetically using the AUTO-DataGenCARS+ tool. These new criminals will be defined with the same attributes as the original ones, but modifying the percentages of appearance of some races; specifically, we will reduce the number of African-American prisoners and increase that of Caucasians, to balance the number of instances of those two races; notice that, by default, the behavior of AUTO-DataGenCARS+ is to generate items with the desired proportions indicated considered as average values, as there is some randomness in the process (the proportions can be seen in terms of probabilities). The reoffense risk (i.e., the "rating") will be generated with this new item data but considering the behavior of the original dataset, based on the statistics and user profiles automatically extracted from the original dataset.

In order to generate new item data containing information of the prisoners, several steps will be taken in the "Generate a synthetic dataset / Items" tab. First, we will define the item profiles to be used during the generation of item data. Then, in the "Generation settings" section, we will select the required number of items (in our specific example, we will generate 59.456 items) and specify the percentage of instances to generate for each item profile type, along with a 10% noise percentage for each type. Finally, we will design the item schema using a form provided by the tool and the attribute information contained in the COMPAS dataset. On the left of Fig. 5, we can see the distribution of reoffense risks according to the race in the original dataset, and on the right of Fig. 5 the distribution in the new dataset. Balancing the proportion of Caucasian and African-Americans races has changed the distribution of risks in an appropriate way. For comparison, we can plot the distributions of the risk of reoffense with both the original and the balanced dataset depending on a specific attribute (e.g., "priors_count", which is the number of previous crimes committed).

The synthetically generated data improves fairness by offering a more balanced racial representation compared to the original dataset, indicating a reduction in bias, which could also be similarly achieved by using an oversampling approach. However, whether the bias reduction technique applied leads to a more realistic dataset or not depends on the particular context and the purpose

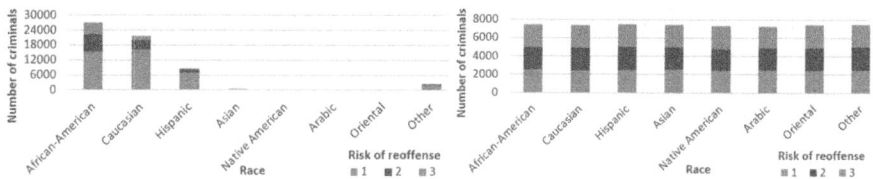

Fig. 5. Risks with the unbalanced COMPAS dataset (left) and with the new COMPAS-inspired dataset (right).

for which the data are intended. The purpose of this example is just to show how we can generate a synthetic dataset inspired by a real one but considering balanced classes, using AUTO-DataGenCARS+. Moreover, a significant research effort has been invested in the development of techniques to handle dataset bias in machine learning (e.g., see [22]), which could be integrated in the tool to enhance it with additional specific ways to handle bias.

4.4 Generate a Completely Synthetic Dataset

In this final example, we create a completely synthetic dataset using the "Generate a synthetic dataset" option of the tool. For the purpose of defining the schema and configuration files of users, items and contexts, we were inspired by the same structure of the STS dataset [3]. It contains information of 325 users (including attributes such as their birthday, gender, openness to experiences, conscientiousness, extraversion, agreeableness, and emotional stability), 249 POIs (Points Of Interest), the context when the user rating was provided (e.g., distance, time available, temperature, crowdedness, knowledge of surroundings, season, budget, daytime, weather, companion, mood, weekday, travel goal, transport), and 2534 ratings (on a scale of 1 to 5) provided by the users. Additionally, for the synthetic dataset's user, item, and context files, we apply the same percentages of unknown values found in the STS dataset. Furthermore, we analyze the distribution of values for user, item, and context attributes within the synthetic dataset by utilizing the "Analyze a dataset / Visualization" option of AUTO-DataGenCARS+.

In order to eliminate missing values in the synthetic dataset, we apply the "Pre-process a dataset / Replace NULL values" workflow on the context file. Then, we evaluated the CM recommendation paradigm on both datasets (see Fig. 6), employing the Naïve Bayes classifier with contextual attributes as features. We considered 5 potential target classes and opted for a 10-fold cross-validation approach. The experimental results reveal a significant difference in performance metrics between the synthetic and STS datasets. The CM approach presents superior performance across all metrics with the synthetic dataset. This enhanced performance could be attributed to the complete and well-distributed context attributes, in contrast to the STS dataset, which suffers from a high percentage of unknown context attributes (89.37%), as highlighted by a recent study [10]. This limitation of the STS dataset underscores the importance and the advantage of using tools like AUTO-DataGenCARS+ to generate more reliable datasets for evaluating CARS, especially given the lack of robust datasets in this research field.

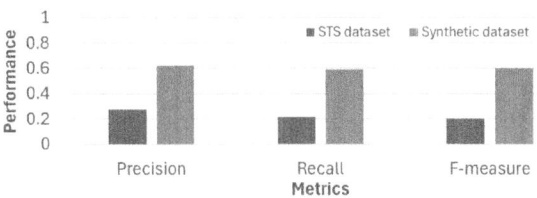

Fig. 6. Performance of Contextual Modelling with STS and the synthetic dataset.

This experiment demonstrates the utility and effectiveness of the AUTO-DataGenCARS+ tool in generating high-quality datasets to facilitate the evaluation of CARS, pointing towards future research where challenges such as data scarcity and dataset reliability are effectively mitigated.

Table 2. Summary of Lessons Learnt.

Category	Key Aspect	Lessons Learnt
Contextual data	Importance	Contextual data is crucial in providing personalized recommendations, especially in sectors like tourism.
Evaluation challenges	Lack of Datasets	Evaluating CARS is difficult due to the scarcity of datasets with rich contextual information.
Synthetic data	Utility	Synthetic data generation tools like AUTO-DataGenCARS+ are valuable for overcoming the limitations of existing datasets.
Tool design	User-oriented	Designing tools with user-friendly interfaces allows broader accessibility and usability for non-experts.
Architecture	Flexibility and extensibility	AUTO-DataGenCARS+ offers a flexible and extendable architecture to support different evaluation scenarios.
Evaluation integration	In-built tools	Integrating evaluation functionalities within the tool facilitates an uninterrupted workflow from data generation to evaluation.
Realistic data generation	Mixing datasets	The ability to mix real and synthetic datasets enables the creation of more realistic data for CARS evaluation.
Research and practice	Contribution	AUTO-DataGenCARS+ contributes to both research advancement and practical development of personalized recommendation systems.
Future directions	Research opportunities	The development and application of AUTO-DataGenCARS+ open new research ways in context-aware recommendation approaches.

5 Conclusions and Future Work

In this paper, we have presented AUTO-DataGenCARS+, a data generation tool that we have developed to help designers of recommender systems to evaluate their proposals in any desired scenario. It is a powerful graphical user interface equipped with a variety of relevant functionalities designed to facilitate the use of all its capabilities. We have illustrated the strengths of AUTO-DataGenCARS+ by considering several example scenarios and using them to extract conclusions. The development of this tool has been motivated by existing challenges that arise to evaluate context-aware recommender systems and we believe that it can be a relevant contribution to the mobile data management research community. In Table 2, we present a summary of key aspects and lessons learned about synthetic data generation for evaluating Context-Aware Recommendation Systems. A demo instance of the tool is available at the tool's website [23].

As future work, we would like to analyze the possible integration with simulation tools that support the simulation of scenarios where users move around a physical space, where different types of events can happen, and interact with recommender systems [9]. The addition of specific techniques to deal with bias, as well as evaluating the tool when dealing with large datasets, are also interesting aspects for future work.

Acknowledgements. This publication belongs to the following project: PID2020-113037RB-I00, funded by MICIU/AEI/10.13039/501100011033. Besides the NEAT-AMBIENCE project, we also acknowledge the Government of Aragon (COSMOS research group; last group reference: T64_23R). We thank Beatriz Franco (researcher at ITA) and Ignacio Palacios (former student of the University of Zaragoza) for providing their efforts and their contribution to develop the Python and Java versions of the GUI tool, respectively. This work has also been partially funded by the Department of Big Data and Cognitive Systems at the Technological Institute of Aragon, under Retech Tourism-Spain Living Lab Agreement within the "PLAN FOR RECOVERY, TRANSFORMATION AND RESILIENCE - FINANCED BY THE EUROPEAN UNION - NEXTGENERATIONEU" and by the Government of Aragon.

References

1. Adomavicius, G., Sankaranarayanan, R., Sen, S., Tuzhilin, A.: Incorporating contextual information in recommender systems using a multidimensional approach. ACM Trans. Inf. Syst. **23**(1), 103–145 (2005)
2. Bobadilla, J., Gutiérrez, A., Yera, R., Martínez, L.: Creating synthetic datasets for collaborative filtering recommender systems using generative adversarial networks. Knowl.-Based Syst. **280**, 111016 (2023)
3. Braunhofer, M., Elahi, M., Ricci, F.: STS: a context-aware mobile recommender system for places of interest. In: 22nd International Conference on User Modeling, Adaptation, and Personalization (UMAP), pp. 75–80. CEUR Workshop Proceedings (2014)
4. del Carmen Rodríguez-Hernández, M., Ilarri, S., Hermoso, R., Trillo-Lado, R.: DataGenCARS: a generator of synthetic data for the evaluation of context-aware recommendation systems. Pervasive Mob. Comput. **38, Part 2**(2017), 516–541 (2017)
5. del Carmen Rodríguez-Hernández, M., Ilarri, S., Trillo-Lado, R., Hermoso, R.: Location-aware recommendation systems: where we are and where we recommend to go. In: International Workshop on Location-Aware Recommendations (LocalRec 2015), vol. 1405, pp. 1–8. CEUR Workshop Proceedings (2015)

6. del Carmen Rodríguez-Hernández, M., Ilarri, S.: AI-based mobile context-aware recommender systems from an information management perspective: progress and directions. Knowl.-Based Syst. **215**, 1–29 (2021)
7. GroupLens Research: MovieLens Dataset (2016). https://grouplens.org/datasets/movielens. Accessed 13 Sept 2024
8. Hug, N., et al.: Suprise – A Python scikit for recommender systems (2009). https://surpriselib.com. Accessed 13 Sept 2024
9. Ilarri, S., Trillo-Lado, R., Arraez, Á., Piedrafita, A.: Simulating scenarios to evaluate data filtering techniques for mobile users. In: Delir Haghighi, P., Khalil, I., Kotsis, G. (eds.) MoMM 2022. LNCS, vol. 13634, pp. 87–101. Springer, Cham (2022). https://doi.org/10.1007/978-3-031-20436-4_9
10. Ilarri, S., Trillo-Lado, R., Hermoso, R.: Datasets for context-aware recommender systems: current context and possible directions. In: First Workshop on Context in Analytics (CiA), pp. 25–28. IEEE (2018)
11. Kaggle: COMPAS Dataset (2017). https://www.kaggle.com/danofer/compass. Accessed 13 Sept 2024
12. Lee, H., Kwon, J.: Personalised TV contents recommender system using collaborative context tagging-based users's preference prediction technique. Int. J. Multimed. Ubiquit. Eng. **9**(5), 231–240 (2014)
13. Leszczynski, M., et al.: Talk the walk: synthetic data generation for conversational music recommendation. CoRR 2301.11489, 1–10 (2023)
14. Liu, F., Cheng, Z., Chen, H., Wei, Y., Nie, L., Kankanhalli, M.: Privacy-preserving synthetic data generation for recommendation systems. In: 45th International ACM Conference on Research and Development in Information Retrieval (SIGIR 2022), pp. 1379–1389. ACM (2022)
15. Monti, D., Rizzo, G., Morisio, M.: All you need is ratings: a clustering approach to synthetic rating datasets generation. CoRR abs/1909.00687, 1–5 (2019)
16. Nguyen, L.V., Vo, N.D., Jung, J.J.: DaGzang: a synthetic data generator for cross-domain recommendation services. PeerJ Comput. Sci. **9**(e1360), 1–16 (2023)
17. Pasinato, M., Eduardo, C.M., Aufaure, M.A., Zimbrão, G.: Generating synthetic data for context-aware recommender systems. In: BRICS Congress on Computational Intelligence and 11th Brazilian Congress on Computational Intelligence (BRICS-CCI & CBIC), pp. 563–567. IEEE (2013)
18. Pedregosa, F., et al.: Scikit-learn: machine Learning in Python. J. Mach. Learn. Res. **12**, 2825–2830 (2011)
19. Polatidis, N., Georgiadis, C.K.: Mobile recommender systems: an overview of technologies and challenges. In: Second International Conference on Informatics & Applications (ICIA 2013). IEEE (2013)
20. Ricci, F., Rokach, L., Shapira, B., (eds.): Recommender Systems Handbook. Springer, Cham (2022). https://doi.org/10.1007/978-1-0716-2197-4
21. Slokom, M.: Comparing recommender systems using synthetic data. In: 12th ACM Conference on Recommender Systems (RecSys 2018), pp. 548–552. ACM (2018)
22. Susan, S., Kumar, A.: The balancing trick: optimized sampling of imbalanced – a brief survey of the recent state of the art. Eng. Rep. **3**(4) (2020)
23. Universidad de Zaragoza, ITAINNOVA: AUTO-DataGenCARS+. http://webdiis.unizar.es/~silarri/prot/AUTO-DataGenCARSPlus/ (2024), online demo at https://auto-datagencarsplus.ita.es/web/ (user: autodatagencars, password: Qxwsx3py). Accessed 13 Sept 2024

24. Yépez, C., Recalde, L., Loza-Aguirre, E.: Preventing group privacy Disclosure Through synthetic data: an evaluation of recommender system methods. Preprint (2022)
25. Zangerle, E., Bauer, C.: Evaluating recommender systems: survey and framework. ACM Comput. Surv. **55**(8) (2022)

A Method for Eliminating False Positives of Acceleration-Based Gesture Recognition Using Eye Tracking

Hinase Kawano and Kazuya Murao(✉)

Ritsumeikan University, Osaka, Japan
hinase.kawano@iis.ise.ritsumei.ac.jp, murao@fc.ritsumei.ac.jp

Abstract. This paper sets up a scenario where a monitor is operated through gestures and proposes a method that excludes false positives in gesture recognition using eye tracking data. A preliminary experiment confirmed that existing gesture recognition using acceleration data often misrecognizes relatively simple gestures like Circle and Check during activities involving significant movements, such as stretching and walking, compared with more complex gestures like Cross and Triangle. Additionally, eye tracking data were collected during daily activities. Analyzing these results, we hypothesized that a user's gaze movements are small during intentional gestures aimed at operating a monitor. By calculating the standard deviation of various gaze features and excluding segments with abnormal values, we aimed to enhance the accuracy of gesture recognition. The results showed that features such as Fixation Movement Distance and Average Pupil Diameter Change are relatively effective in excluding false positives, particularly for simple gestures like Circle and Check.

Keywords: smart watch · gesture recognition · accelerometer · eye tracking

1 Introduction

With the advancement of sensing technology and wearable devices equipped with sensors, research on behavior recognition and gesture recognition using sensor data has progressed. In particular, the widespread adoption of wristwatch-type wearable devices known as smartwatches has led to active research on gesture recognition using acceleration and angular velocity data obtained from these devices.

For example, Kader et al. [3] created a dataset by writing Bengali characters in the air with an accelerometer attached to the wrist and achieved 96.5% accuracy in recognizing these characters using a Gaussian SVM. Furthermore, Ameliasari et al. [2] defined eight gestures and proposed interactions that assign each gesture to the On/Off operation of four IoT lights. Li et al. [4] envisioned scenarios where gesture recognition using a smartwatch could be applied to the On/Off and adjustment of smart home appliances such as air conditioners, proposing smart home interactions. Additionally, Apple's Apple Watch[1] detects gestures such as tapping or double-tapping between the thumb and index finger and assigns these gestures to various operations. This allows a significant portion of the smartwatch's functionality to be operated with one hand, enhancing the user experience. As such, gesture recognition using smartwatches is applicable to various applications and is an increasingly important field for the future.

However, gesture recognition using only acceleration data or angular velocity data has the problem of being unable to distinguish whether a gesture was truly intentional. For instance, when performing gesture recognition using acceleration data, the system cannot differentiate between an acceleration waveform pattern generated when the user intentionally performs a gesture and the waveform pattern generated when a gesture-like movement occurs incidentally in daily life. Thus, if acceleration data similar to a predefined gesture is incidentally generated and recognized by the system, it may mistakenly interpret it as an intentional command, leading to unexpected and undesirable device actions. These false positives not only degrade the usability of the device but also contribute to user frustration.

In this paper, we propose a method that eliminates false positives in gesture recognition by incorporating eye tracking data into acceleration-based gesture recognition. We conducted a preliminary experiment to investigate the situations in which false positives occur during gesture recognition in daily life and the behavior of eye tracking data when users intentionally perform gestures. In the experiment, a scenario was set in which the user operates a monitor using gestures within a one-hour procedure simulating daily life activities. The results revealed a tendency for the standard deviation of gaze data to decrease when the user was fixated on the monitor. On the basis of these findings, we propose the following method: using the SPRING waveform matching algorithm, we detect segments from the acquired stream data that are likely to contain gestures. We then set the standard deviation of the change in each gaze feature across the entire stream data as a threshold. If the change in eye tracking data within the detected segments is below the threshold, we discard those segments as false positives. In this paper, we apply the proposed method using various gaze features and perform comparative analysis.

In this paper, Sect. 2 introduces related work, Sect. 3 explains the experiment for collecting wrist acceleration and gaze data, Sect. 4 presents the proposed method, Sect. 5 describes the evaluation experiment and its results, Sect. 6 discusses the challenges of the proposed method and future directions, and finally, Sect. 7 concludes the paper.

2 Related Work

Existing gesture-recognition methods using accelerometers can be broadly classified into two categories: template matching and machine learning. Template

---
[1] https://www.apple.com/watch/.

matching is a method where gesture patterns are obtained in advance as training data, and matching segments are found in the input data using these patterns. This method has been used for a long time, utilizing algorithms such as Dynamic Time Warping (DTW), which compares the similarity of waveforms and calculates the degree of pattern matching, regardless of differences in the length of the time series data. For example, Akl et al. [1] and Liu et al. [5] built gesture recognition systems using DTW with 3-axis accelerometers installed in Wii remotes.[2]

On the other hand, gesture-recognition methods using machine learning learn from large amounts of data to classify gestures from newly input data. In this approach, existing machine learning techniques such as SVM and random forests are widely used, and methods using convolutional neural networks (CNN) and recurrent neural networks (RNN) have become mainstream in gesture recognition. For instance, Makaussov et al. [6] developed a system that recognizes gestures in real time by inputting the points where the L^2 norm of 3-axis acceleration exceeds or falls below a threshold into an RNN model. Additionally, Kurz et al. [8] achieved over 10% higher accuracy compared with SVM-based methods by using a bidirectional LSTM model to identify five gestures.

However, in both cases, when these gesture recognition systems are applied in daily life, there is a risk that waveform data similar to the data registered or used for training as gesture patterns may cause the system to mistakenly recognize the data as a gesture, leading to false positives. For example, such false positives may cause gesture-assigned operations to activate unintentionally, posing risks of reduced usability and unintended system behaviors.

3 Data Collection Experiment

This section describes the experiment conducted to investigate the characteristics of eye tracking data when performing intentional gestures and to explore the potential for false positives in gesture recognition in daily life.

3.1 Experiment Environment

Information on the subjects is shown in Table 1. Four subjects (A–D, all male, with an average age of 22.25 years) took part in the experiment. As shown in Fig. 1, subjects wore Tobii Pro Glasses 2[3] on their heads as an eye-tracking device, which collected data on Gaze 2D points, Fixation points, Gaze 3D points, Pupil Diameter, Gaze Direction, and Pupil Position. Additionally, to collect wrist motion data, subjects wore an Apple Watch Series 6[4] on their dominant hand, which recorded 3-axis acceleration data from the wrist. Among the subjects, only subject D was right-handed, while the others were left-handed. Subjects performed a series of prescribed routines to simulate typical daily routines. Between

---

[2] https://www.nintendo.co.jp/wii/features/wii_remote.html.
[3] https://www.tobii.com/products/discontinued/tobii-pro-glasses-2.
[4] https://support.apple.com/111918.

Table 1. Subjects information

Subjects	Sex	Age	Wrist with Watch
A	Male	22	Left
B	Male	22	Left
C	Male	23	Left
D	Male	22	Right

Table 2. Experiment routine

Activity or Gesture Type	Duration
Stretching Activity	3 min
Circle Gesture	a few seconds
Walking Activity	10 min
Cross Gesture	a few seconds
Eating Activity	10 min
Triangle Gesture	a few seconds
Playing Game Activity	15 min
Check Gesture	a few seconds
Desk Work Activity	20 min

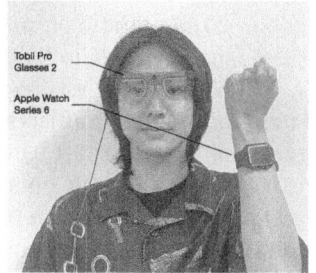

Fig. 1. Subject wearing Tobii Pro Glasses 2 and Apple Watch Series 6.

Fig. 2. Subject performing gesture

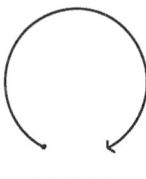 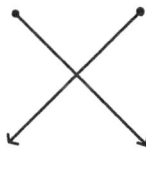 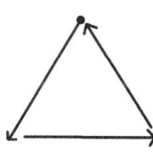 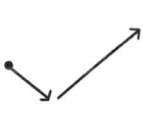

(a) Circle   (b) Cross   (c) Triangle   (d) Check

Fig. 3. Gesture type

activities during these routines, they were asked to perform specific gestures. The flow of this experiment is illustrated in Table 2, and the four types of gestures are shown in Fig. 3. The total duration of the experiment was approximately one hour. Subjects first engaged in a stretching activity for 3 min, during which they were allowed to freely stretch their bodies in place. For the walking activity, subjects walked around the room for 10 min. Following this, they seated themselves for the eating activity, where they ate and drank for 10 min. The playing-game

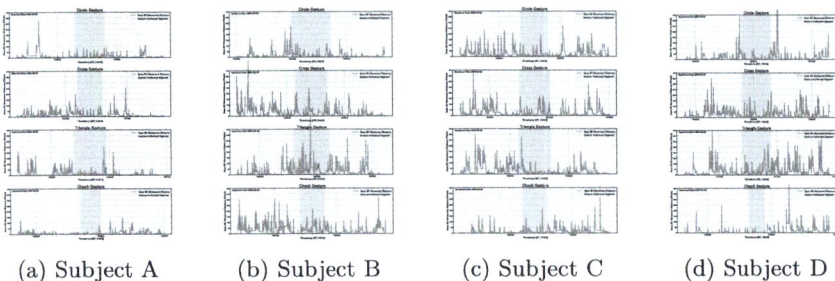

Fig. 4. Gaze 2D Movement Distance in gesture-performed segment: ± 5 s.

activity involved subjects playing a game on a Nintendo Switch for 15 min. In the final desk work activity, subjects were instructed to perform tasks such as document creation on their personal computers for 20 min. Between each of these activities, subjects performed specific gestures, such as the Circle, Cross, Triangle, and Check gestures, each lasting a few seconds. These gestures were performed with the scenario of operating a large monitor in mind. Subjects were instructed to perform the gestures in front of a large monitor (vertical: 1.0 m, horizontal: 1.7 m) positioned 4.0 m away, with the instruction to "imagine operating the monitor in-mind" as shown in Fig. 2. This setup was intended to replicate a real-world scenario involving monitor interaction, ensuring that subjects performed the gestures with appropriate context. Additionally, we collected motion data as training data by having the subjects perform each gesture 5 times, for a total of 20 individual gestures.

3.2 Eye Tracking Data

Among the data that can be measured with Tobii Pro Glasses 2, Gaze point X and Gaze point Y represent the horizontal and vertical coordinates of the averaged left and right eye gaze points, respectively, with the unit being pixels. The range of values that Gaze point X can take is from 0 to 1920 pixels, while the range for Gaze point Y is from 0 to 1080 pixels. The Gaze 2D Movement Distance is calculated using the Euclidean distance, as represented by the following equation:

$$\text{Gaze 2D Movement Distance} = \sqrt{(\Delta x)^2 + (\Delta y)^2} \quad (1)$$

Here, Δx denotes the change in Gaze point X, and Δy denotes the change in Gaze point Y. The Gaze 2D Movement Distance of each subject, within the range from 5 s before to 5 s after performing the gesture, is plotted on a graph and shown in Fig. 4. Similarly, Fixation point X and Fixation point Y represent the horizontal and vertical coordinates, respectively, of the averaged fixation points where the left and right eyes have remained for a certain period, with the unit being pixels. The fixation movement distance within the range from 5 s before to 5 s after performing the gesture is calculated in the same manner as the Gaze

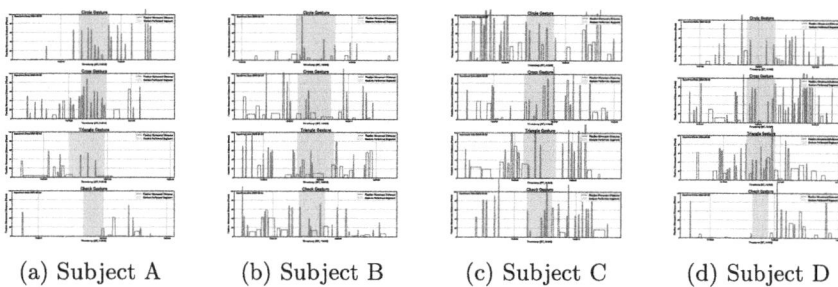

Fig. 5. Fixation Movement Distance in gesture-performed segment: ± 5 s.

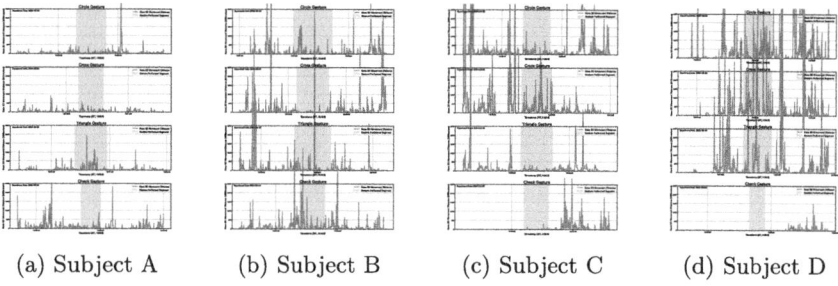

Fig. 6. Gaze 3D Movement Distance in gesture-performed segment: ± 5 s.

2D Movement Distance and is shown in Fig. 5. Gaze point 3D X, Y, and Z represent the vergence point of the left and right gaze vectors, with the unit being millimeters. The changes in the left and right Gaze Point 3D X, Y, and Z coordinates, denoted as Δx, Δy, and Δz, respectively, are used to calculate the Euclidean distance as follows:

$$\text{Gaze 3D Movement Distance} = \sqrt{(\Delta x)^2 + (\Delta y)^2 + (\Delta z)^2} \qquad (2)$$

The average movement distance of the vergence point of the left and right gaze vectors was calculated and plotted on a graph within the range from 5 s before to 5 s after each subject performed the gesture. The results are shown in Fig. 6. The change in the left and right pupil diameters of each subject, within the range from 5 s before to 5 s after performing the gesture, are plotted on a graph and shown in Fig. 7. The unit is a millimeter. The average of movement distance of the left and right gaze directions within the range from 5 s before to 5 s after each subject performed the gesture was plotted on a graph, and the results are shown in Fig. 8. The unit is millimeters. The average movement distance of the pupil position within the range from 5 s before to 5 s after each subject performed the gesture was plotted on a graph, and the results are shown in Fig. 9. The unit is millimeters. In each figure, the segment with the yellow background is the segment where the subject performed the gesture. Next, Table 3 shows the standard deviation of various features for the segments in which the sub-

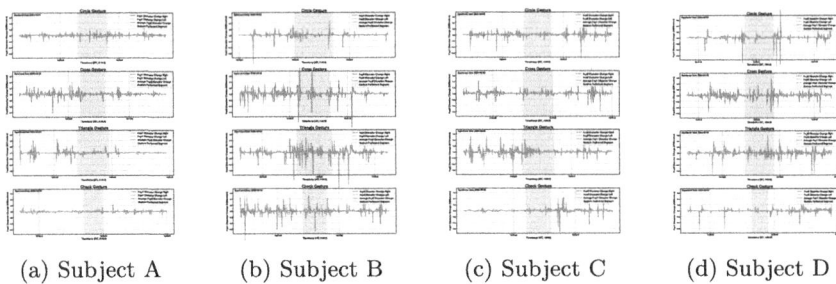

(a) Subject A (b) Subject B (c) Subject C (d) Subject D

Fig. 7. Pupil Diameter Change in gesture-performed segment: ± 5 s.

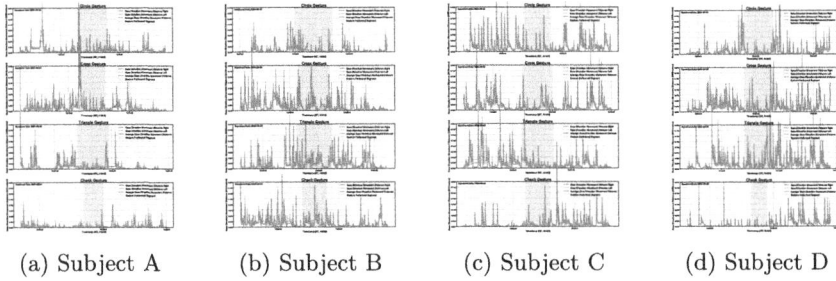

(a) Subject A (b) Subject B (c) Subject C (d) Subject D

Fig. 8. Gaze Direction Movement Distance in gesture-performed segment: ± 5 s.

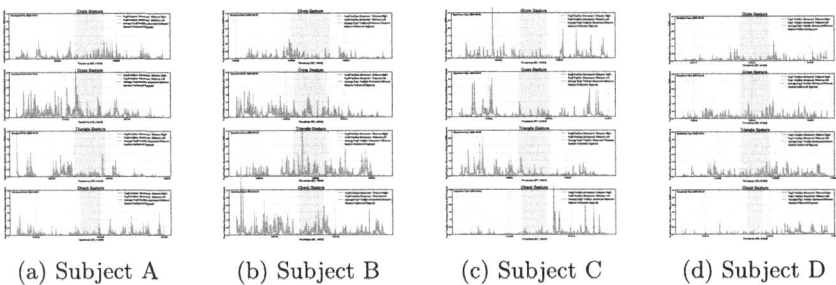

(a) Subject A (b) Subject B (c) Subject C (d) Subject D

Fig. 9. Pupil Position Movement Distance in gesture-performed segment: ± 5 s.

jects performed different activities and gestures. For Average Pupil Diameter Change, values were rounded to the fourth decimal place, while for all other measurements, values were rounded to the third decimal place.

3.3 Results of Eye Tracking Data

Firstly, it can be observed that the standard deviations of Gaze 2D Movement Distance, Gaze 3D Movement Distance, and Fixation Movement Distance were high for all subjects during activities involving significant body movement, such

Table 3. Standard deviation of eye-tracking features in segment of each activity or gesture.

Subjects	Standard Deviation of Features of	Stretch	Circle	Walk	Cross	Eat	Triangle	Game	Check	Desk work
A	Gaze 2D Movement Distance	39.39	19.13	40.30	21.22	35.88	29.64	22.99	11.75	24.65
	Fixation Movement Distance	20.67	15.40	22.45	22.67	15.93	10.05	14.88	0.00	15.03
	Gaze 3D Movement Distance	263.41	62.60	247.79	93.97	486.82	281.69	125.71	144.35	108.62
	Average Pupil Diameter Change	0.052	0.031	0.050	0.028	0.036	0.023	0.026	0.014	0.028
	Average Gaze Direction Movement Distance	0.026	0.015	0.027	0.014	0.018	0.011	0.014	0.008	0.015
	Average Pupil Position Movement Distance	0.299	0.145	0.279	0.164	0.152	0.080	0.129	0.077	0.133
B	Gaze 2D Movement Distance	55.52	24.85	64.00	45.44	58.52	61.37	37.30	40.87	45.48
	Fixation Movement Distance	18.79	14.52	21.69	11.65	21.34	11.39	19.48	15.94	19.37
	Gaze 3D Movement Distance	234.10	240.74	975.64	52.03	436.66	971.86	121.82	592.02	96.26
	Average Pupil Diameter Change	0.065	0.043	0.084	0.074	0.081	0.094	0.057	0.061	0.057
	Average Gaze Direction Movement Distance	0.025	0.016	0.027	0.024	0.029	0.023	0.020	0.021	0.022
	Average Pupil Position Movement Distance	0.192	0.114	0.225	0.189	0.228	0.212	0.166	0.164	0.174
C	Gaze 2D Movement Distance	40.94	29.43	43.29	42.57	43.84	35.94	19.41	31.97	23.99
	Fixation Movement Distance	21.65	23.09	25.71	27.61	21.57	21.18	15.86	26.82	16.92
	Gaze 3D Movement Distance	1423.54	175.63	2457.75	573.42	498.89	57.29	60.34	34.52	464.74
	Average Pupil Diameter Change	0.059	0.020	0.050	0.036	0.057	0.039	0.021	0.018	0.030
	Average Gaze Direction Movement Distance	0.024	0.023	0.026	0.028	0.026	0.023	0.013	0.020	0.016
	Average Pupil Position Movement Distance	0.143	0.106	0.168	0.150	0.169	0.137	0.086	0.083	0.110
D	Gaze 2D Movement Distance	51.25	16.28	52.85	36.56	35.65	53.06	31.29	10.20	40.69
	Fixation Movement Distance	20.15	12.68	25.49	21.85	17.90	29.86	21.21	0.00	25.42
	Gaze 3D Movement Distance	2106.86	627.39	1234.56	2516.98	3692.12	1176.42	425.54	3.15	100.07
	Average Pupil Diameter Change	0.087	0.029	0.089	0.078	0.058	0.077	0.048	0.015	0.058
	Average Gaze Direction Movement Distance	0.030	0.010	0.031	0.025	0.023	0.039	0.021	0.007	0.028
	Average Pupil Position Movement Distance	0.155	0.058	0.148	0.149	0.109	0.168	0.105	0.042	0.123

as Stretching and Walking. This indicates that the subjects' gaze moved considerably during these activities. Notably, subjects C and D exhibited very high standard deviations in Gaze 3D Movement Distance, indicating substantial gaze variation. Conversely, in relatively static activities such as Game and Desk Work, the standard deviations of these features were lower. This suggests that the subjects' gaze movements were minimal as they were focused on the screen or a specific object. In particular, subjects A and B showed significantly lower standard deviations during these activities than others. With respect to gestures, simple gestures such as Circle and Check had relatively low standard deviations of gaze features. This may be attributed to the short duration of these gestures and minimal eye movement. In particular, the Check gesture showed the least amount of eye movement for all subjects. On the other hand, gestures such as Cross and Triangle tended to show higher standard deviations in gaze features. These gestures involve complex movements, and it is believed that the subjects unconsciously followed their hand movements with their eyes. Similar trends were observed for changes in pupil diameter. The standard deviations were higher during activities involving body movement and lower during static activities. Particularly, during Stretching and Walking, significant fluctuations in pupil diameter were noted, which could be influenced by environmental changes and physical movement, reflecting variations in the subjects' arousal and attention levels. When performing gestures while looking at a monitor with the intent to operate it, it is expected that gaze movement would be minimal. Supporting this hypothesis, the standard deviations of gaze features were low during Circle and Check. These gestures are confirmed to have small gaze movements, resulting in lower standard deviations. In contrast, complex gestures such as Cross and Triangle showed higher standard deviations in gaze features. This result suggests that the subjects were likely following their arm movements with their eyes during these gestures. Therefore, while the hypothesis that "feature values become smaller during gestures" is not fully substantiated for all gestures, it is supported for simpler gestures.

3.4 Gesture Recognition Algorithm

We use the SPRING [7] algorithm, which is adapted from DTW (Dynamic Time Warping) for stream data processing, as a gesture recognition algorithm. DTW is a method for measuring the similarity between time-series data of different lengths. It can find the best match between each point by stretching or shrinking two pieces of time-series data along the time axis. SPRING computes DTW for streaming data and is suitable for cases where the waveforms to be recognized are part of long time-series data to be acquired such as in this study. SPRING detects subsequences in streaming data that are similar to the query waveform using disjoint queries, which combine best-match queries and range queries. It operates on a single matrix where the time axis is represented by $X = (x_1, ..., x_n)$ and the value axis by $Y' = (y_0, y_1, ..., y_n)$. This matrix consists of elements (d, i), where d represents the distance, and i is the starting point. For best-match queries, SPRING outputs the most similar subsequence $X[ds : de]$, and for disjoint queries, it outputs all matching subsequences $X[ds : de]$. Let s_i and s'_i be arrays of n distance values and t_i and t'_i be arrays of n integers. Define $s_i = s(d, i)$ and $s'_i = s(d-1, i)$, $t_i = q(d, i)$ and $t'_i = q(d-1, i)$. The DTW distance for each subsequence can be calculated as:

$$s_i = |x_d - y_i| + s_{best}$$
$$s_{best} = \min(s_{i-1}, s'_i, s'_{i-1}) \quad (3)$$
$$s_0 = s'_0 = 0$$

The starting point of the subsequence can be calculated as follows:

$$t_i = \begin{cases} t_{i-1} & (s_{i-1} = s_{best}) \\ t'_i & (s'_i = s_{best}) \\ t'_{i-1} & (s'_{i-1} = s_{best}) \end{cases} \quad (4)$$

Therefore, SPRING updates n distances and integers at each time step. Stream processing for best-match queries outputs the most appropriate subsequence using Eqs. 3 and 4. It updates the distance s_i at each time step for disjoint queries and uses the result to determine the starting point t_i. When the distance is below the threshold ω, it reports the distance for the subsequence and reinitializes the array s_i. Next, it calculates the segments for the X, Y, and Z

Table 4. Threshold for each gesture of each subject.

Subjects	SPRING Threshold	Gesture Type			
		Circle	Cross	Triangle	Check
A	SPRING Threshold	2.8	4.5	4.0	4.0
	gesture min time	1.0	1.5	1.5	0.75
	gesture max time	4.0	3.5	4.0	2.5
B	SPRING Threshold	7.5	7.0	5.0	5.2
	gesture min time	1.0	1.25	1.25	0.75
	gesture max time	4.0	4.0	3.5	3.0
C	SPRING Threshold	3.4	3.3	1.9	3.5
	gesture min time	2.0	1.5	1.0	0.75
	gesture max time	4.0	4.0	4.0	3.0
D	SPRING Threshold	3.8	3.9	4.6	4.7
	gesture min time	1.0	0.75	1.0	0.5
	gesture max time	4.0	3.0	4.0	2.0

Table 5. Segments identified as gesture performed using SPRING algorithm.

Subjects	Gesture Type	Total	Activity Type				
			Stretch	Walking	Eating	Game	Desk Work
A	Circle	7	3	3	0	0	0
	Cross	3	0	2	0	0	0
	Triangle	1	0	0	0	0	0
	Check	13	1	8	3	0	0
B	Circle	3	0	1	0	0	1
	Cross	1	0	0	0	0	0
	Triangle	1	0	0	0	0	0
	Check	6	1	3	0	1	0
C	Circle	3	0	2	0	0	0
	Cross	4	0	0	2	1	0
	Triangle	2	0	1	0	0	0
	Check	12	0	3	5	1	2
D	Circle	2	0	1	0	0	0
	Cross	1	0	0	0	0	0
	Triangle	1	0	0	0	0	0
	Check	13	2	8	1	0	1

axes. Then, we integrate these segments and identify overlapping segments. Initially, we combine the segments for each axis and sort them by their start and end times. Subsequently, overlapping segments are detected, and segments that overlapped on at least two axes are considered segments where gestures are performed. Since the SPRING algorithm, like DTW, is capable of stretching and compressing in the time direction, some of the segments identified as containing gestures may be extremely short or long. Given that gestures are typically performed over a few seconds, segments that are either very short or very long are unlikely to be gestures and are therefore excluded. Specifically, segments that are less than approximately 75% of the minimum duration of each gesture's training data for each subject or longer than approximately 200% of the maximum duration are discarded.

3.5 Threshold Determination

In this section, we describe the preliminary experiment conducted to determine the threshold ϵ mentioned in Sect. 3.4. From the data collected in the experiment, we extracted a segment ranging from 5 s before to 5 s after the gesture was performed. Using all the training data, we applied SPRING while varying the threshold to experimentally determine the minimum threshold at which the gesture could be detected for each subject and each gesture. The results are shown in Table 4.

3.6 Results of Gesture Recognition

Using the threshold ω determined in Sect. 3.5, Table 5 shows the intervals and the number of times gestures were identified when applying the SPRING algorithm to the all of the stream data. After applying the algorithm to each subject's stream data using all five of their training data sets for each type of gesture, we further refined the gesture-performing intervals by detecting overlapping segments from the list of five segments. The total number in the table is the number of times false positives occurred for Stretch ~ Desk Work + 1 correct recognition.

The threshold ω used in applying the SPRING algorithm this time was the ideal threshold for gesture detection determined in Sect. 3.5. Additionally, each gesture was performed only once during the experiment. However, multiple instances of false positives occurred. False positives were particularly frequent in activities involving significant movement, such as Stretching and Walking. In contrast, activities with less hand movement, such as Playing Game and Desk Work, experienced fewer false positives. Further analysis of the false positive instances revealed that simple gestures like the Check gesture had the highest number of false positives across all subjects. This is likely because the gesture is short and simple, making it easily confused with other similar arm movements occurring during activities such as Stretching and Walking. In comparison, more distinctive and complex gestures like Cross and Triangle experienced fewer false positives. These results suggest that while the SPRING algorithm can effectively distinguish complex gestures, it faces challenges in accurately distinguishing gestures from similar movements during activities involving significant body movement.

4 Proposed Method

In this section, on the basis of the results of Sects. 3.3 and 3.6, we describe our proposed method for distinguishing between performed and unintentional gestures among the detected gesture segments.

The flow of the proposed method is shown in Fig. 10. First, gesture recognition is performed using the training data and the SPRING algorithm from the acquired motion data. Then, the segments identified by the SPRING algorithm as performing gestures are cross-referenced with the eye tracking data from the same time period, and gaze features are calculated for each segment. The features used are the same as in Table 3. The standard deviations of various features from the entire stream of eye tracking data obtained in the experiment are calculated, and segments with feature values exceeding these standard deviations are eliminated.

5 Evaluation Experiment

This section describes the experiment conducted to evaluate the effectiveness of the proposed method. The method was applied to the segments incorrectly detected as performing gestures in Sect. 3.6. The results are summarized in a table for each feature, showing how much false positives were reduced.

5.1 Results

The results of the proposed method for each feature are shown in Tables 6, 7, 8, 9, 10 and 11. The reduction in false positives for each method is expressed as (false positive eliminated/all false positives) $\times$ 100% and summarized in Table 12. In

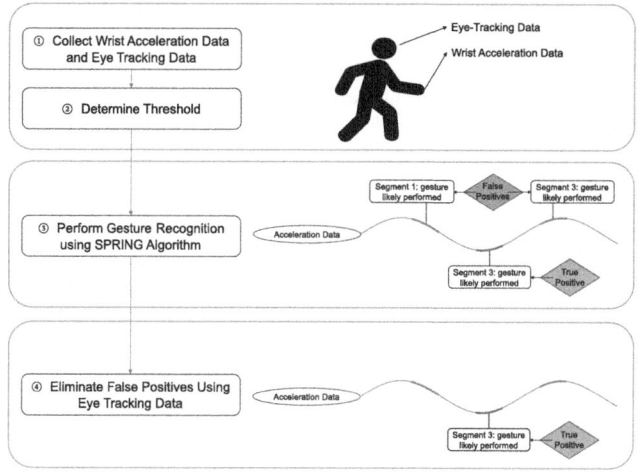

Fig. 10. Flow of proposed method.

Table 6. Segments after eliminating false positives using Gaze 2D Movement Distance.

Subjects	Gesture Type	Total	Stretch	Walking	Eating	Game	Desk Work
A	Circle	5	2	2	0	0	0
	Cross	1	0	0	0	0	0
	Triangle	1	0	0	0	0	0
	Check	5	1	2	1	0	0
B	Circle	3	0	1	0	0	0
	Cross	1	0	0	0	0	0
	Triangle	1	0	0	0	0	0
	Check	4	1	1	0	1	0
C	Circle	1	0	1	0	0	0
	Cross	2	0	0	1	0	0
	Triangle	1	0	0	0	0	0
	Check	10	0	3	3	1	2
D	Circle	2	0	1	0	0	0
	Cross	1	0	0	0	0	0
	Triangle	1	0	0	0	0	0
	Check	6	1	2	1	0	1

Table 7. Segments after eliminating false positives using Fixation Movement Distance.

Subjects	Gesture Type	Total	Stretch	Walking	Eating	Game	Desk Work
A	Circle	3	2	1	0	0	0
	Cross	3	0	2	0	0	0
	Triangle	1	0	0	0	0	0
	Check	4	0	1	2	0	0
B	Circle	2	0	0	0	0	1
	Cross	1	0	0	0	0	0
	Triangle	1	0	0	0	0	0
	Check	5	1	2	0	1	0
C	Circle	2	0	1	0	0	0
	Cross	3	0	0	1	1	0
	Triangle	2	0	0	1	0	0
	Check	11	0	3	5	1	2
D	Circle	1	0	0	0	0	0
	Cross	1	0	0	0	0	0
	Triangle	1	0	0	0	0	0
	Check	6	1	2	1	0	1

Table 8. Segments after eliminating false positives using Gaze 3D Movement Distance.

Subjects	Gesture Type	Total	Stretch	Walking	Eating	Game	Desk Work
A	Circle	7	3	3	0	0	0
	Cross	3	0	2	0	0	0
	Triangle	1	0	0	0	0	0
	Check	11	1	8	2	0	0
B	Circle	3	0	1	0	0	1
	Cross	1	0	0	0	0	0
	Triangle	1	0	0	0	0	0
	Check	6	1	3	0	1	0
C	Circle	2	0	1	0	0	0
	Cross	3	0	0	2	0	0
	Triangle	1	0	0	0	0	0
	Check	9	0	2	3	1	2
D	Circle	2	0	1	0	0	0
	Cross	1	0	0	0	0	0
	Triangle	1	0	0	0	0	0
	Check	12	2	7	1	0	1

the table, the "–" symbol indicates that no false positive occurred during the gesture recognition stage, while "miss" indicates that segments where the gestures were correctly performed were also eliminated. As mentioned, a scenario was assumed in which gestures were performed to operate a monitor. It is based on the hypothesis that gaze movement will be minimal while gestures are performed as the subject looks at the monitor. In Sect. 3.3, this hypothesis was not strongly supported for gestures involving relatively large movements, such as Cross and Triangle. However, these distinctive gestures tended to have fewer false positives in the SPRING algorithm, suggesting that the issue is minimal. Looking at the overall effectiveness of each feature, Fixation Movement Distance and Average Pupil Diameter Change were particularly useful features. For example, for subject A, Fixation Movement Distance reduced false positives for the Check gesture by 75%. Additionally, for subjects B, C, and D, it showed significant effects, particularly for the Circle gesture. On the other hand, Average Pupil Diameter Change reduced false positives for both Cross and Triangle gestures by 100% for subject C and also showed a certain degree of false posi-

Table 9. Segments after eliminating false positives using Average Pupil Diameter Change.

Table 10. Segments after eliminating false positives using Average Gaze Direction Movement Distance.

Table 11. Segments after eliminating false positives using Average Pupil Position Movement Distance.

Table 12. Percentage of false positives eliminated

Subjects	Standard Deviation of Features of	Gesture Type			
		Circle	Cross	Triangle	Check
A	Gaze 2D Movement Distance	33%	100%	–	67%
	Fixation Movement Distance	miss	0%	–	75%
	Gaze 3D Movement Distance	0%	0%	–	miss
	Average Pupil Diameter Change	33%	0%	–	50%
	Average Gaze Direction Movement Distance	33%	100%	–	50%
	Average Pupil Position Movement Distance	33%	100%	–	67%
B	Gaze 2D Movement Distance	0%	–	–	40%
	Fixation Movement Distance	50%	–	–	20%
	Gaze 3D Movement Distance	0%	–	–	0%
	Average Pupil Diameter Change	50%	–	–	20%
	Average Gaze Direction Movement Distance	0%	–	–	0%
	Average Pupil Position Movement Distance	50%	–	–	0%
C	Gaze 2D Movement Distance	miss	67%	100%	18%
	Fixation Movement Distance	50%	33%	0%	miss
	Gaze 3D Movement Distance	50%	33%	100%	27%
	Average Pupil Diameter Change	0%	100%	100%	55%
	Average Gaze Direction Movement Distance	miss	67%	0%	9%
	Average Pupil Position Movement Distance	0%	67%	0%	27%
D	Gaze 2D Movement Distance	0%	–	–	58%
	Fixation Movement Distance	100%	–	–	58%
	Gaze 3D Movement Distance	0%	–	–	8%
	Average Pupil Diameter Change	100%	–	–	33%
	Average Gaze Direction Movement Distance	100%	–	–	58%
	Average Pupil Position Movement Distance	100%	–	–	58%

tive reduction for other subjects. Conversely, Gaze 3D Movement Distance was found to be less useful. This feature did not show a reduction in false positives for most gestures for subjects A, B, and D, and for subject B, it showed no effect at all. However, for subject C, it could eliminate a certain degree of false positives for all gestures. Notably, in the Circle gesture for subject C, there was a case where correctly performed gesture segments were also eliminated. It is possible that during the Circle gesture, subject C was focusing on the monitor, but their gaze was moving in sync with their arm movements. Additionally, there were other cases where true positives were excluded. This suggests that there are limitations to a simple rule-based exclusion method. From a comprehensive perspective, Fixation Movement Distance and Average Pupil Diameter Change were relatively effective features for reducing false positives. In comparison, Gaze 3D Movement Distance showed low effectiveness for subjects other than C, indicating it was less useful compared with the other features. In any case, the useful features will likely vary for each gesture and each subject.

6 Discussion

In this section, we discuss the limitations of the proposed method and future prospects.

6.1 Scenario

We assumed a scenario where an external monitor is operated directly in front of the user from a fixed distance. However, this assumption is too restrictive. In scenarios where gestures are used to control home appliances, such as switching off lights while lying down, operating from various distances and angles during other activities, or controlling devices while walking, it is often necessary to build a system that is robust across a variety of real-world conditions.

6.2 Eye Tracking Data and Gesture Recognition

On the basis of the hypothesis that during gestures performed in the scenario of operating a monitor the user's gaze movement is minimal because they are focusing on the monitor, this method adopts a mechanical threshold classification algorithm utilizing the standard deviation of changes in various gaze features. This approach reduced false positive in activities involving significant eye movements, such as Stretching and Walking. However, it was challenging to reduce false positive in activities with minimal eye movement, such as Game and Desk Work. In some cases, false positives were not reduced at all, depending on the subject and gesture, and even true positives were excluded in some cases. Furthermore, while some subjects may perform gestures by focusing solely on the monitor, others might follow their hand movements with their eyes. We plan to gather more participants to collect data, build a machine learning model, and incorporate inference-based methods. Additionally, we used a waveform matching algorithm called SPRING, assuming post-hoc gesture recognition in a non-real-time setting. In future work, we need to verify whether false positives can occur in everyday life even with machine learning-based methods-which are currently mainstream in gesture recognition-and whether combining real-time gesture recognition with eye tracking data referencing can exclude them.

6.3 Robustness

In this study, each subject's threshold settings for gesture recognition and false positive exclusion were unique. To ensure the system's robustness, it is crucial to use threshold settings that are as user-independent and mechanical as possible. This could involve leveraging machine learning techniques to develop generalized models that can automatically adjust thresholds on the basis of a wide range of user data. Additionally, the system should be capable of dynamically adapting to different users and contexts without requiring extensive recalibration. Future work should focus on creating algorithms that can learn from large datasets and generalize to new users, ensuring consistent performance across various scenarios.

7 Conclusion

In this paper, we proposed a method that incorporates gaze movement information to distinguish between intended and unintended gestures in acceleration-based gesture recognition. In this study, we conducted experiments under the scenario of operating a monitor in daily life, which revealed a tendency for the amount of gaze movement to decrease during gestures. We utilized this characteristic to implement a threshold-based method for eliminating false positives. As a result, we were able to reduce false positives, particularly during stretching and walking activities, to some extent. In the future, we aim to make this method more applicable to a wider range of situations beyond just monitor operation. Additionally, while we used the SPRING algorithm in this study to statically extract the gesture periods from acceleration data after the experiment, we plan to improve the method to allow for real-time gesture recognition.

References

1. Akl, A., Valaee, S.: Accelerometer-based gesture recognition via dynamic-time warping, affinity propagation, & compressive sensing. In: 2010 IEEE International Conference on Acoustics, Speech and Signal Processing, pp. 2270–2273. IEEE (2010)
2. Ameliasari, M., Putrada, A.G., Pahlevi, R.R.: An evaluation of SVM in hand gesture detection using IMU-based smartwatches for smart lighting control. J. Infotel **13**(2), 47–53 (2021)
3. Kader, M.A., Ullah, M.A., Islam, M.S., Ferriol Sánchez, F., Samad, M.A., Ashraf, I.: A real-time air-writing model to recognize Bengali characters. AIMS Math. **9**(3), 6668–6698 (2024)

4. Li, Y., et al.: Control your home with a smartwatch. IEEE Access **8**, 131601–131613 (2020)
5. Liu, J., Zhong, L., Wickramasuriya, J., Vasudevan, V.: uWave: accelerometer-based personalized gesture recognition and its applications. Pervasive Mob. Comput. **5**(6), 657–675 (2009)
6. Makaussov, O., Krassavin, M., Zhabinets, M., Fazli, S.: A low-cost, IMU-based realtime on device gesture recognition glove. In: 2020 IEEE International Conference on Systems, Man, and Cybernetics (SMC), pp. 3346–3351. IEEE (2020)
7. Sakurai, Y., Faloutsos, C., Yamamuro, M.: Stream monitoring under the time warping distance. In: 2007 IEEE 23rd International Conference on Data Engineering, pp. 1046–1055. IEEE (2006)
8. Zhu, P., Zhou, H., Cao, S., Yang, P., Xue, S.: Control with gestures: a hand gesture recognition system using off-the-shelf smartwatch. In: 2018 4th International Conference on Big Data Computing and Communications (BIGCOM), pp. 72–77. IEEE (2018)

Toward the Implementation of a Cooking Support System Complementing Nonexistent Objects with Virtual Objects

Taiki Nihanda[1] and Shoji Sano[2(✉)]

[1] Graduate School of Engineering, Kanazawa Institute of Technology,
Nonoichi, Ishikawa, Japan
c6302078@st.kanazawa-it.ac.jp
[2] College of Engineering, Kanazawa Institute of Technology,
Nonoichi, Ishikawa, Japan
sano@neptune.kanazawa-it.ac.jp

Abstract. Cooking requires the usage of various ingredients and cooking utensils. However, if we lack some of them due to insufficient preparation, we cannot cook as expected. In this paper, we propose a cooking support system that complements nonexistent objects with virtual objects. We developed a prototype for cutting apples to evaluate the differences between using the real object and the virtual one. The results showed that the cutting technique equally enhanced both the cases of using a real knife and a virtual knife.

Keywords: Complement · Virtual objects · Mixed reality · Cooking support system · Cutting technique

1 Introduction

Mixed reality (MR), which overlays virtual contents onto a real space, has been attracting attention in recent years. As MR is utilized to complement real space with virtual objects, it has applications to a variety of contents. One such content, cooking, which is the act of preparing food, requires a certain degree of technique for enjoying delicious food. Therefore, many virtual reality (VR), augmented reality (AR), and MR systems have been developed to support cooking. Two examples are the Cooking Simulator VR application, which supports cooking in a virtual space, and Kitchef [4], which provides a tangible user interface for parents and children to enjoy cooking.

Two fundamental requirements of cooking are ingredients and cooking utensils. Most cooking support systems, including the ones discussed above, are designed under the assumption that everything we need for cooking has already been prepared. However, in reality, we are often lack some of the required items due to insufficient preparation, and as a result, we cannot cook as expected.

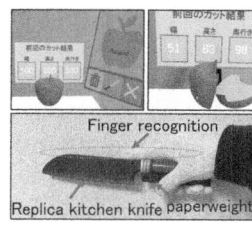 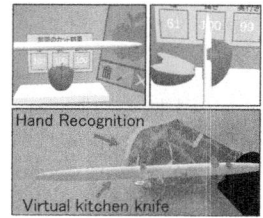 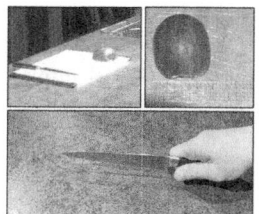

Fig. 1. Prototype system.

We therefore propose a cooking support system that complements nonexistent objects with virtual objects. The proposed system provides virtual ingredients and cooking utensils to stand in for the objects that are missing. In this work, we develop a prototype that cuts apples and evaluate the differences between using real objects and using virtual objects. The results show that the cutting technique equally enhances both the cases of using a real knife and using a virtual knife.

2 Related Work

Many studies have been conducted to integrate real and virtual spaces [5]. These works are similar to our own in that they integrate real and virtual spaces to create a better experience in the real world. In this paper, we incorporate virtual objects into real space in a natural manner as reference.

Research has also been conducted on cooking support systems [6]. Although past studies are similar to ours in that they provide cooking support functions, they are premised on the assumption that all the ingredients and cookware required for cooking are already in place.

3 Proposed System

3.1 Approach

As mentioned above, the previous cooking support systems assume that all of the ingredients and utensils required for cooking have been prepared in advance. However, we sometimes forget to make sufficient preparations. Here, we consider a case in which we want to cook curry rice, which is a popular dish in Japan. Curry rice is made of meat, potatoes, carrots, onions, curry roux, rice, and other ingredients. We also need a pot, ladle, knife, and cutting board. Sometimes, however, we may find that we have forgotten to buy carrots, or in another case, that we have forgotten the onions and the knife.

Our ultimate goal is to complement all objects, but since cooking utensils are the most difficult, we focus on utensils in this work.

3.2 Implementation of Prototype System

We designed and implemented a prototype of the proposed system using Unity (C#) with HoloLens2, as shown in Fig. 1. The prototype implements the function of cutting an apple, which requires the use of a virtual knife and a virtual apple. When cutting a virtual apple using a real knife while wearing HoloLens2, we use a replica knife that does not actually cut for safety reasons. The hand-tracking function of HoloLens2 recognizes the user's fingers, and the Slicer Asset of Unity cuts the apple at the front of the user's index finger. In virtual space, the initial size of the apple is 100, as we assume the size of an actual apple is 100 mm. The width, height, and depth of the apple is measured and then displayed in the prototype.

4 Evaluation

4.1 Evaluation Method

We conducted an evaluation experiment to investigate the difference between using real objects and virtual objects in the prototype system. Ten participants aged 20–23 years cut an apple before and after a 10-minute practice. They were asked to perform two types of cutting: 1) cutting the apple into nine parts and 2) cutting the apple into 5-mm-long strips. In addition, there were three types of practice: 1) cutting virtual apples with a replica knife, 2) cutting virtual apples with a virtual knife, and 3) cutting real apples with a real knife. In the first two practices, the participants used the prototype system while wearing HoloLens2, and in the third practice, they did not use it. We measured the width of the cut apple to evaluate the degree of knife technique improvement (Fig. 2).

4.2 Results

Table 1 shows the width of the cut apples and the cutting time before and after practice. Figure 3 shows the time of cutting in the evaluation experiment and in the practice about participants A, B, C, F, G, and H.

Table 1. Results of evaluation experiment.

		Cutting into 9 parts		
		Virtual apple - Replica kitchen knife		
		Average	Variance	Time
Participant A	Before	34.33	64.22	0:35
	After	34.67	94.89	0:24
Participant B	Before	28.33	30.89	0:25
	After	27.00	32.67	0:26
Participant C	Before	27.00	38.00	0:42
	After	25.67	26.89	0:39
Participant D	Before	27.33	68.22	0:26
	After	26.33	16.22	0:21
Participant E	Before	28.00	8.67	0:13
	After	27.33	3.56	0:10

		Virtual apple - Virtual kitchen knife		
		Average	Variance	Time
Participant A	Before	26.33	29.56	0:27
	After	24.33	6.22	0:21
Participant B	Before	30.33	33.56	0:25
	After	30.00	74.67	0:29
Participant C	Before	29.67	74.89	0:31
	After	30.00	40.67	0:36
Participant D	Before	32.00	50.67	0:21
	After	31.67	22.22	0:19
Participant E	Before	31.33	30.89	0:27
	After	28.67	0.22	0:19

		Real apple - Real kitchen knife		
		Average	Variance	Time
Participant A	Before	25.33	10.89	0:24
	After	26.00	26.00	0:23
Participant B	Before	24.33	67.56	0:24
	After	24.67	24.22	0:26
Participant C	Before	24.67	38.89	0:30
	After	24.67	14.22	0:33
Participant D	Before	26.00	18.67	0:21
	After	26.00	4.67	0:18
Participant E	Before	34.33	108.22	0:19
	After	32.00	4.67	0:25

		Cutting into strips		
		Virtual apple - Replica kitchen knife		
		Average	Variance	Time
Participant F	Before	5.59	6.24	1:10
	After	5.71	3.15	1:01
Participant G	Before	6.33	4.49	0:57
	After	6.62	4.39	1:08
Participant H	Before	6.53	3.32	0:42
	After	7.57	4.10	0:31
Participant I	Before	4.56	5.61	0:45
	After	5.87	4.12	1:06
Participant J	Before	7.67	5.72	0:30
	After	7.54	4.71	0:41

		Virtual apple - Virtual kitchen knife		
		Average	Variance	Time
Participant F	Before	4.87	2.25	0:41
	After	4.93	4.64	0:50
Participant G	Before	5.40	3.84	0:52
	After	5.50	1.54	0:51
Participant H	Before	7.15	11.21	0:46
	After	6.86	2.69	0:45
Participant I	Before	6.38	4.24	0:55
	After	7.36	2.78	0:50
Participant J	Before	7.92	3.74	0:29
	After	9.00	6.00	0:27

		Real apple - Real kitchen knife		
		Average	Variance	Time
Participant F	Before	6.07	5.21	0:42
	After	3.86	2.12	1:32
Participant G	Before	5.60	3.04	0:44
	After	5.80	2.16	0:32
Participant H	Before	5.11	2.99	0:51
	After	6.00	1.47	0:55
Participant I	Before	4.05	2.58	0:58
	After	5.77	3.56	0:54
Participant J	Before	7.60	4.91	0:44
	After	5.53	2.14	0:41

As we can see, the width variance of the cut apples was smaller after the practice than before the practice. In particular, the results of participants D, E, and F indicate a smaller variance, and the results of participants E and f show a smaller variance between the cases of the practice of cutting virtual apples with a replica knife and real apples with a real knife. On the other hand, the speed of cutting the apple did not improve. One reason could be that participants may have been cutting more carefully after practice because they were focused on cutting the apple into equal widths.

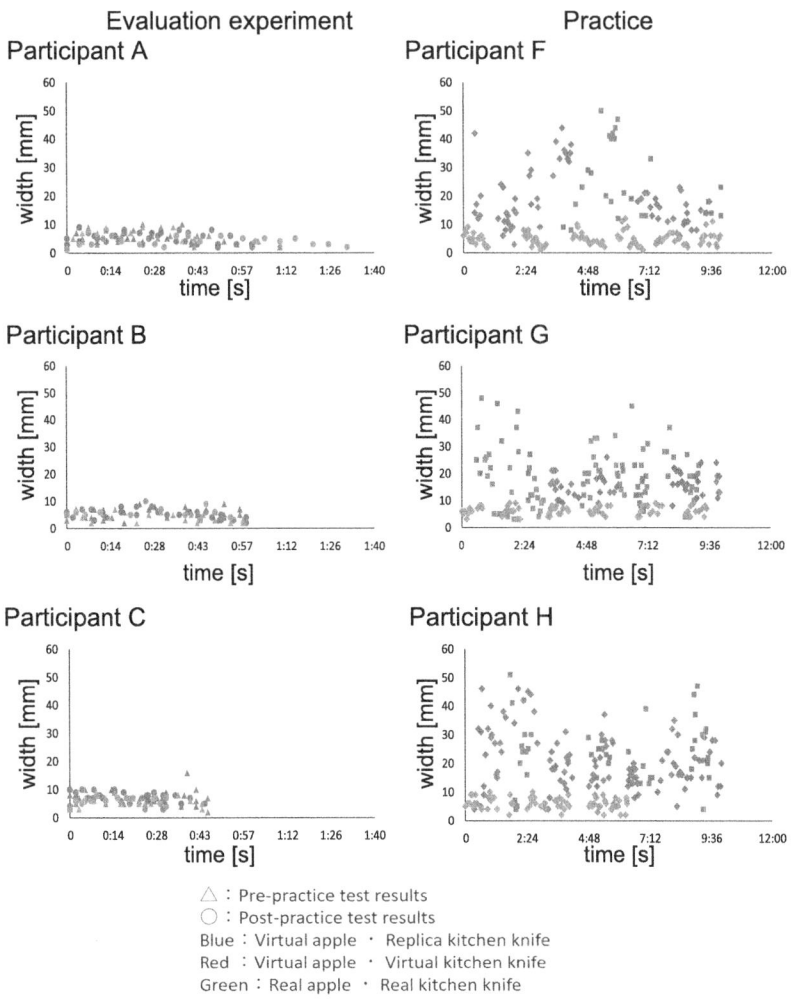

Fig. 2. Time variation (cutting into 9 parts) (Color figure online)

Overall, the results indicate that the cutting technique equally enhanced both the cases of using a real knife and using a virtual knife.

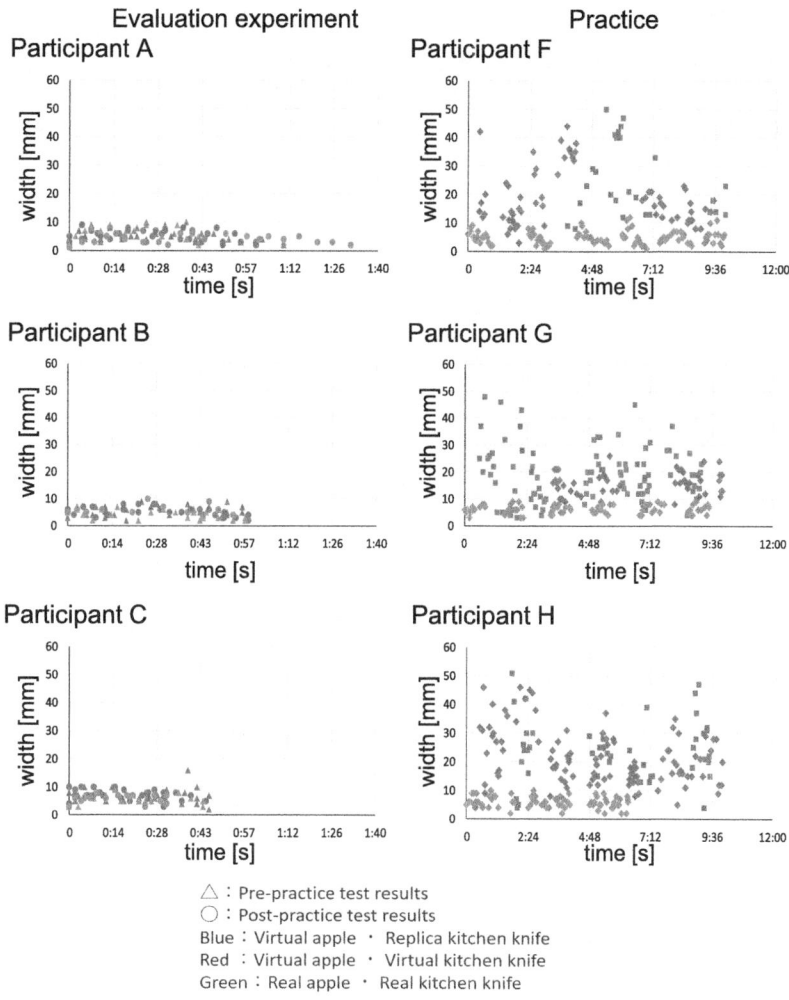

Fig. 3. Time variation (cutting into nine parts) (Color figure online)

5 Conclusion

We have developed a cooking support system that complements nonexistent objects with virtual objects. In this paper, we presented a prototype for cutting apples and conducted an experiment to evaluate the differences between using the real object and the virtual one. The results demonstrated that the cutting technique improved equally in both the cases of using a real knife and using a virtual knife.

In future work, we will expand the proposed system to enable baking, boiling, and other cooking techniques using a pot, a frying pan, and so on. Moreover, in the current system, we can look at virtual objects through the head-mounted display but not smell or taste them, so we also plan to add aroma and taste to the cooked dishes.

References

1. Milgram, P., Takemura, H., Utsumi, A., Kishino, F.: Augmented reality: a class of displays on the reality-virtuality continuum. In: Proceedings of Telemanipulator and Telepresence Technologies, vol. 2351, pp. 282–292 (1994)
2. Fadzli, F.E., Ismail, A.W., Talib, R., Alias, R.A., Ashari, Z.M.: MR-deco: mixed reality application for interior planning and designing. In: Proceedings of the International Conference on Virtual and Mixed Reality Interfaces 2020 (ICVRMR 2020), vol. 979, no.1, pp. 1–12 (2020)
3. Al Janab, H.F., et al.: Effectiveness of the Hololens Mixed Reality Headset in Minimally Invasive Surgery: A Simulation-based Feasibility Study. Surg. Endosc. **34**(3), 1143–1149 (2020)
4. Yaar, N.M., et al.: Kitchef: a TUI for parent-child cooking together. In: ACM CHI 2024 Extended Abstracts on Human Factors in Computing Systems (CHI EA 2024), no. 213, pp. 1–7 (2024)
5. Kanke, H., Takegawa, Y., Terada, T., Tsukamoto, M.: Airstic drum: a drumstick for integration of real and virtual drums. In: proceedings of the 9th Advances in Computer Entertainment Conference (ACE2012), pp. 57–69 (2012)
6. Nakabe, J., Mizumoto, T., Suwa, H., Yasumoto, K.: ParaCook: optimal cooking support system for multiple dishes. In: Proceedings of the IEEE International Conference on Pervasive Computing and Communications (PerCom 2021) Work in Progress (WiP) Session, pp. 368–371 (2021)
7. Miyashita, H.: Norimaki synthesizer: taste display using ion electrophoresis in five gels. In: Extended Abstracts of the CHI Conference on Human Factors in Computing Systems (CHI 2020), pp. 1–6 (2020)

Author Index

B
Becker, Christoph 39

C
Caballero, Marcos 176
Cavallaro, Lucia 101
Chuang, Yi-Fang 95

D
del Carmen Rodríguez-Hernández, María 176
del-Hoyo-Alonso, Rafael 176
Dittrich, Jakob 24
Dzierwa, Piotr 115

E
Erhan, Laura 101

F
Findling, Rainhard Dieter 24

G
Gotoh, Yusuke 107
Grossmann, Niklas 54

H
Hermoso, Ramón 176
Hirakawa, Eiji 107
Hlavacs, Helmut 54
Huang, Wei-Chieh 95

I
Ilarri, Sergio 176

K
Kawano, Hinase 192
Kobiela, Jaroslaw 115, 145

L
Lee, Chien-Cheng 95
Liotta, Antonio 101

M
Mukai, Kae 3
Murao, Kazuya 18, 31, 192

N
Nakajima, Tatsuo 86
Nakao, Ryoma 86
Narahashi, Subaru 107
Nesterchuk, Oleh 161
Nihanda, Taiki 208

O
Oberweis, Andreas 39
Ohashi, Takuro 130
Ohnishi, Ayumi 3

P
Pfeifer, Simon 39

S
Sano, Shoji 208
Sauer, Max 39
Shoji, Yoshiyuki 70
Sürmeli, Jan 39

T
Takeuchi, Momo 70
Terada, Tsutomu 3

Trillo-Lado, Raquel 176
Tsuchida, Shuhei 3
Tsukamoto, Masahiko 3

U
Uchiyama, Akira 107
Urbaniec, Piotr 145

W
Watabe, Ryo 18
Watanabe, Katsumi 3
Watanabe, Ken 3

Y
Yakovyna, Vitaliy 161
Yamamoto, Yusuke 70
Yokoyama, Shohei 130
Yokoyama, Takeru 31

SPRINGER NATURE

GPSR Compliance

The European Union's (EU) General Product Safety Regulation (GPSR) is a set of rules that requires consumer products to be safe and our obligations to ensure this.

If you have any concerns about our products, you can contact us on ProductSafety@springernature.com

In case Publisher is established outside the EU, the EU authorized representative is:

Springer Nature Customer Service Center GmbH
Europaplatz 3
69115 Heidelberg, Germany

The manufacturer's authorised representative in the EU is Springer Nature Customer Service Centre GmbH, Europaplatz 3, 69115 Heidelberg, Germany. If you have any concerns regarding our products, please contact ProductSafety@springernature.com

Printed and bound by CPI Group (UK) Ltd, Croydon, CR0 4YY

25/03/2026

02078195-0009